History

as a

Way

of

Learning

Articles, Excerpts, and

Essays

by

WILLIAM APPLEMAN

WILLIAMS

A Division of Franklin Watts, Inc.
New York

HISTORY

as a

WAY

of

LEARNING

New Viewpoints

1973

Library of Congress Cataloging in Publication Data

Williams, William Appleman.
    History as a way of learning.

    Includes bibliographical references.
        1. United States—History—Addresses, essays,
    lectures.   2. United States—Historiography—
    Addresses, essays, lectures.   I. Title.
    E178.6.W7   1974   973   73-10469
    ISBN 0-531-06362-3
    ISBN 0-531-06491-3 (pbk.)

Cover design by Judie Mills

Text design by Diana Hrisinko

Permissions Acknowledgments

Introduction to History as a Way of Learning from CONTOURS OF AMERICAN HISTORY. Reprinted by permission of Quadrangle Books. Copyright © 1966 by Quadrangle Books.

Brooks Adams and American Expansion. Reprinted by permission of *The New England Quarterly.*

American Intervention in Russia, 1917–1920. Reprinted by permission of *Studies on the Left.*

A Second Look at Mr. X. Copyright © 1952 by Monthly Review Incorporated. Reprinted by permission of the editors of *Monthly Review.*

The Legend of Isolationism in the 1920's. Reprinted by permission of *Science and Society.*

The Frontier Thesis and American Foreign Policy. Reprinted by permission of the *Pacific Historical Review.*

The Age of Re-Forming History. First appeared in *The Nation.* Republished by consent of *The Nation.*

A Note on Charles Austin Beard's Search for a General Theory of Causation. Reprinted by permission of the *American Historical Review.*

Schlesinger: Right Crisis—Wrong Order. First appeared in *The Nation.* Republished by consent of *The Nation.*

The American Century: 1941–1957. First appeared in *The Nation.* Republished by consent of *The Nation.*

Charles Austin Beard: The Intellectual as Tory-Radical from AMERICAN RADICALS: SOME PROBLEMS AND PERSONALITIES. Monthly Review Press, 1957.

The Age of Mercantilism: An Interpretation of the American Political Economy, 1763 to 1828. First appeared in *The William and Mary Quarterly.*

The Large Corporation and American Foreign Policy. First appeared in *The American Socialist.*

Samuel Adams: Calvinist, Mercantilist, Revolutionary. Reprinted by permission of *Studies on the Left.*

The Cuban Revolution Assaulted from Abroad from THE UNITED STATES, CUBA, AND CASTRO. Monthly Review Press, 1962.

Karl Marx's Challenge to America from THE GREAT EVASION. Reprinted by permission of Quadrangle Books. Copyright © 1968 by Quadrangle Books.

The Cold-War Revisionists. First appeared in *The Nation.* Republished by consent of *The Nation.*

An American Socialist Community? Reprinted by permission of *Liberation.*

Contents

Contents

Preface: A Few Personal Thoughts on Reprinting These Selections

Ivan Dee first proposed a collection of early essays a good many years ago, when he was chief editor of Quadrangle Books during that firm's period of courageous and creative independence. I dismissed the suggestion out-of-hand: it struck me as unnecessary; and I had teaching obligations and writing commitments that claimed more than the time I was willing to deny my family.

One of those projects, rather far down my list of priorities, had been underwritten by a shrewdly modest advance from Quadrangle. During the years that I failed to produce that manuscript, moreover, I began to receive regular requests for offprints of various articles that I had written and then largely forgotten, and I discovered that I had none to send in reply. In his lovably sly way, Ivan Dee realized that he had a screw to turn and he began with gentle relentlessness to twist it into my life.

We arranged a friendly compromise. Quadrangle released me from my existing contract in return for my promise to produce a collection of articles, excerpts, and essays.

Then The New York Times Company bought Quadrangle Books as a way of diversifying its economic power base, and in order to publish the books it thought fit to print. The wise men of the *Times* did not consider my books either desirable or profitable —or both—to print. So they flipped them out into the marketplace. The sun of friendly compromise plopped out of sight and the star of eastern conglomerate empire inched another degree toward a zenith.

Thanks largely to Clifford Solway, my work that had been published by Ivan Dee and Quadrangle was kept alive by the New
Viewpoints division of Franklin Watts. He also asked me to honor
the contract for this collection. Fair enough.

I do not know Solway as well as Dee; but in my experience he
is a warm, helpful, intelligent man who is not completely persuaded
that the reforms of late-century liberalism provide solutions to our
problems—let alone guidelines for realizing our aspirations. But
he also wrote, in the old (and by me lamented) *Saturday Review of
Literature,* one of the most informed and thoughtful commentaries-
in-criticism about what is commonly known as New Left or revisionist historiography. It was an essay (unlike many others on the
subject) that made it clear that he was—and is—his own man.

As for this collection, I chose the selections on these grounds:
the personal fun and excitement involved in doing them; the com-
radeship with other men and women during the research and discussion that produced them; the response that they evoked (anger
and evasion, as well as praise and incitement to further exploration); and the sense I have about which issues still cry out for further attention.

I cannot tell you which one means the most to me: the thrill of
early publication is balanced by the pleasure of later discovery. And
I have no warrant even to try to tell you which one is best. That is
your prerogative—and your problem.

But I do remember certain moments with goose-bump intensity.

As a graduate student, I argued with all my power once a week
for nine months with William Best Hesseltine about my exploration of Brooks Adams. Hesseltine (known to us behind his back as
Curly or Wild Bill) was, as he would sometimes admit after a few
shots of *very* good booze, a perfect son of a bitch—speaking intellectually. He did not so much teach you as he infuriated you to
learn. As a human being—well, I simply loved him.

Merrill Jensen and George Mosse: Arkansas honing stones from
Iowa and Germany.

Harvey Goldberg: sitting on the grass at Ohio State within sight of the hippodrome built for Woody Hayes and his circus talking about Karl Marx and Rosa Luxemburg.

The men and women who created our seminar at Wisconsin: to name them in alphabetical order would reduce them to a list, whereas they were the blood of a vital part of my life. I am happy that they know, through our individual personal relationships, and our collective experience, how much I am indebted to them—in the heart as well as in the mind. Yes, including a few who clearly thought I was too far gone to be saved even by their truths.

Charles Beard: I came to my serious confrontation with his mind rather late, and that was good, for others had taught me enough to sense what he was about. Even now, though, I am not sure I wholly understand. He was a long way down the road. Very much of a piece in a time when being only a piece was the way to get to the top.

Yet, in a special way, all the undergraduates: no matter whether they picked the back row to sleep or to feel each other up; whether they read newspapers or posed unanswerable questions; or whether they wrote unnerving papers in lucid prose or drove me up the wall with their incomprehensible meanderings through the thicket of their indifference.

And, of those, at least in this context, a never forgotten few days with the students at Oberlin: they invited me to give some lectures and talk with them, and out of that dialogue came *The Great Evasion.*

Which brings us back to Ivan Dee. He read the manuscript, accepted it, and pushed it into print within a few months. It dropped into the void of the New Frontier. But apparently it stirred up some eddies, for Robert Heilbroner chose to kick it around in *The New York Review of Books.* He made it clear, even more than Adolph Berle's much earlier review of *The Tragedy of American Diplomacy* in *The New York Times,* that we skeptics had somehow slipped a shiv into the rationalizations of those who spoke for the system. Nobody of Heilbroner's impressive talents should otherwise have required all *that* space to dismiss a book that he finally damned as misguided, mistaken, and irrelevant.

Hence the dialogue will continue, even if it turns out that Indochina is allowed to go its own way. If everyone elsewhere *does* deny us the chance to realize ourselves by changing them, we nevertheless have a magnificent fall-back position: we can finally confront the question of what we are going to make of America.

A long forgotten humanist scholar of remarkable insights named T. K. Whipple once put it this way: "We, the people, need remaking worse than the land does." [1] Only we can reconstruct ourselves, and it will require most of our attention and impressive talents—and all of our will and courage.[2]

I have learned more and thought more since I wrote these selections. I could fiddle with all of them, and I could clarify and buttress key points that have been questioned or denied. I have not done so because I consider that kind of revision to be playing tricks upon the living, and because I think this history does help us face vital questions about ourselves—and about our future as a people.

[1] *Study Out the Land* (Berkeley: University of California Press, 1943), p. 57. The essay was written in 1934.

[2] W. I. Susman, in *American Reform: The Ambiguous Legacy* (Yellow Springs, Ohio: The Ampersand Press, 1967), pp. 94–108.

History

as a

Way

of

Learning

Introduction:
History as
a Way of
Learning

> *To study history is always to seek*
> *in some degree to get beyond the*
> *limitations and preoccupations*
> *of the present; it demands*
> *for success an effort of*
> *self-transcendence.*
>
> ARTHUR O. LOVEJOY, 1939

Relieved and exhilarated by their triumph over the Axis Powers in 1945, Americans seemed to have assumed that their traditional dream of becoming a world unto themselves was about to be realized. Far from having become disillusioned (or isolationist), they appeared casually confident that their earlier visions of Manifest Destiny were materializing as the reality of the present. Though vaguely uneasy about the full extent of its powers, most Americans looked upon the atom bomb as a self-starting magic lamp; even without being rubbed it would produce their long-sought City on the Hill in the form of a *de facto* American Century embracing the globe.

It was generally taken for granted that such benevolent Americanization of the world would bring peace and plenty without the moral embarrassments and administrative distractions of old-fashioned empires. And so, having created the most

(5)

irrational weapon known to man, Americans proceeded with
startling rationality to abandon the mass army as their principal
strategic weapon. Armed only with their bomb, they then generously offered to help everyone become more like themselves.
"We are willing to help people who believe the way we do," explained Secretary of State Dean Acheson, "to continue to live
the way they want to live."

Had Americans applied their intelligence, humanitarianism,
and power to the paradox of plenty without purpose within
their own society and to the needs and aspirations of their fellow humans throughout the world, it is possible that their self-
centered dream would have been transformed into a vision of
brotherhood among men. Instead, they calmly asserted that they
had disarmed, a confusion of the truth so complete as to befud-
dle even their opponents. On the one hand, American leaders
explained that The Bomb kept the barbarian at bay while he
was collapsing under the economic and political pressures exerted by the United States. On the other hand, they righteously
condemned his failure to disarm while they kept a monopoly of
nuclear weapons. Their promises of self-restraint served only to
add a touch of arrogance to the double standard of their morality, a morality as dangerous and destructive as their weapon.

Some years later, after the Russians accepted the American
logic of disarmament-by-nuclear-fusion and produced their own
hydrogen bomb, the United States was forced to confront its
own dilemmas with more candor and concern. But even earlier,
throughout an era which might be called The Years of Babbitt's
Confidence, Americans had become increasingly perplexed, anxious, and frustrated. Not even McCarthyism, a particularly viru-
lent epidemic of the anti-intellectualism of the frontier, could
cope with the harsh realities of a world in revolution. In attempting to exorcise their fears, overcome their spiritual and in-

tellectual malaise, and resolve their dilemmas, Americans in surprising numbers next turned more formally and directly to history for an explanation of their predicament and a program (if not a panacea) for the future.

As a result, and despite the natural charms and cultivated coquetry of psychology, sociology, and economics, Clio became involved in another of her many affairs with a society in search of reassurance and security. American foreign service officers retired to write memoranda for today's diplomacy in the form of history books while historians took leaves of absence to become acting foreign service officers. Many businessmen underwrote the reconstruction of selected portions of their past, while some historians made a thriving business of carefully culled segments of the heritage of America. And convinced of the validity of the underlying assumptions of such activities, numerous communities legislated history into the curriculums of their schools.

Many observers interpreted this enthusiasm as a sign that America was solidly afoot on the road to salvation. Without denying the virtues and values of history, there is nevertheless considerable reason to doubt whether the evidence is that persuasive. Even the most casual review of this particular renaissance reveals the persistance of two phrases, "history shows" and "history proves," used to establish *ex post facto* the validity of a policy or attitude already entertained by the writer. Instead of being treated as the study of the past and present in which thinking, reasoning, and reflection might lead to insights and perception, history appeared more often to be viewed as a grab bag from which to snatch footnotes for an a priori opinion.

But History is one of the most misleading—and hence dangerous—approaches to knowledge if viewed, or practiced, as a process of reaching back into the past for answers sufficient unto the present and the future. For although historical consciousness can be a powerful tool with which to improve our lives and our world, it is little more than a demonic sorcerer's apprentice unless the history of which we become conscious is something more than a brief in defense of some particular proposal. The purpose of history is not to explain our situation so that we settle down as what C. Wright Mills has called Cheerful Robots in This Best Possible of All Worlds. Neither is its function to propel us into orbit around some distant Utopia. Indeed not. History's great tradition is to help us understand ourselves and our world so that each of us, individually and in conjunction with our fellow men, can formulate relevant and reasoned alternatives and become meaningful actors in making history.

Considered in this light, History is a way of learning. As such, it begins by leaving the present; by going back into the heretofore, by beginning again. Only by grasping what we were is it possible to see how we changed, to understand the process and the nature of the modifications, and to gain some perspective on what we are. The historical experience is not one of staying in the present and looking back. Rather is it one of going back into the past and returning to the present with a wider and more intense consciousness of the restrictions of our former outlook. We return with a broader awareness of the alternatives open to us and armed with a sharper perceptiveness with which to make our choices. In this manner it is possible to loosen the clutch of the dead hand of the past and transform it into a living tool for the present and the future. . . .

The tool used in the present study is the concept of *Weltanschauung,* or definition of the world combined with an explanation of how it works. Every sane adult has such an inclusive conception of the world which cuts across and subsumes personal motives, group interests, and class ideologies. This point needs to be emphasized, for in recent years many historians have relied extensively on the psychology of the irrational in developing their analyses and interpretations. As a result, they seem to have confused consciousness of purpose with conspiracy. Now neither contingency nor madness is absent from history, but the vast majority of significant figures on the stage of history act consciously and purposefully (if usually routinely) within their conceptions of the world. Hence to assert, or assume, that the choice of interpretations lies between irrationality, chance, and conspiracy is to distort the nature of history almost beyond recognition. History written from that point of view becomes little more than a bag of tricks dumped upon the living.

This essay reviews and attempts to make sense out of American history by reference to three conceptions of the world which are traditionally associated with economic thought and action. The approach is open to two criticisms: it can be charged that this means that all thought is economic, and it can be claimed that it implies that ideas have no life of their own. There are two answers to these caveats.

First, some ideas which originate as instruments of specific interests ultimately break their narrow bounds and emerge as broad, inclusive conceptions of the world. Herbert Spencer made this point in convincing fashion. "I do not think," he answered a critic, "that *laissez-faire* is to be regarded simply as a politico-economical principle only, but as a much wider principle— the principle of letting all citizens take the benefits and evils of their own acts: not only such as are consequent on their industrial conduct, but such as are consequent upon their conduct in general."

Secondly, it should be obvious that ideas persist for a long time after their immediate relevance is gone, and therefore may act as independent variables in later circumstances. For this reason, and because of the practical problem of organizing any written history, it is always an arbitrary choice as to which— reality or existing ideas—will be discussed first. . . . Though it is possible and indeed accurate, therefore, to speak of an over- riding outlook, an equal emphasis is placed on conflict and change, upon the efforts of men to recognize and direct or in- hibit such changes, and upon the development of new explana- tions of reality which come ultimately to replace the formerly accepted order.

The method of history is neither to by-pass and dismiss nor to pick and choose according to preconceived notions; rather is it a study of the past so that we can come back into our own time of troubles having shared with the men of the past their dilemmas, having learned from their experiences, having been buoyed up by their courage and creativeness and sobered by their shortsightedness and failures. We shall then be better equipped to redefine our own dilemmas and problems as oppor- tunities and possibilities and to proceed with positive rather than negative programs and policies. This enrichment and im- provement through research and reflection is the essence of being human, and it is the heart of the historical method.

· · · · ·

History as a way of learning has one additional value be- yond establishing the nature of reality and posing the questions that arise from its complexities and contradictions. It can offer examples of how other men faced up to the difficulties and op- portunities of their eras. Even if the circumstances are noticeably different, it is illuminating, and productive of humility as well, to watch other men make their decisions, and to consider the consequences of their values and methods. If the issues are simi- lar, then the experience is more directly valuable. But in either case the procedure can transform history as a way of learning into a way of breaking the chains of the past.

For by watching other men confront the disparity between existing patterns of thought and a reality to which they are no longer relevant, the outsider may be encouraged to muster his own moral and intellectual courage and discipline and undertake a similar re-examination and re-evaluation of his own outlook. Whether the student of history follows the responses of earlier men remains a matter of his own choice, and even if he accepts their views he is obtaining his answers from men, not History. History offers no answers per se, it only offers a way of encouraging men to use their minds to make their own history.

This essay in the review and interpretation of American history has suggested that several elements have emerged as the major features of American society, and that those have in turn defined the central issues faced by contemporary Americans. One is the functional and syndicalist fragmentation of American society (and hence its individual citizens) along technological and economic lines. The personal and public lives of Americans are defined by, and generally limited to, their specific functional role. To an amazing extent, they share very little on a daily basis beyond a common duty as consumers and a commitment to anti-communism. The persistent cliché of being "caught in the rat-race" dramatizes that alienation, as does the attempt to "play it cool" in order to maintain some semblance of identity and integration.

The second theme is the persistence of a frontier-expansionist outlook—a conception of the world and past American history—which holds that expansion (or "growth," as Walter Lippmann put it in 1960) offers the best way to resolve problems and to create, or take advantage of, opportunities. A third is a commitment to private property as the means of insuring personal identity, and of thereby guaranteeing democratic politics, and of creating material well-being. And finally, Americans have displayed a loyalty to an ideal of humanity which defines man as more than a creature of property; which defines him as a man by reason of his individual fidelity to one of several humane standards of conduct and by his association with other men in a community honoring those codes.

None of those themes is unique, or even of recent origin, in American history. One example will suffice to establish that. Bernard Baruch raised in 1944 the specter of a dangerous fragmentation of American society into functional groups bent on pursuing the short-run satisfaction of their interests to the detriment of the general welfare, and his report was followed by many related or separate comments on the same problem. But Herbert Hoover had discussed the same issue at great length in the 1920s; the founders of the National Civic Federation had been motivated in large part by a similar concern at the turn of the 20th century; Abraham Lincoln had come to stress the same issue after he became President in 1861; James Madison and other Founding Fathers had grappled with the identical problem in the late 18th and early 19th centuries; and others had struggled to provide a resolution of the same dilemma during the Restoration Era in England. Hence it was not the issues that were new in 1944. The crisis was of a different nature, being instead defined by the progressive failure of the approach that Americans had evolved to solve the problems. That approach no longer provided a satisfactory resolution.

From [the early 17th century] forward, the solution developed by Americans had been compounded of two conflicting themes or answers. One was the interpretation of Christianity advanced by the Levellers during the English Revolution, and later reasserted wholly within that tradition by Karl Marx in the form of a secular socialism. It held that the problems raised by faction, interest, fragmentation, and alienation could only be resolved—and man restored to a true wholeness and identity —by de-emphasizing private property in favor of social property and through the co-operative building of a community rather than the mere construction of an organized collective system. Save for the first two decades of the 20th century, that outlook never played a large and direct role in American history. Indirectly, however, it did exert a sustained influence.

The other approach accepted private property as necessary and desirable. For guidance in defining and honoring the ideal of a commonwealth, its followers looked to different religious and secular traditions. One of these was Calvin's conception of a corporate Christian commonwealth in which the trustee accepted and discharged the responsibility for the general welfare; at the same time, all men were charged to honor the axiom that their choice between callings should be made in favor of the one that contributed most to the common good. Another tradition involved the ideal and practice of feudal *noblesse oblige.* That view had of course arisen within the Christian world, but by the 17th century had developed a secular life of its own. Finally, such men also relied upon a secular argument which held that expansion offered the only feasible way of underwriting private property while at the same time improving the general or collective welfare.

Put simply, the mercantilists . . . sought to integrate those three themes into a coherent and consistent *Weltanschauung.* That outlook on the world was, and remained, the essence of all class consciousness among upper-class groups in England and the United States from the Age of Elizabeth I. Thus [they] accepted the responsibility of those who enjoyed the possession of consolidated property for maintaining the general welfare and viewed the state as the natural and appropriate instrument for implementing that obligation. At the same time, [their key leaders] tried to organize political affairs on the basis of parties which included men of all functional interests (or factions) who accepted a broad conception of the general welfare and the means to achieve it. By thus coming together as men who shared an ideal of community—a Utopia—they would be able to override the tendency of functional activity to fragment and divide them—both internally (or personally)—from their fellow men.

[They] extended that outlook into foreign affairs, accepting the necessity of expansion and acting vigorously to co-ordinate the various aspects of commerce and colonization. But [they] also sought to build such an empire as a mutually beneficial and responsible commonwealth. [They] had few qualms about waging war against outsiders to protect or extend the empire, and certainly intended to control its members; but they did have a strong sense of partnership that guided their actions toward the colonies. [Such] mercantilists made many false starts, and they failed to control all factions (or to subordinate their own particular interests) at all times. It is nevertheless true that they did to a rather remarkable degree develop and act upon such a class-conscious outlook that combined a defense of private property with a belief in the necessity of expansion, and with an ideal of community and commonwealth.

That outlook was carried to America by the Puritans, by other emigrants, and by the empire directives prepared by [England's leaders]. It was thereby established, in various versions, in every colony. In many respects, moreover, it continued to mature and develop beyond its English origins and precedents. Indeed, Jonathan Edwards integrated its various themes perhaps more successfully and infused them with a more noble vision of Christian community than any English or American philosopher either before or after his time. His corporate Christian commonwealth was one of the few American visions worthy of the name Utopia.

But in any of its versions, that outlook was a demanding *Weltanschauung*. As Frederick Jackson Turner pointed out three centuries after the colonies had become firmly established (and in doing so offered a revealing insight into his own generation), the urge to escape the responsibilities of that ideal of a corporate Christian commonwealth was powerful, persistent, and without regard for the direct and indirect costs of such flight. In England, for example, expansion offered a progressively more appealing substitute for the self-discipline and fidelity to ideals that was essential in maintaining the general interest against the factional. And in America the presence of a continent defended only by weaker souls made that solution even more convenient. Americans proceeded in the space of two generations to substitute the Manifest Destiny of empire for the Christian Commonwealth of Jonathan Edwards. Thomas Jefferson was the great epic poet of that urge to escape, to run away and spend one's life doing what one wanted—or in starting over time after time. Jackson, Benton, and Polk were but the type-cast protagonists of that dream, and through his early years even Lincoln was a man who charted his career by that same western star.

James Madison was the theorist of the outlook, and in offering expansion as the way of controlling faction, he articulated the guiding line of American history from the end of the 18th century through the 1950s. Yet unlike most who followed his theory, Madison recognized the grave implications of the solution; along with such men as Calhoun, Monroe, Clay, and especially John Quincy Adams, he sought to prevent the complete devaluation of the self-restraint and other ideals that [his British predecessors] and Edwards had stressed. The continent was too much for them. By making escape so easy, it produced an unrestrained and anti-intellectual individualist democracy that almost destroyed any semblance of community and commonwealth. Even before the continent was filled up, the frontier had become a national Utopia and Madison's theory the New Gospel. Men largely ceased to think about problems, and merely reacted to them by reciting the frontier catechism and pushing the Indians off another slice of the continent. Following the general lines of Seward's reformulation of Madison's argument to fit the conditions of an industrial society, Hay's Open Door Notes merely restated the principle in terms appropriate to the 20th century.

Less than 60 years later, however, the open door of escape was no more than ajar. Two forces had combined to all but close it: Russian and Chinese industrial and nuclear power and potential; and the growing refusal by societies that had formerly served as the frontier to continue in the role any longer. As a result, the frontier Utopia had ceased to offer a practical substitute for the more demanding *Weltanschauung* of class-conscious leadership and responsibility. *Expansion as escape meant nuclear war.* Yet the cold war was essential to those who still, consciously or unconsciously, saw expansion as the means of adjusting and controlling factions and at the same time providing some measure of welfare. In typical frontier fashion, such people saw defeat or war as the only other solutions.

Expansion of a vastly different character and drastically more limited nature was still possible, but even that could be sustained only by strengthening the self-discipline necessary to honor the commonwealth ideal that [some Englishmen], Edwards, and Adams had tried to sustain. Expansion of any sort was only possible without war, and that is to say, only possible if the frontier were abandoned as a Utopia. Expansion of that kind would of necessity be channeled through the United Nations, without political or economic strings, in an effort to help other societies solve their own problems within their own traditions. Hence the possibility of any full maturation of the class-conscious industrial gentry that had slowly been created by the corporation between the 1890s and the 1950s turned on one very simple test. Did that gentry have, or would it manage to muster, the nerve to abandon the frontier as Utopia, to turn its back on expansion as the open door of escape?

It is of course fair to ask whether any precedents exist for encouraging such a display of intelligence and courage. For while it is helpful to find examples in the past, it is too much to ask that contemporary corporation executives and political leaders model themselves on [17th century mercantilists] or John Quincy Adams. Very few, if any of them, are men of sufficient empathy. Nor would it be wise for them to follow such a course even if they could. Not only are the circumstances different, but it is the attitude and the ideals that are important, not the personal styles or the specific policies. But there is no need to return to the past in that sense, for some of the very Americans who restated the expansionist outlook in the 20th century also realized that there was another choice.

Brooks Adams, for example, admitted that America did not have to embark upon a program to control China and Siberia. It was merely the easier way out of the dilemma, and one which in his opinion offered more glory and riches. And as late as 1944, Dean Acheson acknowledged that he and his colleagues in government could invest an indefinite amount of energy and time in discussing alternatives to expansion as a way of building "a successfully functioning political and economic system."

Acheson dismissed such approaches, however, on the grounds that they would weaken the rights of private property, require modifications of the Constitution, and limit the frontier-style liberties to which Americans had become accustomed.

Herbert Hoover and Charles Beard had more intellectual courage and imagination than either Adams or Acheson. They argued that it was possible to build a community—a commonwealth—based on private property without relying on imperial expansion. Whatever his other failings, Hoover did at least refuse to go to war for the Open Door in Asia, and did try very hard to change the character of America's overseas economic expansion. In some ways, at least, Beard advocated an even more rigorous effort to restore the ideal of a commonwealth as the American Utopia. But in its commitment to the frontier as a Utopia of escape, the American public refused to give that approach a serious or a fair trial.

Finally, the mid-century industrial gentry might draw even more encouragement from the example provided by the southern Negro. During approximately a century after the Civil War, the Negro modeled his aspirations and ideals on the white society in which he existed. Briefly at the end of the Civil War, again in the 1890s, and then with a rush during World War I, the Negro adapted the frontier-expansionist outlook to his own position. He defined northern urban centers as his frontier of escape from the conditions of survival in the south. For a generation or more, Negroes streamed into that supposed Utopia only in the end to discover that it was largely a mirage. Then, under the leadership of deeply religious and courageous men like the Reverend Martin Luther King, Jr., they broke with that traditional view of the frontier as escape and defined the south, the cities and the states where they lived, as the only meaningful frontier that existed.

Having made that magnificently courageous and deeply intelligent decision, they stood their ground and faced the issue in the present, reasserting as their solution the ideal and the practice of a Christian community or commonwealth. In a way that dramatized their abandonment of the frontier outlook, they organized themselves in such groups as "the Montgomery Improvement Association." No longer did they rally under the old slogan of the frontier, "Kansas or Bust," merely changing Kansas to read New York or Chicago or Detroit or Cleveland or Pittsburgh. They made no mention of the frontier: they simply talked about the here and the now, and set about to improve it guided by the Utopia of a Christian commonwealth. And to do so they chose the appropriate weapon—nonviolent resistance. Within one year they had effected more fundamental progress than in a century of following the white man's theory of escape through the frontier. Not merely did they begin to obtain food in formerly closed cafés: that was really a minor point. What they really won was respect for themselves as men who no longer ran away. The frontier never had and never could give a man that kind of self-respect.

But while Reverend King and the Montgomery Improvement Association offered the class-conscious industrial gentry inspiring proof that wealth and welfare were obtainable without running off to some new frontier, they also posed some crucial questions. Even if the gentry could regenerate such a Christian vision of a corporate commonwealth, would corporation capitalism be able to function if operated according to its precepts? Perhaps it would not. Perhaps the corporation economy could not function without the indirect but vital help of the citizen in the form of taxes paid to the government and then handed on to the corporation in the form of subsidies. If that were the case, then how and by what secular ideal and hierarchy of values—

by what Utopia—would the class-conscious industrial gentry transform such double jeopardy into a system of true equity in which every citizen, along with the corporations, received a fair share of wealth and welfare? It might be rather difficult to convince the citizen that his sacrifices were worthwhile on the grounds that the gentry would then take an honest interest in him. For even under the best of circumstances, is having an interest taken in one a sufficient substitute for active participation in the present and future affairs of one's own society?

Those are fundamental and very difficult questions. Even to ask them is to understand why the frontier as a Utopia of escape has been so attractive in the past, and why it still exerts such influence in the middle of the 20th century. But to ask these questions is also to raise the issue as to whether Americans have any other traditions that are appropriate to the present. Is it really a choice between, on the one hand, a continuance of government by a syndicalist oligarchy relying on expansion or, on the other, a government by a class-conscious industrial gentry? To be sure, the choice does offer some measure of meaningful difference; for a class-conscious industrial gentry with the nerve to abandon the Utopia of frontier expansion would clearly provide at least the chance of a more equitable, humane, creative, and peaceful future. But if that is all Americans can offer themselves, then they are apt to become unique in the sense of becoming isolated from the mainstream of 20th-century development.

For the rest of the world, be it presently industrial or merely beginning to industrialize, is very clearly moving toward some version of a society modeled on the ideal and the Utopia of a true human community based far more on social property than upon private property. That is what the editors of *The Wall Street Journal* meant in 1958 when they candidly admitted that the United States was on "the wrong side of a social revolution."

That socialist reassertion of the essence of the ancient ideal of a Christian commonwealth is a viable Utopia. It was so when the Levellers asserted it in the middle of the 17th century, and it remains so in the middle of the 20th century. It holds very simply and clearly that the only meaningful frontier lies within individual men and in their relationships with each other. It agrees with Frederick Jackson Turner that the American frontier has been "a gate of escape" from those central responsibilities and opportunities. The socialist merely says that it is time to stop running away from life.

And in Eugene Debs, America produced a man who understood that expansion was a running away, the kind of escape that was destructive of the dignity of men. He also believed and committed his life to the proposition that Americans would one day prove mature and courageous enough to give it up as a child's game; that they would one day "put away childish things" and undertake the creation of a socialist commonwealth. Americans therefore do have a third choice to consider alongside that of an oligarchy and that of a class-conscious industrial gentry. They have the chance to create the first truly democratic socialism in the world.

That opportunity is the only real frontier available to Americans in the second half of the 20th century. If they revealed and acted upon the kind of intelligence and morality and courage that it would take to explore and develop that frontier, then they would have finally broken the chains of their own past. Otherwise, they would ultimately fall victims of a nostalgia for their childhood.

The Contours of American History
(New York: Quadrangle Books, 1966)

Brooks Adams and

American

Expansion

Long slighted as a somewhat eccentric brother of the more famous Henry Adams, Brooks Adams has received less attention than he deserves. Brooks Adams not only influenced Henry Adams; he also made a significant impression on such leading public figures as John Hay, Henry Cabot Lodge, and Theodore Roosevelt. Of particular consequence was Brooks's rôle in the development of United States foreign policy in Asia—and toward Russia in particular—from 1895 to 1908.

The Panic of 1893 brought Henry Adams into close and extended contact with his brother for the first time in several years. Henry, perplexed by the problems posed by the new industrialism, was quick to benefit from Brooks's researches and insight. By 1893 Brooks Adams had completed some ten years of exhaustive inquiry upon which he had formulated a broad theory of history. And as the two brothers waited out their fortunes that summer Brooks gave Henry the full argument of his thesis, which was shortly published as *The Law of Civilization and Decay.*[1]

In the course of this tutoring it is clear that Henry acquired from Brooks "certain fundamental conceptions of history, explicit in *The Law,* which subsequently bulked large" in his own writing.[2] By Henry's own admission it was Brooks who "discovered or developed" the law: "The book," Henry wrote, "is

wholly, absolutely, and exclusively yours." [3] Of equal significance, however, is the fact that both Brooks and Henry Adams
considered *The Law* to be the central problem of their life.

Brooks Adams sought a law of history but in effect rediscovered the sine curve. From the laws of mass, energy, and acceler-
ation, he formulated a concept of society's oscillation between
"barbarism and civilization." In the decentralization of the
former, Brooks argued, fear bred imagination, which in turn
begot the religious, artistic, and military types. But as the centralization of wealth (stored energy) proceeded, the "economic
organism" tended to replace the emotional and martial man;
and ultimately the pressure of economic competition reached a
critical point and the society either reverted to barbarism or
collapsed—its energy exhausted.[4]

Brooks was appalled by his conclusions—that rational
thought played "an exceedingly small part . . . in moulding the
fate of men," and that a society's decline was marked by intense
centralization and "economic competition." The first was personally unacceptable, but on every hand he saw evidence that
such deadly concentration was well advanced in the United
States. Desperate for a way out, Brooks brushed aside Henry's
warning that he was beginning "to monkey with a dynamo,"
and from 1895 on primarily concerned himself with the search
for a formula that would avert chaos.[5]

Brooks inclined to two conclusions: that the next concentration of economic power would occur in New York, and that the
expansion of the United States into Asia was the only technique
by which *The Law* could, in effect, be repealed. The problem
then became Russia, since in his view England was already becoming an economic vassal of the United States. But Brooks did
not believe that Russia would acquiesce in American control of
Asia; and so the key question was how to defeat St. Petersburg

and take control of China. Well aware of his brother's new interest (Russia is mentioned but once in *The Law*), Henry's first reaction was one of fear and curiosity. "I fear Russia much!" he admitted to Brooks; and concluded that "you ought to be,— like your grandfather,—minister to St. Petersburg." [6] As for Brooks's plan to preëmpt Asia as a colony, Henry was dubious. "Russia," he advised Brooks, "as yet seems too far to reach. We have not come to that point. Probably we shall never get there." [7]

For his part, Brooks proceeded to round out a detailed program for the repeal of *The Law*. That the job was completed during the winter of 1897–1898 is clear from Henry's correspondence. Henry wrote from Athens in April, 1898 (where he was visiting the American minister to Greece, William Woodville Rockhill), to offer Brooks two jingles: one for the "wording of your Law," and the second for "your other formula." The latter documents Brooks's preoccupation with Asia.[8]

> *Under economical centralization, Asia is cheaper than Europe.*
> *The World tends to economic centralization.*
> *Therefore Asia tends to survive, and Europe to perish.*

But Brooks was concerned with action, not jingles, and soon published a policy recommendation.

In February, 1899—eight months before Washington enunciated the Open Door in Asia—Brooks Adams presented his proposals in an article in the *Fortnightly Review*. In the past, he began, American industry's "liberal margin of profit" had been "due to expansion" across the continent. In the drive to control that market, however, industry had been "stimulated" to produce a surplus. "The time has now come," Brooks went on, "when that surplus must be sold abroad, or a glut must be risked." Those who failed to expand, he warned, were "devoured by the gangrene which attacks every stagnant society and from which no patient recovers." "Eastern Asia," he then pointed out, "now appears to be the only district likely soon to be able to absorb any great increase of manufactures." There was no choice, Brooks Adams concluded, but to compete for that "seat of empire." [9] This strident call for expansion fell on important ears.

Soon after his seminar with Brooks in 1893, Henry Adams became obsessed with *The Law*. Not only did it arm him with a rational defense for his pessimism and disillusionment, but it became the theme of his endless discussions with John Hay, Henry Cabot Lodge, William Woodville Rockhill, and Theodore Roosevelt. As one witness recalled: "Henry sincerely admired his brother's intellect; he quoted him the way Saint Augustine quoted Aristotle, only more frequently." As for the book itself, Henry took pains to see that it reached "all the hands worth considering," including those "of the Supreme Court and the Cabinet." [10] Henry's rôle in the propagation of Brooks's ideas was particularly important prior to the date (September, 1901) that Theodore Roosevelt became President. Those years were especially significant because of Henry's intimate association with Hay and Rockhill, who directed United States foreign policy in Asia.

Henry Adams and John Hay had known each other since 1861, but prior to Henry's summer with Brooks their relationship was primarily of a gay social and intellectual nature. The character of the friendship changed noticeably, however, after Henry was apprised of *The Law*. In 1891, for example, Henry complained that French "painting and sculpture" made him "sea sick." But in October, 1893, Henry Adams suddenly began to discuss the fate of the world in terms of "universal bankruptcy," and by January, 1898, he was "more immediately curious about Russia." [11] This new concern remained the central feature of their subsequent correspondence.[12] During these same years, moreover, Henry extended his friendship with William Woodville Rockhill.

Henry's acquaintance with Rockhill was of later origin because of the latter's duty as a State Department official in China and Korea, and his subsequent expeditions to Mongolia and Tibet. But after 1890 their contacts were extended and together with Hay they formed a seminar on foreign affairs. The group was temporarily disrupted, however, in 1897. First Hay was sent to London as United States Ambassador. That left Henry "quite alone . . . except for Rockhill, in the atmosphere of foreign affairs." [13] A bit later Rockhill was again sent abroad, but this time Henry trailed along, and the two of them enjoyed a trip through the Balkans.[14] Not much later, however, Hay returned to take up his duties as Secretary of State under President William McKinley and these friendships took on added importance.

The first task which confronted Secretary Hay and Henry Adams was to get Rockhill home from Athens, where he was serving as United States Minister to Greece. "Everything will be done," Henry assured him, "to bring you back." After some difficulty Hay secured Rockhill's appointment as Director of the Bureau of American Republics, and the circle was again complete.[15] Hay had already "expressed a wish" to have Henry as "an associate in his responsibilities"; but Henry preferred to function in a more confidential manner. They began their routine of daily walks at four in the afternoon, time spent "discussing the day's work at home and abroad." [16]

These discussions, it is clear, were carried on within the frame of reference supplied by Brooks Adams. They "diagnosed

the whole menagerie," as Henry recalled, and "killed and bur-
ied, in advance, half the world and the neighboring solar systems." But Russia plagued them constantly. "What *can* you
do?" Henry challenged bluntly; and Hay confessed, in moments
of despair, that the "only comfort after all is in your cheerless
scheme of the correlation of forces." [17] But obviously, Hay did
not really believe himself in such moments of fatalism, for all
the while he actively sought to implement Brooks Adams's answer to the dilemma.

The remarkable correlation between Secretary of State Hay's
"Open Door Notes" of September, 1899 (and his later policy toward Russia), and Brooks Adams's detailed blueprint of the
proper policy to be followed by the United States in Asia was not
a coincidence. That is not to say that Brooks Adams was directly responsible for that policy. The Secretary not only leaned
heavily on Rockhill for advice concerning China, but both of
them were strong Anglophiles who lent a ready ear to British
proposals to coöperate against Russia in the Far East.[18]

Most significant of all, of course, was the eager enthusiasm
with which American economic interests responded to the lure of
new markets in China. American capital, represented by the
American Trading Company, the Bethlehem Iron Works, the
Chase National Bank, other syndicates of American bankers, industrial corporations and railroads, and the American China Development Company began to move into Asia as early as
1895.[19] The latter organization was one of the first to cross
swords with the Russians, but of more immediate importance
was the pressure exerted on the State Department by the Pepperell Manufacturing Company of Boston, cotton textile exporters. Their petition of January, 1899 (endorsed by other business
interests and supported by Senator Lodge), requested action to

remove the "danger of being shut out from the markets of that portion of North China which is already occupied or threatened by Russia." A bit later the South Carolina mill owners declared that their "prosperity" depended "on the China trade." [20] This was the overseas economic expansion on which Brooks Adams based his analysis.

Yet these factors—vital as they were—do not fully explain the readiness with which Secretary Hay disregarded the advice of his representatives who warned that the English were America's "worst antagonists" in Asia and recommended that "our friendly relations with Russia should be enhanced." [21] Or, more significantly, his instructions to "act energetically" in behalf of those who signed the Pepperell petition.[22] It seems clear that he had been conditioned to an acceptance of Brooks Adams's broad analysis through his long and intimate association with Henry. Small wonder that Brooks Adams thought that "the only minister of foreign affairs in the whole world who grasped the situation was John Hay." [23] Nor did the influence of Brooks Adams decline in subsequent years.

Henry Adams, however, ultimately declined to support such vigorous expansion. True, for a time he thought "that the world has got to be run by us, or not at all"; but he soon changed his mind.[24] "I incline strongly now to anti-imperialism," he warned Brooks, "and very strongly to anti-militarism. . . . If we try to rule politically, we take the chances against us." [25] And as time went on, the old intimacy with Hay became "very awkward indeed," as Henry was "dead opposed to all his policy. . . . He is one wheel in the old machine of Hanna and Pierpont Morgan, and Root is the other." Not disposed to put his "fingers into the machinery," Henry Adams turned away to study the "dynamic theory of gases" and cultivate his "twelfth-century instincts." [26]

But Brooks—who thought Henry (like his grandfather) only "disappointed because he was not supernatural"—stepped up the tempo of his campaign to repeal *The Law.*[27]

After 1901, Brooks Adams exerted his influence more directly—as adviser to President Theodore Roosevelt. Their intimate relationship was founded on a common determination to disprove the validity of *The Law.* They shared an incidental friendship prior to 1885, but during the following ten years the men developed a warm understanding. When Brooks married the sister of Henry Cabot Lodge's wife in September, 1889, the friendship was further strengthened. A bit later, for example, Lodge and Brooks collaborated to organize the Commonwealth Club; and throughout the period, of course, Roosevelt was "always welcome" in the inner sanctum at 1603 H Street.[28] By 1895 Brooks and Roosevelt were not only cordial friends, but the latter was well acquainted with the thesis of *The Law.*

That such was the case need not be doubted, for early in November, 1896, Roosevelt acceded to Brooks's request to review the volume. Early that same spring, moreover, Roosevelt revealed that the study disturbed him considerably. He took particular care to advise Lodge that Gustave Le Bon was guilty of "fundamental errors . . . quite as vicious in their way as Brooks Adams's." Nor had he found solace in Le Bon's conclusions, which "contained a sweeping prophecy of evil quite as gloomy as Brooks's." [29] Roosevelt's review of *The Law* was written in the same vein.

"Few more powerful and . . . melancholy books have been written," declared Roosevelt; but though he picked at the thesis and its proof, his review is remarkable for its acceptance of much of Brooks's argument and phraseology. Friend Theodore considered Brooks "at his best in describing . . . the imaginative man whose energy manifests itself in the profession of arms." But TR, who had a "very firm faith" in the philosophy of steady progress, entered a strong dissent when Brooks denied that any individual or group could "influence the destiny of a race for good or bad." "All of us admit," Roosevelt conceded, "that it is very hard . . . but we do not think it is impossible." [30]

Other factors intensified Roosevelt's response to *The Law*. A practicing Social Darwinist, Roosevelt was also a close friend of Captain Alfred Thayer Mahan. And the Captain's theory of an industrial mercantilism enforced by control of the sea not only influenced TR considerably, but also supplemented the views of Brooks Adams. Likewise important is the fact that Roosevelt was a strong Anglophile. These aspects of Roosevelt's personality and thought help explain his ready response to Brooks Adams's ideas and friendship.[31]

Roosevelt was one of the first to whom Brooks Adams revealed his own concern with *The Law*. "The whole world," he admitted early in 1896, "seems to be rotting, rotting." But at an early date Brooks recognized that Roosevelt was the perfect medium through which to act, and he began to play on TR's admiration for the military. "You are an adventurer," he wrote, "and you have but one thing to sell—your sword." Brooks went on to point out that the essence of life was to live; and then bluntly challenged Roosevelt to join him in an assault upon *The Law*. "Why not live," he asked, "and be hired by a force which masters you, rather than be crushed in a corner to no purpose?" [32]

Roosevelt gave ready assent to Brooks's plan to re-emphasize the "martial man," who in turn would dominate the centralization and economic competition that threatened disintegration. "Peace is a goddess," TR declared in June, 1897, "only when she comes with sword girt on thigh." Later, when Roosevelt became Governor of New York, Brooks journeyed to Albany to warn TR of the dangers in militant trade-unionism and the eight-hour day. But neither of the men ever lost sight of the real goal—to repeal *The Law*. On that occasion, as Roosevelt advised Hay, they discussed the possibility of "heading some great outburst of the emotional classes which should at least temporarily crush the Economic Man." [33] That Brooks had also briefed TR on his full program became apparent shortly thereafter.

The following year (1900) Brooks Adams published his detailed plan to destroy *The Law*. Entitled *America's Economic Supremacy*, it was merely an expansion of the article in the *Fortnightly Review*. From a careful review of the concentration and disintegration of England's economic power, Brooks drew one major conclusion: expansion into Asia must be pressed. The obvious enemy was Russia ("the vast monster"), but if Japan should prevail "the situation would remain substantially unaltered." Nor did the means pose any serious problem. Martial man was to be reinvigorated, and the United States, concluded Brooks, must "reduce" Asia "to a part of [its] economic system." [34] That the book was either ignored or misunderstood (and sold but a few copies) was unimportant; for Theodore Roosevelt became President of the United States less than a year later.

Roosevelt had already given the public a preview of what was to come. Writing in the *Independent* of December 21, 1899 (a mere six months after Brooks's summer visit), TR announced that "on the border between civilization and barbarism war is generally normal." It naturally followed, argued Roosevelt, that only "the mighty civilized races which have not lost the fighting instinct" could, "by their expansion," gradually secure peace through the defeat of the "barbarians." With reference to the Pacific, moreover, Roosevelt was careful to note that "the great progressive colonizing nations are England and Germany." The inference was clear; doubly so since Brooks declared that Russia was "peopled by an archaic race." [35]

And Roosevelt's State-of-the-Nation message on December 3, 1901, must have sounded familiar to anyone who had read *The Law* and *America's Economic Supremacy.* TR stressed two themes: military might and the "permanent establishment of a wider market for American products." With reference to China, he declared, the latter meant "not merely the procurement of enlarged commercial opportunities on the coasts, but access to the interior." For a summary, the President merely paraphrased Brooks (by whom, he took care to acknowledge, it had "been well said") in a categorical warning. "The American people," Roosevelt admonished, "must either build and maintain an adequate navy or else make up their minds definitely to accept a secondary position in international affairs, not merely in political, but in commercial, matters." [36]

Despite such influence, Brooks Adams was impatient. Henry offered encouragement. "I rather incline," he wrote in April, 1902, "to suspect that, another year, your friend in the White House may feel more grateful for your support than in the years now passing, even if he is not more active in rewarding it. . . . Teddy's luck is not to be forgotten." [37] Brooks, of course, had not long to wait. Senators Henry Cabot Lodge and Jonathan P. Dolliver publicly acknowledged their debt to Brooks Adams and urged the public to support both economic expansion in Asia and opposition to Russia.[38] And Roosevelt soon gave his undivided attention to China—for Brooks "the great problem of the future." [39]

The Far East was "uppermost" in Roosevelt's mind and it was, moreover, the "corrupt, tricky, and inefficient" Russians (Brooks termed them "ignorant, uninventive, indolent, and im-

provident") who early "aroused and irritated him." [40] This open
and vigorous opposition to Russia, however, tends to obscure the
fact that "at no time" did TR favor Japan's complete ascen-
dancy. In the struggle between those two nations his plan—
in close harmony with Brooks's—was "to exhaust both
Russia and Japan" and thereby secure America's supremacy in
Asia.[41] But their undue emphasis on the Russian menace caused
Brooks and Theodore to lose the initiative to Japan.

Both men recognized their dilemma. What the Japanese
"will do to us hereafter," worried TR, "when intoxicated by
their victory over Russia, is another question." [42] Roosevelt was
also ready to stop the whole affair on another count. Both
Brooks Adams and TR's diplomatic trouble-shooter, businessman George von Lengerke Meyer (the President, in his growing
fear, had transferred him from Italy to St. Petersburg) warned
that a revolution in Russia would be disastrous no matter what
the final result.[43] A weakened Russia would further strengthen
Japan while a reinvigorated Russia might threaten the Manchurian claims of all the interested powers. Yet either possibility
seemed imminent as Tsarist bureaucracy began to crack under
the strain of war. Roosevelt confided his fear to some; to others
his problem was obvious.

Henry Adams, for one, was near hysteria lest his brother
("who runs about and instructs the great") would precipitate a
full-scale catastrophe. "We shall sink or swim" with the Tsar,
he cried, "half crazy" over the prospect of a revolution in Russia.[44] Roosevelt, too, was afraid. "I earnestly hope," he admitted
to Meyer, that "the Tsar will see that he must at all hazards
. . . make peace . . . and then turn his attention to internal
affairs." [45] But Henry was not encouraged. Theodore, in his
opinion, had "touched nothing which he has not deranged." It

was not so much his fault, however, as it was "the rotten old machinery of society." [46]

Brooks Adams still argued, however, that the machinery "must be made to run"; a notion to which Henry replied that Brooks "had better just make his own, and the public's mind run, for the trouble is here." [47] And finally, his patience exhausted, Henry charged Brooks with full responsibility. "All you can do," he thundered, "is vapor like Theodore about honesty! —Damn your honesty! And law!—Damn your law! And decency!—Damn your decency! From top to bottom the whole system is a fraud—all of us know it, laborers and capitalists alike—and all of us are consenting parties to it." [48]

Clearly, the plan to repeal *The Law* had gone awry. But Brooks Adams and Theodore Roosevelt struggled on. The United States would be safe, TR assured Lodge, "if the Navy was strengthened." But "if as Brooks Adams says, we show ourselves 'opulent, aggressive and unarmed,' " a disaster might well occur. This phrase seems to have been a Roosevelt favorite, for he had also used it in his message of December 3, 1901. And after a guarantee for the Philippines had been negotiated (the Taft-Katsura Memorandum of July 29, 1905), Roosevelt staged a great show of force. The intent behind his dispatch of the fleet on a world cruise is clear—TR thought it "time for a showdown." [49] That the Japanese reaction might be something less than awe seems never to have been considered.

Brooks Adams and Theodore Roosevelt confessed their temporary failure but never abandoned their effort to get the world on a down-hill pull. Both men blamed the public for their failure, saying that it lacked the strength to carry through.[50] But Henry Adams, among others, viewed the performance with grave misgivings. "I still see our Theodore," he confided to Elizabeth Cameron, "as before, in the guise of a rather droll Napoleon who thinks that the laws are not made for him." [51] And, in a moment of brilliant insight, he also rebuked Brooks. One of his own efforts, Henry found it necessary to explain to Brooks, was a joke; and then, almost as an afterthought, Henry added: "It can't help you in the least. Jokes never do." [52] For Brooks Adams, who thought his brother pathetic in that he was "disappointed because he was not supernatural," was even more so —Brooks thought himself to be just that.

American Intervention

in Russia,

1917–

1920

I. The Weltanschauungen of
American Policy Makers

Official American leaders significantly involved in making policy toward Russia in 1917 ranged from slightly left of center well over toward the right wing of the philosophical, ideological, economic, and political coalition known as the Progressive Movement. Some of them, like Robert Lansing, had been initially appointed to government service by Republican presidents. Others, such as Ambassador to Russia David Roland Francis, were men of established influence in the Democratic Party. As a group, however, they were either members of, or served as advisors and administrators for, the upper strata of the American political economy.

Basil Miles and Frank Polk were the members of the State Department general staff who exercised some influence on Russian policy during the first years of the Bolshevik Revolution. Miles had made a career of Russia. He served first as personal secretary to businessman George von Lengerke Meyer while the latter was Ambassador to Russia under President Theodore Roosevelt, and then stayed on as Third Secretary of the embassy until May 1907. He then resigned to become head of the Washington, D.C. office of the United States Chamber of Commerce. He returned to Russia, appropriately enough, as special assistant to Ambassador Francis, whose first objective was to negotiate a new trade treaty. Then, later in 1917, he was recalled to Washington to become the Department's resident expert on Russian affairs. His anti-Bolshevik attitude appeared immediately in November 1917, and never changed. "My view has not changed since 1917," he once reminded Lansing; "that we should support any reputable and sound elements of order wherever they may be found." [1] Should there be any doubt, the phrase "reputable and sound elements of order" was the chief euphemism of the time for anti-Bolshevik forces.

Frank Polk was more of a late-comer to the official scene whose career began with his study of the law at Yale and Columbia. His abilities and connections helped him move rapidly toward the top in that key profession, and in the Democratic Party organization of New York State. President Woodrow Wilson brought him into the Department of State as counselor when Lansing became Secretary upon the resignation of William Jennings Bryan in 1915. Together with Miles, Polk drafted many of the routine dispatches concerning Russia; and, on his own, enjoyed access to private and informal discussions with Wilson and Lansing. He, too, was anti-Bolshevik, and often exerted his influence for a more vigorous and direct expression of that policy.

Maddin Summers, the American Consul General in Russia, was the most influential career man involved in the day-to-day events of the Russian Revolution. He had been a foreign service officer since 1899. Detailed to Russia in 1916 after a long tour of duty in Latin America, he soon thereafter married the daughter of a Russian noble. His own conservative ideological outlook was intensified, and given an emotional edge, by the effects of

Bolshevik policies on the wealth, position, and personal style of life of his wife's family. He was confident that "communism cannot find a place in modern times," and did his best to prevent himself from being proved wrong in Russia.[2] Ambassador Francis said it all in his observation that Summers "bitterly hates Bolsheviks." [3]

The Ambassador himself was a self-made wealthy Missouri businessman who had also acquired considerable political influence. From humble origins, he had become a millionaire by the mid-1890's through his activities as a grain merchant, banker, and railroad investor. One of his remarks to Albert W. Klieforth, another member of the State Department group in Russia, beautifully captures Francis's own conception of himself. "I sold newspapers as a boy in Kentucky; I made a fortune later in life; I was Mayor of St. Louis and governor of Missouri; I was a member of Cleveland's cabinet; and I was the president of the St. Louis Fair."

Francis had served as Secretary of the Interior under President Grover Cleveland, and his loyalty to the principles of the Gold Democrats cost him dearly in Missouri and national politics when Bryan took over the party. Wilson discriminated less against such economic orthodoxy, and first offered Francis the post as Ambassador to Argentina. Francis declined the job, but made a strong impression on the President during an interview at the White House. Then, when the President began his search for the right man to negotiate a new trade treaty with Russia, Wilson turned immediately to Francis. This time Francis accepted. He vigorously supported overseas economic expansion, and ultimately became very critical of the House of Morgan for its policy of working through British connections instead of undertaking independent operations in Russia.

Francis enjoyed his poker, and other manly pleasures, and

he was getting on in years, but he was neither as incompetent nor as senile as he has sometimes been pictured. He was actually a shrewd Missouri conservative politician who saw the Bolsheviks for what they were—radical social revolutionaries. He told Lansing as early as May 21, 1917, for example, that they advocated "extreme socialist" measures.[4] He opposed them for that reason, and did his best to weaken, disrupt, and replace their authority in Russia.

Ambassador to Japan Roland Morris and Minister to China Paul S. Reinsch played contributory roles in the evolution of American intervention. Both men were anti-Bolshevik on philosophical grounds, and because they saw the radicals as a direct and indirect threat to the development of American economic and political influence in the Far East under the general strategy of the Open Door Policy. Wilson and Lansing valued their reports and advice, and relied upon their analyses in developing a way of intervening against the Bolsheviks without at the same time giving Japan an opportunity to extend and consolidate its position on the mainland of Asia.

Reinsch's most important activities in the development of intervention involved his part in the early decision to support Chinese military operations against the Bolsheviks at Harbin, Manchuria, and his later analysis of the conflict between Bolshevik and Czecho-Slovakian forces in Siberia which provided Wilson with the central idea for a tactical approach to intervention.[5] For his part, Morris provided extensive reports and warnings about Japanese policy and action, analyzed the progress of the Revolution as it developed in Siberia, and later undertook special investigations for Wilson concerning the character and strength of various anti-Bolshevik forces.[6]

Though both men enjoyed firm personal standing with Wilson, they were not of course as important or as influential as

Secretary of State Lansing. Eastern urban upper-class by birth and education, Lansing evolved in a family tradition of corporation lawyers who became influential in government affairs that had been initiated by John W. Foster, and which later produced Allen W. and John Foster Dulles. Like a good many other Wilson appointments, Lansing was a Cleveland rather than a Bryan Democrat, and in religion a conservative Presbyterian who often read the Bible late into the night after completing his official and social duties.

Lansing's ideology and politics involved a conservative adaptation of classic 19th century liberalism to the realities of 20th century industrialism. He believed in democracy, and considered its extension throughout the world as the key to prosperity and peace. The democracy itself was defined in terms of individualism and private property. He understood that the government had to accept more responsibility for planning and directing the political economy during a war, but he worried a good deal about the consequences.

A close lawyer friend wrote Lansing in December 1917, as the Secretary was helping make key decisions toward the Bolshevik Revolution, to commiserate about the dangerous drift of affairs in the United States itself, and Lansing's reply offers a valuable insight into the basis of his opposition to the Revolution. "The whole tendency of the government is socialistic," the confidant fretted; "we may become measurably in the condition of Russia." In a "private and confidential" reply, Lansing was sympathetic. "From our discussions years ago on political principles, you know that by conviction I am an individualist rather than a nationalist (that is, in my opinion, a luke-warm socialist) and am naturally disposed to support individualism as the paramount principle in our national life." [7] Concerned as he was by the "centralization of power and control of business" in Amer-

ica, Lansing nevertheless accepted and sought to work within
the new institutional framework being established by the convergence of the corporation and the national government. He
was far less inclined to compromise, however, in dealing with
the Bolsheviks.

Though not as extreme or grandiose in his rhetoric as either
Reinsch or Wilson, Lansing firmly accepted both the necessity
and the morality of American overseas economic expansion.
Thus he sought in his diplomacy to "reaffirm explicitly the principle of the 'Open Door'." [8] Lansing's generally more cautious approach, and his less moralistic and crusading temperament, did
serve to limit intimate, personal collaboration with Wilson. Ultimately, of course, it led to an open break. But that final rupture should not be interpreted to mean that they were constantly at odds with each other, or that Wilson ignored
Lansing's policy advice.

Thus, on the eve of the Russian Revolution, and as the
United States was preparing to enter the war, Lansing was engaged in helping Wilson tighten-up the President's early formulation of the essentials in a post-war settlement. A deep and fundamental concern for overseas economic expansion was apparent
in the thinking of both men. Wilson's short outline of February
7, 1917, concerning the crucial points in any peace program,
laid particular emphasis on freedom of the seas, territorial guarantees, and security for trade expansion—"equal opportunities
of trade with the rest of the world."

In reply, Lansing offered two keen suggestions. Instead of a
vague treaty involving the principle of the open door, he proposed a very specific "mutual agreement not to form any international combination or conspiracy to interfere with the commercial enterprises or to limit the equal trade opportunities of

any nation." The secretary was equally upset by the implications of Wilson's moratorium on territorial changes and expansion. He wanted to leave the way open for expansion "as a result of increased population or an accumulation of capital desiring investment in territory under national control." Wilson saw the point. He changed his formulation so that it opened the door for "natural expansion peaceably accomplished." [9]

As this episode indicates, Wilson's moralism did not exclude an early, persistent, and hard-headed concern for America's overseas economic expansion. This emphasis was not surprising in view of his assumptions that "society is an organism," and that "we have not a large enough market or the means of disposing of the surplus product"—"Our domestic markets no longer suffice. We need foreign markets." [10] Amplifying and projecting his axiom that society was "an organism," Wilson argued that business "is the foundation of every other relationship, particularly of the political relationship." Since "the organic cooperation of the parts is the only basis for just Government," it followed that "the question of statesmanship is a question of taking all the economic interests of every part of the country into the reckoning. Just so soon as the business of this country has general, free, welcome access to the councils of Congress," he concluded, "all the friction between business and politics will disappear." [11]

"If America is not to have free enterprise," Wilson stated flatly, "then she can have freedom of no sort whatever." [12] The integration of economic and political freedom in an organic whole was the ideal to be realized, and Wilson viewed the office of the President as the agency of such integration, and the overseas economic expansion of the American system as a crucial means of achieving that goal. He was deeply impressed by Frederick Jackson Turner's frontier thesis as an explanation of

America's past prosperity and democracy, and took it over as a guide for policy to maintain those desirable conditions. Having entered upon the course of commercial empire after the closing of the frontier, Wilson saw the United States inexorably involved in a struggle to "command the economic fortunes of the world." The prize was control of the overseas market to soak up the surpluses—"the market to which diplomacy, and if need be power, must make an open way." [13]

"It is evident," he concluded in 1901, "that empire is an affair of strong government." [14] Then, as he began his campaign for the presidential nomination in 1912, he noted that this had become particularly true "now that we see some possibility of flinging our own flag out upon the seas again and taking possession of our rightful share of the trade of the world." [15] He amplified the argument in his speech accepting the nomination. "Our industries have expanded to such a point that they will burst their jackets if they cannot find a free outlet to the markets of the world." If elected, Wilson promised to do his utmost to see that the United States attained its "deserved supremacy in the markets and enterprises of the world." [16] "The Government," he added in December 1919, "must open these gates of trade, and open them wide; open them before it is altogether profitable to open them, or altogether reasonable to ask private capital to open them at a venture." [17]

As though in microscopic illustration of his macroscopic theory about society as an organism, Wilson's economic ideas were integrated with his political ideology, and with his moral views and moralistic temperament. Expansion which produced well-being and constitutional government for its practitioners was by definition moral. The more so, indeed, because it carried the same benefits to others. Americans were thus the "custodians of the spirit of righteousness, of the spirit of equal-handed justice." [18] Wilson was candidly prejudiced in favor of "those who act in the interest of peace and honor, who protect private rights, and respect the restraints of constitutional provisions." [19] This inclined him strongly against helping those who "show that they do not understand constitutional processes." [20] Yet his Christianity, and the demands of American foreign policy as he defined them, made it extremely difficult for Wilson actually to dismiss any society from any and all consideration. But the competing demands of Christian ethics and national expansion created tremendous moral tension, and Wilson's commitment to the principle of self-determination served only to intensify the dilemma.

His basic approach to resolving the conflict is of central importance to any understanding of his ultimate decision to intervene in Russia. "When properly directed," he noted, "there is no people not fitted for self-government." [21] Such being the case, the role of the United States was to discipline, educate, and guide the laggards and the mistaken. Wilson thus set about to "teach the South American republics to elect good men," and to use the power of the United States to establish a government in Mexico "under which all contracts and business and concessions will be safer than they have been." [22]

This integrated moral and economic expansionism provides the root explanation of Wilson's extensive political, economic, and military intervention in various Caribbean countries (Haiti, Nicaragua, and the Dominican Republic), and in the Mexican Revolution. Paradoxically, it also was the basis of his decision in 1913 to forego open and vigorous support for the American bankers involved in the reorganization loan to China. Wilson wanted to return to a pure version of the Open Door Policy under which Americans would act independently for their own and Chinese benefit.

Simultaneously with his refusal to back the bankers, therefore, the President acted to push American penetration of China. The government and the private entrepreneurs, he explained to American officials who might have misunderstood his earlier action, "certainly wish to participate, and participate very generously, in the opening to the Chinese and to the use of the world the almost untouched and perhaps unrivalled resources of China." He went on to "urge and support" such activity, and promised government assistance in providing "the banking and other financial facilities which they now lack and without which they are at a serious disadvantage." [23]

This determination to participate in "the economic development of China" prompted the Wilson Administration to move firmly (if in the beginning somewhat deliberately) against Japan's threat in 1915 to establish extensive control over China. Wilson not only expressed "grave concern" over the specific challenge, but candidly and forcefully spoke of his commitment in the basic issue of "the maintenance of the policy of an Open Door to the world." [24] This explicit and unqualified statement of his foreign policy strategy goes far beyond explaining Wilson's response to Japan's Twenty-One Demands. It provides the central definition of his diplomacy, and reveals the underlying nature of his conception of the League of Nations. That institution was in his mind, and from the very beginning, conceived and designed to establish and guarantee the principle of the Open Door Policy as the basis of international relations.

Given the nature of his integration of morality, politics, and economics around the Open Door Policy, Wilson's opposition to revolutions becomes quite comprehensible. Such social upheavals were immoral disruptions of America's program. The President's thought, concludes Professor Harley Notter, "disclosed itself as anti-pathetic to unsettled political conduct and to revolution as a method of government." Nor was there any question concerning Wilson's position on socialism. He analyzed it as "either utterly vague or entirely impracticable." His conclusion was unequivocal. "I do not believe in the programme of socialism." The danger it posed, however, could "be overcome only by wiser and better programmes, and this is our duty as patriotic citizens." [25]

Anti-socialism was thus defined as an essential component of American patriotism. But such an approach did not really resolve the contradiction and dilemma in Wilson's integrated liberal outlook. It only served to infuse one casuist solution with the emotions of nationalism. For, by the logic of the *principles* he avowed, Wilson was bound to accept and tolerate socialism as a legitimate expression of self-determination and as a respectable Christian heresy. By those principles, therefore, his commitment to American free-enterprise expansion as the engine of general peace and prosperity, and of political and moral salvation for mankind, had to be restrained in the face of socialist efforts to accomplish the same objectives. By defining anti-socialism as a manifestation of patriotism, however, Wilson distorted the Christian and liberal doctrine of the right of self-defense into a justification of—if not a rallying cry for—militant and righteous opposition to socialism. As will be seen, Wilson's personal understanding of this conflict defines the tragic core of the whole story of American intervention in Russia.

This review of the outlooks of the key officials involved in making American policy toward the Bolshevik Revolution suggests several further generalizations. First, none of them were naive or innocent. They very seldom blundered into either success or failure. Many more times than not they won because

they shrewdly picked their spots and deployed their power effectively; and when they lost it was because they were bested in
tough competition in the course of which they gave almost as
good as they took. All of them, furthermore, had extended experience in business and politics, and many of them had participated in the demanding labor of thinking inclusively and inci-
sively about those matters. They were also men who had to
come to terms with—and practiced—the kind of routine
casuistry that often seems to be inherent in the conduct of big
business, big law, domestic politics, and diplomacy. They were
not dishonest in the usual meaning of that term, and they were
not hypocrites. They were simply powerful and influential men
of this world who had concluded, from hard experience and
close observation, that all of the truth all of the time was almost
always dangerous. Hence they did not use all of the truth all of
the time.

Secondly, these American decision-makers viewed economics
as of extremely great, if not of literally primary, importance in
the dynamic operation of the American system. This does not
mean that they were motivated by personal pocketbook considerations. It means that they thought about economics in a *national* sense; as an absolutely crucial variable in the functioning
of the system per se, and as the foundation for constitutional
government and a moral society. And all of them viewed overseas economic expansion as essential to the continued successful
operation of the American free-enterprise system.

Finally, these men shared a central conviction that the good
society—and the good world—were defined by the forms
and the substance of Western Civilization as they had manifested themselves in the United States at the hour of the Bolshevik Revolution. Some were conservatives concerned to preserve
aspects of the status quo that they considered particularly valu-

able. Others were reformers more interested in improving the existing order. But all of them shared a fundamental belief in, and a commitment to, the established system. This is by no means surprising, but an explicit awareness of it is essential to understanding their policy toward the Bolshevik Revolution.

II. The Crucial Decision of Principle

The Bolshevik Revolution challenged American leaders, both as individuals and as a group, in many central areas of their beliefs, ideas, and objectives. And they knew it—every one. Inherently and explicitly opposed to the Revolution, they found themselves in a veritable thicket of dilemmas as they approached the broad policy problem. These difficulties can be summarized as follows:

How was it possible to oppose the Bolsheviks effectively and yet—
1. not compromise their own moral values and ideological precepts?
2. not risk the successful conduct of the war against Germany?
3. not allow Japan to establish itself in a position from which it could bolt and bar the open door in China?
4. and not unite other Russians behind the Bolsheviks?

Such was the problem. It was an extremely difficult one, and there should be no surprise that Lansing was occasionally depressed, or that Wilson repeatedly complained about "sweating blood" over the Russian question.

American leaders were not totally unprepared for the Bol-

shevik coup on November 7, 1917. Francis and others had described the Bolsheviks as radicals, and had kept Washington relatively well-informed of their activities throughout the summer
and early autumn. And everyone was aware that the general
Russian situation had become increasingly unstable.

Lansing gave considerable thought to the dangers of the situation on August 8, 1917. He knew of "the strong opposition
developing against" the Kerensky Government, and was hence
"very skeptical" of the Premier's chances to survive as the leader
of the general Russian Revolution. The revolution, Lansing concluded, was a fundamental one, and would therefore go through
what he considered to be the usual historical cycle of such upheavals: "First, Moderation. Second, Terrorism. Third, Revolt
against the New Tyranny and restoration of order by arbitrary
military power." For the moment, at any rate, the situation was
"demoralized." That meant, at least to the Secretary, that the
United States "should therefore prepare for the time when Russia will no longer be a military factor in the war," and await
the opportunity to act during the third stage of the revolution.[26]

This conclusion was reinforced by a memorandum on war
strategy that Lansing received in October. The Army War College discounted any possibility of "action through Russia." Routine logistics difficulties and the classic admonition against di-
viding one's forces explained part of the decision. More
important was the judgment that "the invasion of Russia is, in
itself, not a definite objective on the part of Germany." The
issue "will be settled on the Western Front." In addition, "certain political considerations render advisable the presence of English troops in Mesopotamia and in Egypt, and of French and
Italian troops in Greece." Hence it would be difficult to muster
an effective force for action in Russia. And finally, and perhaps
as important as any reason in the minds of those who made the

decision, "the English and the French, rather than the Russians, are our natural allies." [27]

On November 7, the day the Bolsheviks took power, Lansing was giving serious attention to a dispatch from Consul Summers. Having apparently given up on Kerensky even before he was finally toppled, Summers was casting about for acceptable and reliable replacements. He was concerned for "all classes of Russians standing for law and order." Lansing was alerted by the warning, and sent it on to Secretary of War Newton D. Baker with a covering letter that reinforced the consul's report.[28] This episode indicates the early date at which Americans were concerned with strengthening conservative elements in Russia, but some of the most revealing evidence about the immediate reaction of American leaders to the triumph of the Bolsheviks was provided by reporters of *The New York Times.*

It was "thought certain," one of them learned after a Cabinet meeting of November 9, that the United States and its Allies would recognize and extend aid to the anti-Bolshevik forces. One official said the Bolsheviks would be treated as "international outcasts." And another noted, in an amazing preview of what ultimately happened, that Vladivostok would probably be used as the main base for operations against the Bolsheviks.[29] On the next day, moreover, the reporter was told that it was "a logical deduction" that aid shipments to Russia would be stopped until the Bolsheviks were overthrown.[30] In this case, in any event, the logic pointed the way toward policy and the assistance was terminated.

President Wilson's speech to the annual convention of the American Federation of Labor on November 12 provided the next public clue to administration thinking and policy. His broad theme was the need to strengthen and accelerate the war effort, and he specifically wanted labor to buckle down and produce mountains of arms and other supplies. Radicals who fomented labor unrest were troublesome enough, but radicals who wanted to end the war before Germany was overwhelmed were particularly dangerous. The President explicitly mentioned the Bolsheviks in this connection and called them "ill-informed." Then he smeared American pacifists (and other critics of the war) by the demagogic device of describing them as being "as fatuous as the dreamers of Russia." [31] There would seem little reason to speculate about Wilson's early attitude toward the Bolsheviks. He was antagonistic.

Intervention as a consciously anti-Bolshevik operation was decided upon by American leaders within five weeks of the day Lenin and Trotsky took power. On November 19, for example, Ambassador Francis appealed publicly to the Russian people to "remove the difficulties that beset your path." [32] A week later Summers warned Lansing that, true to their radical socialism, the Bolsheviks were "inciting the Proletariat against law-abiding citizens." Action was imperative: "strongly advise . . . protest against present regime." [33] And on December 1, 1917, the Inter-Allied Conference in Paris began a three-day discussion of intervention in Siberia as a means of keeping the supply lines open to anti-Bolshevik forces organizing in southern Russia.

At this juncture, when overt anti-Bolshevism was clearly on the rise, the British made a suggestion which became the basis of the grand strategy of talking about action against the Bolsheviks in terms of something else. London warned on November 22 that "any overt step taken against the Bolsheviks might only strengthen their determination to make peace, and might be used to influence anti-Allied feeling in Russia, and so defeat the very object we were aiming at." [34] Colonel Edward House, one of the most influential advisors in Wilson's personal entourage, agreed with this strategy. He was specifically upset and worried about the consequences of various straightforward anti-Bolshevik remarks in the United States, and other attacks on the revolutionaries as enemies. He therefore advised Wilson and Lansing on November 28 to change the form of expressing such sentiments. "It is exceedingly important," he explained, "that such criticisms should be suppressed. It will throw Russia into the lap of Germany if the Allies and ourselves express such views at this time." 35

These developments serve to raise the general question of the interrelationship between the fighting of the war and the evolution of intervention against the Bolsheviks. More precisely defined, the issue concerns the way the commitment to defeating Germany affected American policy toward the Bolsheviks. It is true, of course, that the war against Germany limited the number of troops that the United States (and the other Allies involved in combat in Europe) could deploy for direct intervention. And America's top military commanders consistently opposed intervention because it would weaken the Western Front.

But the crucial point is that President Wilson overruled this purely military argument once he decided to intervene. He did so, moreover, in the late spring and early summer of 1918, at a time when American forces were being committed against the big German push as a preliminary to a major counter-offensive. It can hardly be over-emphasized, indeed, that Wilson made the decision to intervene in Russia with American troops *before* the Germans were stopped in the Second Battle of the Marne (July 18–August 6, 1918).

It is also undeniable that the Allies and the United States wanted to sustain military pressure on the Germans from the

East. To this end they had exerted heavy influence on the Kerensky Government right up to the hour of its collapse. But the leaders of the United States persistently refused to seek that objective through even short-run collaboration with the Bolsheviks. In this sense, and it is an important one, a strategic objective of the war took second priority behind strategic opposition to the Bolsheviks.

It should be clear that neither the British nor Colonel House were attacking, or suggesting a change in, the policy of opposition to the Bolsheviks. The advice was to suppress—to knowingly hide—the fact that the policy was anti-Bolshevik because general awareness of that fact could cause grave consequences. Furthermore, the Bolsheviks were treated as revolutionaries. There was no assumption, implication, or assertion that they were agents of the Imperial German Government. Colonel House and the others were simply afraid that open opposition might *drive* the Bolsheviks into some kind of a bargain with the Germans.

Lansing saw the point of this argument and momentarily agreed with the advice. But nobody giving the advice offered any concrete suggestion as to a different mode of referring to the Bolsheviks in public. Lansing solved the problem in a very natural way. He began to talk about the Bolsheviks in terms of "German intrigue." [36] As his diary reveals, however, Lansing did not actually think that the Bolsheviks were literally German agents. In one sense, he was merely using the possible danger as a weapon to forestall its realization. In another, the psychological, he was projecting the fear about what the Bolsheviks might do in response to American action as a description of what the Bolsheviks were in fact doing—a description that provided a legitimate basis for American action. This was perhaps the first instance of such behavior in American-Soviet relations, but it certainly was not the last.

This approach led American officials into the confusing practice of using two sets of terminology with reference to the Bolsheviks—they were "German agents" in public discourse and "dangerous social revolutionaries" in private discussions. American leaders also tended to see the Bolsheviks as men who indirectly furthered German purposes, at least when considered within the framework of the war, and sometimes talked of them in those terms. But they never abandoned their basic definition of the Bolsheviks as radical revolutionaries.

For that matter, Lansing very quickly began to question the wisdom of the advice from House and the British. He really preferred to attack the Bolsheviks publicly for the real reasons they were being opposed, and thereby bring the basic issue out into the open. Sometime between December 2 and 4 (and probably on the 3rd), he prepared a long memorandum stating the basis of American anti-Bolshevism. It contained no nonsense about Lenin and Trotsky as agents of German intrigue. They were defined and discussed as radical socialist revolutionaries bent upon a general revolution in keeping with their beliefs. As far as Lansing was concerned, therefore, they could be understood and dealt with only in terms of "a determination, frankly avowed, to overthrow all existing governments and establish on the ruins a despotism of the proletariat in every country." Including Germany.

Hence it was "unwise to give recognition to Lenin, Trotsky and their crew of radicals." The United States was dedicated to "the principle of democracy and to a special order based on liberty." The Bolsheviks openly challenged that unique system and should be dealt with accordingly. The first step, Lansing argued, was to prepare and issue a ringing public declaration of opposition and follow through with an announcement that the Bolshevik government would not be recognized.[37]

Lansing carried his argument to Wilson on December 4. According to the Secretary, Wilson "did not think it was opportune to make a public declaration of this sort at the time it was suggested. He nevertheless approved in principle the position I had taken and directed that our dealings with Russia and our treatment of the Russian situation be conducted along those lines." Ray Stannard Baker, one of Wilson's intimate associates and his official biographer, supports Lansing's account.[38] So do subsequent developments. On December 6, for example, Lansing advised Francis (and other American officials abroad) that "the President desires American representatives withhold all direct communication with Bolshevik Government." [39]

Some commentators, most notably George Frost Kennan, have explained Wilson's refusal to act on Lansing's request by referring to the President's speech of that day (December 4) asking the Congress to declare war on Austria-Hungary. Kennan's argument is that Wilson did not want to blunt the impact of that performance. There is some point to this comment, but the President could have made such a statement on Russia in a few days. The reason he did not do so is very probably bound up in the way that Wilson had followed House's advice in referring to Russia in the war message. He called the Bolsheviks "masters of German intrigue" who "lead the people of Russia astray." [40]

It seems very likely that Wilson had reacted favorably to the suggestion from House because it offered him a way to ease the very pressing contradiction and dilemma in his ideology. The Bolshevik Revolution caught Wilson between two central axioms of his outlook, and the resulting pressure must have been very severe and painful. On the one hand, he fundamentally opposed socialism. On the other hand, he avowedly "stood resolutely and absolutely for the right of every people to determine its own destiny and its own affairs." [41]

By referring to the Bolsheviks as German agents, however, the President could define the issue of self-determination in a way that excluded the program of the Bolsheviks. He thereby categorized the Bolsheviks as instruments of external influence rather than as agents of internal revolution. Wilson could thus oppose the Bolsheviks on the grounds of their having violated the right of self-determination instead of having to acquiesce in—or even assist—their efforts to determine Russia's "own destiny and its own affairs."

But such public rhetoric did not serve to change the facts —or to resolve the real dilemma. There is persuasive evidence to indicate, moreover, that Wilson knew this as well as, if not better than, anyone else. As he admitted to Lincoln Colcord on December 6, for example, the great bulk of the information reaching him defined the Bolsheviks as radical social revolutionaries rather than as German agents.[42] And his next action was predicated upon that knowledge, and upon his estimate that such radicalism threatened vital American interests in the Far East.

This decision was a response to Bolshevik agitation in Harbin, Manchuria, which served as the headquarters for the joint Russo-Chinese management of the Chinese Eastern Railway. The United States had been involved, ever since 1905, in a struggle with Japan for predominant influence over that railroad and the associated opportunities for trade and investment in Manchuria and China. And it seemed, at the time of the Bolshevik Revolution, that America would succeed in reasserting the kind of influence it had enjoyed in that area prior to the Russo-Japanese War.

This opportunity to consolidate the traditional strategy of the Open Door Policy was threatened when the Bolsheviks challenged the authority of the existing Russian manager of the Chinese Eastern, General Dmitri L. Horvat, who was a man amenable to American influence. The first warning went from the American consul in Harbin to Reinsch in China.[43] Three weeks later the developments had verified the storm signal. "Situation Harbin serious," Reinsch cabled Lansing. "General Horvat ready to conduct joint administration with Bolsheviks." Reinsch then advised support for a plan to send Chinese troops to counter the Bolshevik pressure. That would block the radicals and also prevent Japan from moving in with troops and thereby threatening the American position.[44]

Actually, of course, the Bolsheviks had a legitimate claim to control or replace Horvat. He was the Russian representative on the railroad board under the terms of a Russo-Chinese treaty. A new government in Russia (or China) had a legal right to exercise its authority under the terms of that agreement. With some reason, however, Reinsch and his superiors feared that Bolshevik participation in the management of the railroad might conflict with the realization of American objectives under the Open Door Policy.

Wilson and Lansing approved the basic idea of denying treaty rights to the Bolsheviks. Their only concern was that China might fail in the specific operation, or initiate general military operations, and thereby give the Japanese an excuse to march in as the saviors of the Chinese Eastern. Hence they offered a strong warning against allowing the Chinese to open any military action they could not handle. All went well. By the end of the month, Reinsch (who had referred to the Bolsheviks as "revolutionaries" throughout the crisis) reported that the Chinese had deployed over 3,000 men and that the operation was a success. The Bolsheviks were checked, and Harbin became a center of anti-Bolshevik intrigue.[45]

By that time, Lansing and Wilson had worked out the basic strategy of American intervention against the Bolsheviks. On December 7, as he considered the crisis in Harbin, Lansing again reviewed the general Russian situation.[46] The Bolsheviks represented "a despotism of the proletariat." Thus "the correct policy for a government which believes in political institutions as they now exist and based on nationality and private property is to leave these dangerous idealists alone and have no direct dealings with them." The Bolsheviks, he judged, "are wanting in international virtue." They sought "to make the ignorant and incapable mass of humanity dominant in the earth." For such reasons, he discounted the rumors that they were German agents: "I cannot make that belief harmonize with some things they have done."

Lansing then evaluated the existing situation in the light of his general theory that revolutions progressed through three phases: "First, Moderation. Second, Terrorism. Third, Revolt against the New Tyranny and restoration of order by arbitrary military power." The Bolsheviks represented the second, "black period of terrorism" of the general Russian Revolution which had started in March 1917, while Generals Alexeev and Kaledin were the chief candidates "for a strong, commanding personality to arise . . . gather a disciplined military force . . . restore order and maintain a government" which could carry Russia on into the post-Revolutionary era.

Lansing's urge to act in line with this analysis was shortly reinforced by advice from two men whose views he respected. First, during regular working hours on December 9, he received a report from Summers reviewing a long discussion of the anti-Bolshevik problem that the Consul had held with a close associate of Generals Alexeev and Kaledin. Summers was convinced that they had strength "sufficient to reestablish order" if they received official encouragement and material support from the United States and its allies. He strongly recommended such assistance.[47] Then, after supper, Lansing had a long discussion of the situation with Major Stanley Washburn. The major reinforced the Consul. Their combined effect was to convince Lansing that there was a chance to accelerate affairs in Russia into phase three of the revolution.

On the following morning of December 10, therefore, Lansing proposed such action to Wilson. The Secretary's operational plan involved breaking "Bolshevik domination" by supporting "a military dictatorship backed by loyal disciplined troops." Following the advice of Summers (which he sent along to Wilson), Lansing cast his vote for Kaledin. The "only apparent nucleus for an organized movement sufficiently strong to supplant the Bolsheviki and establish a government would seem to be the group of general officers with General Kaledin." He would "in all probability obtain the support of the Cadets and of all the *bourgeoisie* and the land-owning class." "Nothing is to be gained by inaction," Lansing concluded, "that is simply playing into the Bolsheviki's hands . . . I do not see how we could be any worse off if we took this course because we have absolutely nothing to hope from continued Bolshevik domination." [48]

Wilson responded favorably. He spent an hour and twenty minutes discussing the proposal with Lansing on the night of December 11. The Secretary's diary tells the story: "went over the Russian situation particularly strength of Kaledin movement." [49] They decided to aid the anti-Bolshevik forces, and the next day Lansing asked for clearance on the financial side from Secretary of the Treasury William G. McAdoo. The money was available: "This is O.K. so far as I am concerned." [50] The President, who wanted action "immediately," quickly authorized the operation: "This has my entire approval." [51]

As should be apparent from the language of American policy-makers, this decision to intervene was based on their opposition to the radical nature of the Bolshevik Revolution. The *strategy,* that is to say, was anti-revolutionary. Any opposition movement, Lansing explained in his action dispatch, "should be encouraged even though its success is only a possibility." [52] The decision to intervene, as even Kennan has acknowledged, was "a major decision of principle." [53]

Lansing was not able, however, to persuade Wilson to oppose the Bolsheviks openly on the fundamental issue of their radicalism. As a result, the *rhetorical tactics* of intervention followed the suggestions offered at the end of November by House and the British. The operation was to be kept secret, and was cast in the idiom of strengthening the Eastern Front against Germany.[54]

But this tactic of intervention should not lead to confusion about the strategic grounds on which the decision was based. To ask whether the intervention was not *really* anti-German or anti-Japanese is to misconceive the nature of the problem. Action through Russia aimed at Germany or designed to check the Japanese in the Far East—or both—could have been formulated and implemented through cooperation or collaboration with the Bolsheviks. American leaders were aware of that option and upon occasion skittishly considered it as a basis for policy. But they always rejected it on the grounds that opposition to the Bolsheviks claimed first priority. Anti-Bolshevism was the central causative and determining element in American intervention in Russia, an intervention which was in principle decided upon between December 10 and 12, 1917.

III. *Validating the Decision to Intervene*

Various Americans raised fundamental questions about the policy of opposing the Bolsheviks. Two of the most significant and influential of these critics based their opposition on their experiences in Russia. One was Colonel William V. Judson, the American military attaché. The other was Raymond Robins, a devoted midwestern follower of Theodore Roosevelt who had gone to Russia as the Rough Rider's personal selection on the Red Cross mission to supply non-military aid—and political advice and support—to the Kerensky Government. Robins later became head of the mission and quickly established himself as a quasi-official liaison man between the United States and the Bolsheviks.

Robins and Judson were convinced that America's central objectives—the defeat of Germany and a long-range strategic relationship with Russia—depended upon recognizing and supporting the Bolsheviks. Neither man was a radical or what in later years came to be called a fellow-traveler. But they did understand the scope of the revolution, they did correctly estimate the odds in favor of the Bolsheviks retaining power, and they did realize that the Bolsheviks were inclined, as their difficulties became increasingly serious, to turn to the United States for aid. Robins and Judson wanted to exploit the opportunity thus offered to achieve immediate and future benefits.

Judson had personal discussions with Francis concerning policy matters; and, through various official channels and the influence of his friend Postmaster General Albert Burleson, his ideas also came directly to the attention of Lansing and Wilson.

Robins talked policy with Francis almost every day, and his views and suggestions entered the State Department and the White House through that channel as well as through the efforts of his many personal and political friends in New York and Washington.

Both men knew of the plan to aid Kaledin and opposed it vigorously. Judson warned on December 17 that it "would be absolutely futile and ill-advised." The Bolsheviks were not German agents, and they realized that their revolution was mortally threatened by German ambitions in Russia. Hence the proper and effective strategy was to support the Bolsheviks against the Germans.[55] Combined with similar arguments advanced by Robins, Judson's efforts led Francis to offer to modify his own anti-Bolshevik position.

It is probably impossible to establish with full certainty the precise meaning of this offer by Francis. He later maintained that he was playing a double game all along, intending to strengthen the Red Army only to turn it against the Bolsheviks.[56] That may have been the case. He may, however, have simply been maneuvering to provoke a strong reply from Washington that would serve to put a check-rein on Robins and Judson. It is also possible that he was entirely serious, if only temporarily so, in his doubts about the official line. In any event, he advised Lansing on December 24 that "Bolshevik power is undoubtedly greatest in Russia." For this reason, and because of the growing Bolshevik fear and antagonism toward the Germans, and the indications that Lenin was interested in American aid, Francis said he was "willing therefore to swallow pride, sacrifice dignity, and with discretion . . . [establish] relations with Soviet Government . . . [to] influence terms of peace." [57]

This dispatch serves to date the beginning of a period of some ambivalence and drift in American policy that lasted until

mid-February 1918, when Wilson and Lansing firmly reiterated
the principle and the policy of intervention against the Bolsheviks. This hiatus was caused by the convergence of three principal difficulties: the practical problem of translating the principle
of intervention into action without creating serious dangers to
other aspects of American policy; the power and persistence of
the argument that American objectives could best be attained
through some kind of cooperation with the Bolsheviks; and
Wilson's exhausting bout with the inescapable realization that intervention contradicted the principles of both his personal ethic
and his liberal ideology.

In the face of these difficulties, Lansing's first response when
he received the cable from Francis offering to open talks with
the Bolsheviks was to carry on in the spirit of the decision to intervene. He promptly conferred with "Polk on Bolshevik menace to the world," warned his agent in South Russia to be particularly discreet in negotiations to support Kaledin, and then
turned to the problem of checking Japan's desire to use the
anti-Bolshevik policy as a springboard for further expansion in
Asia.[58]

The Secretary confronted the Japanese Ambassador on December 27, and his argument speaks for itself. "I told him that
the view of this Government was that it would be unwise for either the United States or Japan to send troops to Vladivostok as
it would undoubtedly result in the unifying of the Russians
under the Bolsheviks against foreign intervention." [59] Whatever
one's judgment of the strategy of anti-Bolshevism, it cannot be
denied that Lansing used considerable finesse in acting on the
chosen tactical approach. He used the threat of Bolshevik victory to block Japanese maneuvers with the intention and expectation that the refusal to intervene directly would keep the
Bolsheviks from consolidating their power.

This tactic for implementing the strategy of anti-Bolshevism had much to recommend it, especially its objective of blocking a Bolshevik appeal to Russian nationalism. But there were many difficulties involved in putting it into operation effectively. For one thing, Washington policy-makers were being bombarded by requests for more overt action against the Bolsheviks.[60] And Francis did not ease the tension and uneasiness when he sent along a Bolshevik appeal for world revolution.[61] Neither did Miles offer much concrete assistance. The Departmental expert started off the new year with a long memorandum, but it was nothing more than a verbose recommendation to stick with the decision of principle that had been made in December. His particular formulation—"continue . . . support of elements of law and order in the south, but . . . not exploiting Russia to carry on a civil war"—may very well have served mainly to dramatize the dilemmas of the agreed upon policy.[62]

Wilson could say, as he did, that the memo outlined "a sensible program," but that did not solve the problems.[63] And the pressures to act were increasing each day. In response to the entreaties to give active support to the anti-Bolsheviks, therefore, Wilson shortly approved sending the cruiser *Brooklyn* to Vladivostok as a show of force against the radicals (and as a cautionary hint to the Japanese). That was no more done, however, than Lansing was back with another plea to bring the anti-Bolshevik policy into the open.

Prompted by the Bolshevik appeal to the world that Francis had transmitted, Lansing attacked "the fundamental errors" of the radicals and asked for prompt and effective counter-measures. The Bolsheviks, the Secretary warned, are appealing "to a class and not to all classes of society, a class which does not have property but hopes to obtain a share by process of government rather than by individual enterprise. This is of course a di-

rect threat at existing social order in all countries." The danger
was that it "may well appeal to the average man, who will not
perceive the fundamental errors." Furthermore, the Bolsheviks
threatened to subvert the principle of nationalism by advancing
"doctrines which make class superior to the general conception
of nationality . . . Such a theory seems to me utterly destructive
of the political fabric of society and would result in constant
turmoil and change. It simply cannot be done if social order and
governmental stability are to be maintained."

Nor were the Bolsheviks merely talking about the "aboli-
tion of the institution of private property." They had "confis-
cated private property" in Russia. That could lead only to "the
worst form of despotism." "Here seems to me," Lansing concluded, "to lie a very real danger in view of the present social
unrest throughout the world." "In view of the threat against existing institutions," the Secretary asked Wilson to consider a
blunt counter-attack. He was "convinced" that it was impossible
to cooperate in any way with the Bolsheviks.[64]

Lansing had written a powerful letter. Had it reached the
President under different circumstances, it is possible that Wilson would have accepted it outright as a guide for policy. And it
may have exerted a less dramatic but vital kind of influence,
quietly working away in Wilson's mind during the next two
months. But it had immediately to compete with a resurgence of
the argument to oppose the Germans by aiding the Bolsheviks,
a logic that served additionally to remind the President of his
moral and ideological dilemma.[65] Hence Wilson again deferred
making a bold move.

Lansing promptly launched a counter-attack against this
competing advice. He first conferred with the Secretary of War
"on Russian situation." Lansing was anxious, among other
things, to expedite Judson's recall from Russia. The military at-

taché was an effective critic of official policy, and the Secretary wanted him removed from a position which gave his views some standing and influence inside the government. Then Lansing and Baker joined Secretary of the Navy Josephus Daniels for another discussion of the Russian question with President Wilson. It lasted 40 minutes, and was the first of several which took place during the next 10 days.[66]

The ultimate result of these and associated conferences was a validation of existing policy (and Judson's recall), which, however, did not occur until Wilson had endured another of his periodic crises over the moral and ideological issues of anti-Bolshevism. This developed as the Bolshevik international appeal intruded itself upon Wilson's long-term project of announcing his peace program to the world. When the President would have delivered his now famous Fourteen Points Speech (of January 8, 1918) in the absence of Bolshevik competition for leadership of the peace movement is a moot point; but there is no doubt that, in its given form, the address was intimately bound up with policy toward the revolution in Russia.

As Wilson admitted in a striking and oft-quoted phrase, policy toward Russia was "the acid test" of American and Allied ideas and intentions. He laid bare the central elements of his dilemma. The United States should give Russia "an unhampered and unembarrassed opportunity for the independent determination of her own political development and national policy," and provide "assistance also of every kind that she may need and may herself desire." Only in that way could America and its Allies demonstrate "their comprehension of her needs as distinguished from their own interests, and of their intelligent and unselfish sympathy." These remarks provide classic evidence of the President's intense personal awareness of the crucial dilemma defined by the contradiction between his principles and his preferences.

Considered in isolation from other documents bearing on its nature and meaning, Wilson's speech can be interpreted as a manifestation of his ambivalence and anguished inability to come to a hard decision to implement the anti-Bolshevik decision of December 12, 1917. In context, however, the speech is a document in evidence of Wilson's willingness to modify his principles when they threatened to limit American power and expansion. For as Colonel House noted at the time, the President "resented" the Bolsheviks and was trying to use them in order to appeal through and over their authority to the Russian populace. House's analysis was shortly verified in the course of a public argument over the meaning of the speech for policy toward the Bolsheviks.

The fight developed when William Boyce Thompson, an industrialist and financier who was a powerful and influential friend of Robins, asserted in a newspaper article that the speech meant that Wilson would seek some accommodation with the Bolsheviks. This claim was promptly and vigorously denied by William English Walling, who had access to Wilson's views on the Russian issue. "It is utterly impossible," he asserted in explaining the President's remarks, that the Bolshevik government "should be recognized by America." And a bit later, when Walling advised Wilson that aid to the Bolsheviks would be "playing with fire," the President remarked to Lansing that the warning contained "an unusual amount of truth" and furnished "a very proper basis for the utmost caution" in making policy decisions.[67]

The reason American intervention against the Bolsheviks took such a deceptively passive form for many months was not

that Wilson drew back from the policy, but that it was deemed
necessary to keep the way clear for anti-Bolshevik forces within
Russia to defeat the radicals. As Lansing told the Allies on January 16, American leaders still feared that direct, military intervention might "offend those Russians who are now in sympa
thy with the aims and desires which the United States and its
cobelligerents have at heart in making war and might result in
uniting all factions in Siberia against them [and in support of
the Bolsheviks]." [68]

Wilson continued to be bothered when anyone raised the alternative of maintaining pressure on the Germans, and checking
the Japanese, by collaboration with the Bolsheviks, but his basic
attitude was revealed by his very positive response to a militantly anti-Bolshevik policy recommendation submitted by Samuel Gompers, President of the American Federation of Labor,
and Walling.[69]

The Gompers-Walling memorandum, dated February 9,
1918, arrived at a time when Wilson was particularly weary of
the constant strain connected with the war effort and the Russian problem. "I do not know that I have ever had a more tire-
some struggle with quicksand," he had just written Senator
John Sharp Williams, "than I am having in trying to do the
right thing in respect of our dealings with Russia." [70] Hence it
may have been particularly encouraging to have Gompers come
forward in vigorous and determined opposition to recognition of
the Bolsheviks and to any kind of dealings with them.[71] Here
was the same advice Lansing had been offering, and it was coming from the other side of the class line. And the Secretary was
unquestionably pleased by the President's reaction: the memorandum "deserves a very careful reading" as "a very proper basis
of the utmost caution in the conduct of the many troublesome
affairs" connected with Russian policy.

"It is really a remarkable analysis," Lansing replied, "of the dangerous elements which are coming to the surface and which are in many ways more to be dreaded than autocracy; the latter is a despotism but an intelligent despotism, while the former is a despotism of ignorance . . . It is a condition which cannot but arouse the deepest concern." "I am more than ever convinced," the Secretary concluded, "that our policy has been the right one and should be continued." [72]

Lansing promptly acted to sustain that policy in the face of evidence that his critics were gaining ground. Francis had upset the Department considerably with his dispatch of February 7, advising his superiors that he was "endeavoring to establish gradually working relations" with the Bolsheviks. Whatever the Ambassador had in mind, Miles interpreted the news as the sign of a dangerous development. "This indicates," he warned, "that the Ambassador is getting in touch with Bolshevik government. Does he need instruction?" As one who had always seen Robins as an outsider who ought to be put back in his proper place, Miles had no doubts about the source of the trouble. "I gather Ambassador is being strongly influenced by Robins and he may splash over if we don't look out." [73]

Lansing moved quickly to prevent such an eventuality, and to sustain the right policy. He bluntly told Francis that the United States was "by no means prepared to recognize Bolshevik government officially." [74] Then he again explained to the British that military action in Siberia would be "particularly unfortunate" because it would "tend to estrange from our common interests [a] considerable portion of the people in Russia." [75] But in reiterating that argument, the Secretary entered the qualifying comment that such action would be unwise *"now."* [76] As the caveat indicated, the form of intervention was a tactical matter. Tactics are altered with changing circumstances, and

American leaders were shortly to change their tactics and begin the search for an effective way to undertake more active, overt intervention against the Bolsheviks.

IV. *The Moral and Practical Dilemmas of Action*

The vigorous reassertion in February 1918 of the fundamentally anti-Bolshevik attitudes of American leaders placed President Wilson under increasing pressure from the logic of his own outlook to intervene directly in Russia. His problem henceforward was to find a way to act against the Bolsheviks that would enable him to resolve or rationalize his moral dilemma, that would be effective against the revolutionary forces and that would offer a way of preventing Japan from exploiting intervention to weaken or even subvert the Open Door Policy in Asia.

It is not surprising, therefore, that Wilson and Lansing slapped aside a serious and dramatic French proposal to try collaboration with the Bolsheviks, or that they did so in an instantaneous and ruthless refusal. This striking reversal of earlier French policy, which favored military intervention, evolved in response to the clear indications that the Bolsheviks needed and wanted Allied assistance against the Germans. Renewed German operations in northern Russia prompted Trotsky to advise the coalition of revolutionaries in Murmansk on March 1 and 2, 1918, that it was "obliged to accept any help from the Allied Missions." Lenin supported that decision and later issued general orders to resist the Germans.[77]

American and French representatives in Moscow knew of these decisions, and interpreted them as verification of their own estimates of Bolshevik policies. The American military advisors, who had been seeing Trotsky almost as often as Robins, filed strong recommendations in favor of supporting the Bolshevik effort against the Germans. Coupled with his continuing evaluation of the nature and meaning of the Revolution per se, this convergence of events led the French military attaché, Jacques Sadoul, to extend even further his own talents and energy in an effort to convince his superiors in Russia and Paris that cooperation was both the most rational and the most promising policy for France to follow.

Combining strong emotion and powerful logic with persuasive language, Sadoul's argument momentarily carried the day. The French Government reconsidered its heretofore militant anti-Bolshevism, supported Sadoul's negotiations with the Bolsheviks, and formally asked the United States if it would join in general collaboration with Lenin and Trotsky.[78] American leaders considered the French proposal on February 19, conducting their talks in the context of a militantly anti-Bolshevik memorandum prepared by Miles.

The United States, Miles argued, defined democracy in terms of "the political freedom of its people." On the other hand, the Bolsheviks held that democracy was based on "equal economic freedom." His conclusion was unequivocal. "Fundamentally, these two conceptions are as different as black from white. It is idle to attempt to reconcile them as so many do. They are wholly different and cannot be reconciled." The Bolshevik view was "revolutionary in the deepest sense," and its advocates "have hitherto lived in the shadow." [79] It is apparent, and should be made explicit, that American leaders were every bit as inflexible and deterministic as they accused the Bolsheviks of being; and, further, that it was the Bolsheviks who proved to be the more willing to diverge from the dictates of their theoretical and general opposition to collaboration with capitalist nations.

The decision on the French proposal was wholly in keeping with the logic and tone of the memorandum by Miles. He had not, of course, changed anybody's mind. But his analysis did reinforce the existing anti-Bolshevik consensus. Lansing personally took the French request to President Wilson. His brief pencilled notation documents their attitude: "This is out of the question. Submitted to Pres't who says the same thing." [80] American leaders were of course interested in re-establishing resistance to the Germans on the Eastern Front, but they were not sufficiently anti-German to overcome their anti-Bolshevism.

Robins had no direct knowledge of this mid-February decision, and his efforts to arrange such cooperation with the Bolsheviks came to a climax between February 22, when the Bolshevik Central Committee voted to accept aid from the Allies (with Lenin casting the crucial vote), and March 5, when Trotsky and Lenin gave Robins a written and specific inquiry designed to initiate a serious discussion concerning aid from the United States. [81]

There is some evidence that a full copy of this document failed to reach Washington until after the Bolsheviks ratified the Brest-Litovsk treaty of peace with Germany. Even if this is true, and the evidence is not wholly convincing, the delay is far less significant than such writers as George Frost Kennan have made it appear. *Top American leaders already had explicit knowledge of the Bolshevik interest in obtaining assistance from the United States.* Furthermore, and as Washington was advised by several American military representatives in Russia, ratification of the treaty with Germany did not prevent the Germans from reopening their offensive—or the Bolsheviks from opposing that new attack as best they could. As late as March 26, for example, Francis told Lansing that the Red Army "is the only hope for saving European Russia from Germany." [82] American policy-makers *could* have responded favorably to the overture from Lenin and Trotsky whenever it actually did arrive. For that matter, they could have offered such negotiations on their own initiative. They did neither.

Wilson's message to the Congress of Soviets of March 10 made it clear beyond any question that he had no intention even of exploring the possibilities of such cooperation.[83] He bluntly told the Russian people that the United States, despite its great sympathy for their travail, was not going to help them through the Bolshevik Government. His words further carried the strong implication that the Bolsheviks were in league with the Germans. This document was prepared, moreover, in the course of continuing discussions designed to evolve a plan of intervention which would resolve the moral and practical dilemmas confronting Wilson and other American leaders. By February 26, for example, Lansing was referring in his conversations with Wilson to "our proposed policy." [84] The resulting decision seems to have been produced by several convergent pressures, and was based upon a rather subtle strategy for controlling the variables involved in intervention.

After their proposal to collaborate with the Bolsheviks had been dismissed out of hand, the French returned to nagging Wilson for some kind of intervention in Siberia. The British supported this campaign to break down the President's resistance. And the Japanese, of course, continued their own push for permission to move onto the mainland of Asia. These pressures on the United States were powerful in and of themselves, and gained additional strength from the political and psychological circumstances. Wilson was opposing other Allied suggestions, for example, and he seems to have felt that he might gain some political ground by agreeing to some form of intervention. The psychological factor involved the fatigue which was apparent in Wilson and Lansing. They were tired men, and were no doubt particularly weary of the Russian issue. The inclination to go on in and be done with it may have become quite strong once they had turned their backs on the idea of working with or through the Bolsheviks.

Even so, there was more than political higgling and ennui involved in Wilson's decision in February to approve Japanese intervention. For one thing, Lansing and Wilson seem to have concluded that Japan might do something regardless of American or Allied approval. "My own belief," Lansing fretted in a letter to the President on February 27, "is that Japan intends to go into Siberia anyway." [85] This raised the very difficult question of how to limit and control the Japanese. Lansing first encouraged the Chinese to hold the line in Manchuria. He told them that the United States wanted "the Chinese Government to take over and guard that part of the Trans-Siberian Railroad system [i.e., the Chinese Eastern Railway] which passes through Manchuria." [86] And, since the Chinese already had troops near Harbin, and could send more, this was not an empty gesture.

A second move was based on the old adage of publicly committing a suspect to a self-denying pledge as a way of preventing the crime. Wilson and Lansing had a perfect opportunity to do this: a Japanese spokesman had voluntarily offered such assurances.[87] It is not so often realized, however, that France and the other Allies were also concerned to check Japan. Perhaps the intensity of the French desire to act has obscured this point. While it is true that neither France nor England were as sensitive to Japanese operations in Manchuria, or in North China, as the United States was, it is *not* true that they were indifferent to the implications of an unrestrained Japanese move onto the mainland—particularly in view of Tokyo's seizure of Shantung Province, and its Twenty-One Demands of 1915. And, because it was a late-comer to the scramble for concessions in Asia, and because it was rather self-conscious about its lack of success prior to the war, Italy manifested an even stronger resistance to unilateral, unchecked Japanese intervention.

Lansing had clear evidence of this concern before Wilson acted between February 27 and March 1. The French were "very emphatic" and very explicit: "A full understanding and agreement would have to be had with Japan by all the other leading Allied powers, providing for the retirement of Japanese troops from Russian soil after the war, in addition to certain other guarantees." As if to make doubly sure that the meaning was understood, the French "evinced a keen curiosity as to the reason for the United States Government's opposing exclusive Japanese intervention." [88]

France ideally preferred to bind Japan with a treaty, but Lansing demurred: that approach would involve the Senate, and the ensuing debate would cause jarring complications.[89] A full, public discussion of policy toward Russia was not desirable from the point of view of the Wilson Administration. That would open the way for Robins, Thompson, and other critics to force modifications in—or perhaps even a major change of—existing policy. The European powers acquiesced, and expressed themselves as being "quite satisfied with the way the matter is being handled by the President." [90]

This support from England, Italy and France for the maneuver to control the Japanese encouraged Wilson and Lansing to feel, at least temporarily, and in conjunction with reports from Reinsch, Summers, and other American agents, that they could move in behind the Japanese and influence events in Russia along American lines through the use of economic power and diplomatic influence.[91] Wilson's memorandum of the night of February 27 was a device to commit the Japanese to their own professions of moderation by announcing them publicly as the basis for American acquiescence in intervention. The United States, Wilson explained, "wishes to assure the Japanese Government that it has entire confidence that in putting an armed force into Siberia it is doing so as an ally of Russia, with no purpose but save Siberia from the invasion of the armies and intrigues of Germany with entire willingness to leave the determination of all questions that may affect the permanent fortunes of Siberia to the Council of Peace." [92]

This sly but all-inclusive caveat was intended to trap the Japanese. On the one hand, they dared not reject such a pleasant essay in praise of their integrity. On the other hand, it would do them no good to ignore it because in that contingency the United States could use it as an aide memoire of an understanding based on earlier Japanese assurances. And, armed with the support of its European associates, America could feel confident of winning its point at the peace conference. In a real sense, Wilson was warning Japan to observe the conditions he specified or face united opposition.

Within 72 hours, however, Wilson withdrew even this support for Japanese intervention. The change, he told Polk, was "absolutely necessary." [93] Several reasons account for the abrupt shift. The President was repeatedly and vigorously warned that the United States could not count on controlling Japan through the stratagem of a self-denying pledge. The critics, such as Colonel House, argued that Wilson's approach risked creating an awful choice for the United States if the Japanese should decide to stay in Siberia, or turn their troops southward into China. If either of those conditions developed, the United States would have either to abandon the Open Door Policy or go to war against Japan. This analysis served to dramatize the second negative consideration, which was simply that Wilson was not ready to move immediately with a program of economic aid that would buttress American influence and also strengthen Russian and Chinese opposition to Japan.

In addition, the President also seems to have reconsidered the broad situation and, as a result, to have fallen back on the original strategy of December 1917, which was based on the axiom that direct intervention would provoke the Russians to support the Bolsheviks. Some Americans felt this would be particularly apt to occur if the Japanese went in alone; their reasoning being that racial antagonisms would be intensified by the memory of the Russian defeat in the Russo-Japanese War. And, finally, Wilson's central moral dilemma about intervention had been sharpened by reminders from men like Colonel House. They emphasized the loss of American influence if the principle of self-determination was so blatantly ignored.

All in all, the reversal of policy may well have been Wilson's finest moral hour. Torn by the conflict between his opposition to the Bolsheviks, which involved his entire political, economic, and social philosophy, and his deep involvement with the essential right of self-determination, the President chose to honor the moral axiom. Wilson's moral courage was no doubt reinforced by the fear that, given the existing circumstances, the Japanese outlook would triumph instead of his own. But that consideration should not be allowed to obscure either the intensity of Wilson's moral turmoil over intervention, or the central relationship between that agony and the change in policy. A man so essentially moralistic as Wilson could hardly be expected to view the Bolsheviks as anything but heretics, and to such men the heretic is even more dangerous than the non-believer. In this sense, at any rate, the surprise lies not so much in Wilson's final intervention, but rather in the strength and persistence of his moral qualms about such action. The liberal conscience ultimately broke down, but its initial resistance was greater than sometimes seems to be the case long after the crisis.

While it did not cause Wilson's change of mind, the Italian opposition to unilateral Japanese action may well have encouraged the President as he reconsidered the issue. Clearly seeking to creep in under the umbrella of the Open Door Policy, Italy made "three conditions" for its support of any Japanese move. Tokyo's action "should be satisfactory" to the United States, the intervention "should be *not* by Japan alone," and "guarantees should be given by Japan that they do not intend to hold territory." [94]

Wilson's circular note of March 5 announcing that he now opposed unilateral Japanese intervention provides what is almost a diagram of his thinking on the general subject. He remarked first on the "most careful and anxious consideration" that he had given "to the extreme danger of anarchy" in Siberia. This social and political situation was the root cause of the crisis, and intervention might in the end be necessary to control matters before they got completely out of hand. But he was "bound in frankness to say that the wisdom of intervention seems . . . most questionable." Then, in what was at once a veiled expression of his fears about Japan and his commitment to the right of self-determination, he warned that all the assurances in the world would not prevent what Germany is doing in the West."

In conclusion, Wilson revealed that he had fallen back on the strategic estimate evolved early in December 1917. Military intervention would generate "a hot resentment" in Russia, "and

that whole action might play into the hands of the enemies of
Russia, and particularly the enemies of the Russian Revolution,
for which the Government of the United States entertains the
greatest sympathy in spite of all the unhappiness and misfortune
which has for the time being sprung out of it." [95]

And to Wilson, as to American leaders in general, the Bolsheviks were both the cause and the substance of that unhappiness and misfortune. In their minds, at any rate, the Bolsheviks
were not considered part of the Russian Revolution for which
the United States entertained "the greatest sympathy." As Assistant Secretary of State Long put it in a personal letter to
Reinsch, American policy was concerned with supporting "the
original revolution." [96]

V. *The Decision to Intervene*

Wilson did not abandon the idea of intervention on March 5;
he merely refused to support one of many tactics of intervening.
The President continued his search for some way to go into Siberia as the dominant power in an Allied force including Japan
and then begin economic and political operations in support of
the anti-Bolshevik movement. There is no evidence that the discussions to evolve an effective way to accomplish this objective
had been significantly influenced by the occasional rumors about
German military operations in Siberia. Lansing reviewed these
stories in a memorandum to Wilson on March 19, and concluded that Admiral Knight's evaluation was valid.

Knight concluded that it was "impossible" for any significant part of the military stores in Vladivostok to be destroyed;
that there was "absolutely no danger" they would reach the
Germans; and that there was "no evidence" of any serious Ger-

man influence in Siberia. He added that Lenin and Trotsky, and their Bolshevik followers in the Far East, were revolutionaries —not German agents. And he concluded with a strong recommendation that it was "of first importance" that Japan "should not be permitted to act alone." [97]

Lansing did become somewhat concerned, between March 21 and 24, 1918, over a new flurry of reports that the Bolsheviks were converting some German and Austrian prisoners-of-war to their radical ideology, and then using them in military operations against the anti-Bolshevik forces in Siberia. If this turned out to be true, the Secretary anticipated that "we will have a new situation in Siberia which may cause a revision of our policy." His reference to a "new situation," makes it clear that neither the Bolshevik-as-German agent theory, nor the fear of a German campaign in Siberia, was a causative factor in the discussions of intervention that took place between November 7, 1917, and March 20, 1918. Lansing's approach to the new reports, furthermore, was wholly conditional. He was merely doing what any responsible official would have done: "we should consider the problem on the hypothesis that the reports are true and be prepared to act with promptness." [98]

Wilson commended the Secretary for his foresight, but did not think the situation called for action. "I do not find in them," he replied, "sufficient cause for altering our position." [99] The stories reappeared from time to time, but decisions were not made on the assumption that they were true. In April, for example, both Reinsch and the Czech leader Thomas Masaryk advised Wilson and Lansing that the tales were not worth serious attention, and most certainly were not a reliable basis for policy decisions. Reinsch's estimate was based on extensive first-hand information. He put "much work" into his efforts to find out what was going on in Siberia, and his chief agent in the field,

Major Walter S. Drysdale (the American military attaché in Peking) was a man with "a great deal of good sense." [100]

An early report to Reinsch, prepared by a Colonel Speshneff on March 9, told of finding the prisoners employed "as clerks, [and] some of them work as painters, carpenters, shoemakers, tailors, hair-dressers, etc." Speshneff wanted American intervention "in the internal affairs directed against the Bolsheviki," but he did not base his plea on the danger from the prisoners-of-war. He was simply against the Bolsheviks. Drysdale's review on March 19 of the evidence he had collected during a field trip was unequivocal: "not a single armed prisoner was seen and there is little probability that any of the prisoners are armed." Three weeks later, on April 10, he reaffirmed that estimate. "Some very few of the prisoners" at Chita were being converted politically, and were "fighting as workmen, for the workmen's cause, against the Bourgeoisie."

As one Austrian explained to Drysdale, "they were helping their brother laborers in Russia against Semenoff and the Bourgeoisie." [101] This situation might with some accuracy have been described under the heading of Austrians-as-Bolsheviks, but it was positive disproof of the argument that the Bolsheviks were German agents. And, as the men on the scene reported, there were no other armed prisoners. These on-the-spot dispatches, and Reinsch's summary of them for Washington, put an end even to Lansing's conditional and hypothetical worry about the prisoners-of-war.

On the other hand, the idea of supporting the Bolsheviks against Germany continued to show life. Robins sustained his campaign for that policy to the point of antagonizing Consul Summers beyond his endurance. But, when Summers asked for a transfer, Lansing promptly and effectively exerted pressure on the Red Cross directors to recall Robins from Russia. That did not put an end to the advice to collaborate with the Bolsheviks, however, for American military representatives continued to recommend the same policy after Robins was ordered to return to the United States.

These men, who had agreed with Judson's estimate of the situation in November and December 1917, had no illusions about a political honeymoon with the Bolsheviks. They understood that Lenin and Trotsky were fighting the Germans to save the Revolution—not as a disinterested favor to the Allies. Some of them also had sensed, as Robins did, that the Bolsheviks were becoming aware that they—or any Russian government, for that matter—needed allies against Japan and Germany. Even before World War I, Robins had concluded from a general analysis of the world political system that an American-Russian entente offered security for both countries.

The military representatives may not have gone that far in thinking, but they did argue that short-run collaboration was the most intelligent and practical course of action. Ambassador Francis allowed them to continue their discussions with Trotsky, and even to offer some technical assistance, even though he intended that any army organized by Trotsky would be "taken from Bolshevik control" and used against the revolutionaries.[102] He thought any agreement with the Bolsheviks would help sustain them in power, and considered that "cost will be too dear." [103]

Sometime in the second or third week of April, at a stage when the German prisoner-of-war scare had been thoroughly discredited, President Wilson began an active search for some anti-Bolshevik group through which he could inject American power directly into the Russian situation. "I would very much value a memorandum," he advised Lansing on April 18, "containing *all* that we know about these several *nuclei* of self-governing authority . . . in Siberia. It would afford me a great deal of satisfaction to get behind the most nearly representative of them if it can indeed draw leadership and control to itself." Like the decision of December 10, 1917, to aid Kaledin in southern Russia, this letter makes it clear that American policy-makers were thinking of intervention as an anti-Bolshevik operation. The problem in the spring of 1918 was to find a winner; not only, of course, in order to defeat the Bolsheviks, but also to block the Japanese.

Further conversations between the two men seem almost certainly to have taken place during the next few days, even though no written record survives. This is strongly suggested, for example, by a dispatch Lansing sent to the American Ambassador in France on April 23. For, in briefing the Ambassador so that he would be able to discuss intervention with the French authorities, the Secretary clearly implied that such talks had occurred. Belgium and Italy, Lansing explained, had requested the United States to move a total of 450 officers and men, along with some armored cars, from Nagasaki and Vladivostok to the Western Front. *Acting on its own,* the American government had suggested in reply that it would be wise to leave the troops in the Far East.

That reply, Lansing explained, "was predicated upon the possibility of intervention in Siberia. It seemed inadvisable to bring away from there troops carrying flags of co-belligerents when it might be embarrassing to send back there other such troops." This action did not commit Wilson and Lansing to intervention, but it certainly indicates that they were discussing it seriously enough to keep non-Japanese troops in readiness. This conclusion is reinforced by Lansing's final cautionary word to the American Ambassador in France: "it is felt to be highly desirable that the matter should not be discussed with other persons." [104]

Lansing and Wilson kept a sharp watch on the progress of the anti-Bolshevik leader Grigori Semenov during the ensuing month. Semenov was a Cossack who had served first as a Tsarist officer; then, after the March Revolution, he had gone to Siberia to raise a volunteer force of Mongols to battle the Germans. Caught in the east when the Bolsheviks took power, Semenov promptly began to fight them. He was vain, arrogant, and undemocratic, but his nerve and ruthlessness made him effective in the field—at least for a long enough time to attract the attention of American policy-makers. And, since neither Wilson nor Lansing favored negotiating any understanding with the Bolsheviks about intervention in Siberia, Semenov attracted their interest and concern.

The Secretary of State made it clear that he opposed any agreement with the Bolsheviks, even for the purpose of checking the Germans or the Japanese, because that "would array us against Semenov and the elements antagonistic to the Soviets." That should not be done. Wilson agreed, and on May 20 reiterated his instructions of April 18: "follow very attentively what Semenov is accomplishing and whether or not there is any legitimate way in which we can assist." [105]

The President's clear and persistent concern to evolve some way of aiding the anti-Bolsheviks was reinforced during these weeks by an increasing campaign involving various anti-Bolshevik groups in the United States. They wanted to move in with economic aid, and then stay for a share in the post-Bolshevik economic pie.[106] Wilson was interested in such plans, but his own thinking about intervention ran along the more narrow and specific line of aid to the anti-Bolshevik groups in their mil-

itary operations. The door had to be opened, as it were, before
the economic benefits—and influence—could flow through
it. The President's approach of course involved economic assistance, but not in the precise form then being advocated by the
various clusters of opinion in the United States. This difference
between their outlooks became apparent in a second letter of
May 20 from Wilson to Lansing.

A dispatch from Reinsch urging action prompted Wilson to
ask the Secretary if the moment for intervention had arrived.
"Situation in Siberia seems more favorable than ever," Reinsch
judged on May 16, "for effective joint action of Allies and
American initiative . . . Should America remain inactive longer
friendly feeling is likely to fail." Lansing was definitely interested in Reinsch's argument, perhaps even partially persuaded,
but not wholly convinced.

He was aware that Semenov's "policy is to keep the Siberian
Railway open and overthrow the Bolsheviki," and that his suc-
cesses offered "the prospect of forcing an amalgamation of all the
different elements seeking reconstruction in Siberia." But the
Secretary still worried about the danger of antagonizing the
rank and file anti-Bolshevik Russians, even though support for
Semenov could be combined with assistance to the Czecho-Slovak troops that were in Siberia. Lansing concluded, therefore,
that the time was not yet "opportune" for direct intervention.[107]

Wilson admitted the importance of not antagonizing the
non-Bolshevik Russians, and of checking the Japanese, but those
tactical difficulties did not lead him to abandon the search for a
way to implement the strategy of anti-Bolshevism. He was prepared, as he told the British, to "go as far as intervention
against the wishes of [the Russian] people knowing it was
eventually for their good providing he thought the scheme had
any practical chance of success." Joint intervention offered good

possibilities of rallying the people against the Bolsheviks, but unilateral Japanese action would probably antagonize all the Russians "excepting for a small reactionary body who would join anybody to destroy the Bolsheviks."

Asked if this meant that the Allies should "do nothing at all," Wilson replied "No." "We must watch the situation carefully and sympathetically and be ready to move whenever the right time arrives." While waiting for an invitation to intervene from a successfully organized anti-Bolshevik group, Wilson wanted to prepare the way for effective operations by strengthening the economic situation in the non-Bolshevik areas of Siberia.[108] Even as the President was thus reiterating his commitment to the fundamental strategy of anti-Bolshevik intervention, Lansing was modifying his tactical caution.

The Secretary received on May 26 a long letter from George Kennan, an old friend who was generally considered to be one of America's leading experts on Russian affairs. Kennan's advice and recommendations were militantly anti-Bolshevik. Lansing was impressed. "I have read the letter with especial interest because it comes from the highest authority in America on Russia." The Secretary naturally found it "gratifying" that his own views were "very similar" to those expressed by Kennan. The only significant disagreement concerned the "wisdom of intervention in Siberia."

Kennan was convinced that intervention was tactically workable as well as strategically desirable. Lansing wholly agreed on the strategy of anti-Bolshevism, but was "not so sure" that the tactic of direct intervention would prove successful. He explained, however, that the issue was receiving "very careful consideration" by the administration. And, because Kennan "had so clearly analyzed the state of affairs," Lansing promised to "lay it [the letter] before the President." [109]

Lansing received more of the same kind of advice when he
returned to the Department of State the next morning. A dispatch from Ambassador Page in London advised the Secretary
that a League for the Regeneration of Russia in Union with Her
Allies had been established in Rome, and was receiving support
from Russians in England. It was militantly anti-Bolshevik, appealed directly to the United States for aid and suggested a
"strong central government around which all sane elements
would group themselves against Bolsheviks and Germans." [110]

As he considered this development, the Secretary learned
that the Allied ambassadors in Paris had agreed on the necessity
and wisdom of intervention. They argued that it "must take
place with or without the consent of the Bolshevik government," which in itself "has become far less important." [111] Next,
on May 30, Reinsch added his "urgent appeal" to act on the
"extreme need for Allied action in Siberia." Russia, he explained, "is craving for order and will follow those who establish it. Only if established through Allied assistance will order
be compatible with development of democracy." [112]

All this was enough to prompt Lansing to warn Francis
once again of the extreme care required in any ad hoc dealings
with the Bolsheviks. "I am confident," the Secretary hopefully
reminded the Ambassador, "you will appreciate the delicacy
with which your actions . . . must be conducted." The Bolsheviks must not be allowed to receive or create any impression of
American collaboration or assistance that would "alienate the
sympathy and confidence of those liberal elements of Russian
opinion which do not support Bolsheviki." [113] As these instructions suggest, policy-makers in Washington were moving ever
more rapidly toward overt intervention in support of their established anti-Bolshevism, and they wanted to rally all possible
Russian support for the action.

On the next day, June 2, Lansing learned that a unit of Czecho-Slovak troops in Siberia had engaged the Bolsheviks. These men had fought with the Russians after deserting from the Austrian Army, but the Treaty of Brest-Litovsk left them without a war, and arrangements had been made by the French and the embryonic Czech government-in-exile, in negotiations with Lenin and Trotsky, for them to proceed via Siberia to the Western Front. Given the tensions in Russia, it would have taken a combination of great patience, extraordinary discipline, excellent communications, and unusual luck for such a contingent to avoid some clashes with the Bolshevik regional authorities. The odds against a peaceful remove to Vladivostok were simply too great, and a series of bitter outbreaks occurred along the Trans-Siberian Railway.

Lansing's first response in this situation was to assure Ambassador Page of the administration's sympathy and concern with the anti-Bolshevik League for the Regeneration of Russia. "Deeply interested in program for regeneration of Russia," he replied, "with which this Government, in the main, agrees." Then he alerted Francis to the increasing possibility of intervention through the subtle device of telling the Ambassador that the Department was "considering carefully" his own proposal of May 2 for such action.[114] Assistant Secretary Long shortly thereafter reviewed for Lansing the advantages offered by intervention in liaison with the Czechs. They were "antagonistic to the Bolsheviks," and "available to be used as a military expedition to overcome Bolshevik influence, and under Allied guidance to restore order." [115] As indicated by these and other dispatches of the period, American policy-makers straightforwardly discussed intervention as an anti-Bolshevik operation.

As the momentum for intervention increased among government policy-makers, Lansing became somewhat worried by a growing public discussion of the issue. The Secretary was afraid that the agitation would force the government to move before it was ready. Referring to the criticism of the government for the breakdown and failure of the aircraft construction program, Lansing warned against losing control of the intervention issue in a similar manner. "I see signs," he wrote Wilson on June 13, "in Congress and outside of a similar situation arising in connection with Russia." The Secretary's idea was to have Herbert Hoover take charge of an economic commission that would in turn provide an excellent public image of intervention. "Armed intervention to protect the humanitarian work done by the Commission," Lansing noted, "would be much preferable to armed intervention before this work had begun." [116]

Wilson probably appreciated the political finesse inherent in Lansing's suggestion, but the President was strongly inclined to proceed first with armed intervention in support of the Czechs and other anti-Bolshevik forces. In that frame of mind, he responded favorably to Reinsch's analysis of June 13. Reinsch was very high on the Slavs: with "only slight countenance and support they could control all of Siberia against the Germans." The minister's reference to Germans did not mean that he had changed his mind about the nature of the Bolsheviks or about the danger of a German conquest of Siberia. He knew from Drysdale that the Czechs were anti-Bolshevik, and agreed with his subordinate that it was crucial to keep the Bolsheviks from mounting an effective counter-attack.

The reference to Germany concerned his fear that an increasing number of prisoners-of-war might side with the Bolsheviks in view of the Czech attacks. He did not anticipate a German offensive in Siberia.[117] Neither Wilson nor Lansing misread Reinsch's dispatch to mean that the nature of the danger had become German instead of Bolshevik. The President saw the Czechs as a strong, effective force which he could support against the Bolsheviks, and one which was also anti-Japanese and anti-German. That was precisely the kind of a nucleus he had been looking for since at least as early as the middle of April.

Wilson's central line of thought, and its anti-Bolshevik nature, was clearly revealed in his reaction to a favorable review and estimate of the All-Russian Union of Co-operative Societies. The leader of that organization, after expressing his opposition to the Bolsheviks, asked the United States to take the lead in intervention.[118] The President's comment of June 19 on the report indicates not only his anti-Bolshevik objectives, but suggests very strongly that he had made his personal decision to intervene. The co-ops, he remarked, should be considered "instruments for what we are now planning to do in Siberia." [119]

This interpretation is reinforced by another move Wilson made on the same day. He asked Secretary of War Baker to prepare a campaign plan for Siberia, using as a starting point a memorandum which proposed to undertake intervention by gathering and organizing support from the bourgeoisie in Siberia and the rest of Russia.[120] The Army's reply was drafted by Chief of Staff General Peyton C. March. The war, he argued, would "be won or lost on the western front." Siberian intervention, "considered purely as a military proposition," was "neither practical nor practicable"—"a serious military mistake." [121]

Wilson overruled this argument during a White House conference on July 6, 1918. He did so in full knowledge of the German assault on the Western Front. He also knew that the Czechs had overthrown the Bolsheviks in Vladivostok, and that they offered a general base of operations against the Bolsheviks throughout Siberia. Lansing had the same information. He noted on June 23 that the Czechs were "fighting the Red

Guards along the Siberian line," and added on July 2 that they were fighting "to eject the local Soviets." As he commented in a private memo in July, the Secretary did "not think that we should consider the attitude of the Bolshevik Siberians." [122]

The White House conference made it clear that intervention was *not* designed to establish an eastern front against the Germans. That was "physically impossible." Furthermore, the discussion of the basic "proposition and program" made no reference to aiding the Czechs against either the German or the Austrian prisoners-of-war. That phrasing appeared only as part of the "public announcement" to be made in conjunction with Japan, and in the section of the memorandum enumerating the conditions which Japan would have to meet.[123]

Neither was there any mention of German or Austrian prisoners-of-war, or of Bolsheviks as German agents, in Wilson's aide memoire of July 17, 1918. Though the document has often been described as rambling, fuzzy, and even contradictory, the truth of the matter is that Wilson was both lucid and candid. He discounted intervention as a maneuver to restore the eastern front, "even supposing it to be efficacious in its immediate avowed object of delivering an attack upon Germany," as "merely a method of making use of Russia." That would not help the Russians escape "from their present distress." The Bolsheviks were responsible for that distress.

As far as Wilson was concerned, the purpose of intervention was "only to help the Czecho-Slovaks consolidate their forces and get into successful cooperation with their Slavic kinsmen and to steady any efforts at self-government or self-defense in which the Russians themselves may be willing to accept assistance." [124] The full significance of the word *only,* and of the phrase *Slavic kinsmen,* should not be missed. The *only* was a throwaway word for the simple reason that the Czechs supplied all that was necessary from the American point-of-view. For that reason, the *only* was directed at Tokyo and designed to specify American opposition to Japanese aggrandizement. In a similar vein, the phrase *Slavic kinsmen* was designed to reassure the Russians that the Japanese would be kept under control.

Since Wilson and other top American leaders knew the Bolsheviks to be radical social revolutionaries, and had repeatedly stated their opposition to them on that ground, the meaning of Wilson's aide memoire should be clear. American intervention in Russia was a long-debated and long-delayed tactical move in support of the basic anti-Bolshevik strategy that had been established in December 1917. "I don't think you need fear of any consequences of our dealings with the Bolsheviki," he wrote Senator James Hamilton Lewis on July 24, 1918, "because we do not intend to deal with them." [125]

Lansing added his explicit documentation a bit later. Absolutism and Bolshevism were the "two great evils at work in the world today," and the Secretary believed Bolshevism "the greater evil since it is destructive of law and order." [126] It was, indeed, the "most hideous and monstrous thing that the human mind has ever conceived." That estimate led Lansing in 1918 to recommend a course of action that was to plague Western statesmen for at least two generations. "We must not go too far," he warned, "in making Germany and Austria impotent." [127]

VI. President Wilson's Last Agony

President Wilson continued to aid anti-Bolshevik forces in Russia well into 1919. For that matter, the last American troops did not leave Siberia until April 1, 1920. During those years and months, Wilson avowed his concern not only with the radicals in Russia, but also with "the dangers of Bolshevism" in the United States. "It will be necessary to be very watchful and united in the presence of such danger," he warned on the morrow of Armistice Day, 1918.

As for the difficulties which prevented intervention from attaining its objectives, both the President and Secretary Lansing left terse but sufficient comment. Wilson's explanation to Winston Churchill during a discussion of the issue at the Paris Peace Conference contained all the essentials. "Conscripts could not be sent and volunteers probably could not be obtained. He himself felt guilty in that the United States had in Russia insufficient forces, but it was not possible to increase them. It was certainly a cruel dilemma." Lansing made the same point to George Kennan in a "personal and secret" letter. "I wish you to know that it was not lack of sympathy which prevented the employment of a large active force in Siberia . . . We were bound hand and foot by the circumstances." [128]

American intervention in Russia does not present the historian with an insuperable problem or an impenetrable mystery. It did not involve any dark conspiracy among American leaders. Considered as history, and leaving the question of its wisdom as policy for each reader to decide to his own satisfaction, the record indicates that the action was undertaken to provide direct and indirect aid to the anti-Bolshevik forces in Russia. It was thus anti-Bolshevik in origins and purpose. The men who made the decision viewed the Bolsheviks as dangerous radical social revolutionaries who threatened American interests and the existing social order throughout the world. They did not consider them to be German agents, nor did they interpret the Bolshevik

Revolution as a coup engineered by the Imperial German Government.

Despite their concern to defeat Germany and to check Japan in the Far East, American leaders repeatedly refused to explore the possibility of attaining those objectives through collaboration with the Bolsheviks. *This was not a hypothetical alternative.* In spite of their theoretical doctrine, and the suspicion and hesitance it created in their minds, the Bolshevik leaders made persistent efforts to establish such cooperation. This flexibility created one of those turning points in history at which no one turned. The primary reason this opportunity was never exploited was because American leaders proved in action to be more doctrinaire and ideologically absolutist than the Bolsheviks. What might have been can never be known, but it is clear that American leaders proved less concerned with those possibilities than with the preservation of the status quo. As had so often been the case in the past, the United States defined Utopia as a linear projection of the present.

The only central question that remains unanswered about intervention concerns Wilson's personal authorization for the official publication of the infamous Sisson Documents, which purported to prove that the Bolsheviks were German agents. Neither the British Government nor the American State Department accepted the documents as proof of that allegation. Both therefore refused to publish the material. The President bears sole responsibility.

This becomes even more impressive when it is realized that *Edgar Sisson himself discounted the documents as proof that the Bolsheviks were German agents.* He said this explicitly on February 19, 1918, in a cable to George Creel, his superior in the Committee on Public Information. "These are wild internationalists," Sisson explained, "who not only in the beginning but until lately were willing to have German support for their own ends of Revolution. Germany thought she could direct the storm but the storm had no such intention." [129]

One can only wonder, since no documentary evidence has ever been found, if Wilson knew of and read this dispatch which was transmitted through the State Department. It would certainly help to know; for, early in March, the President privately and personally ordered Sisson to proceed straight to Washington without any further discussion of the documents he had purchased in Russia. We do know that Lansing refused to accept and publish the material under the seal of the Department of State, and that Sisson was an angry man when he left his confrontation with the Secretary at the end of the first week in May. And we know that Lansing later called Sisson "a dangerous person" in a warning about dealing with him in connection with official business. [130]

Finally, of course, we know that Sisson prevailed upon Wilson to publish the forgeries. He did so behind Lansing's back, and despite the Secretary's explicit opposition. It is possible, but unlikely, that Sisson simply persuaded the President that the documents were genuine. Wilson's own estimate of, and attitude toward, the Bolsheviks belies such an explanation. And while it is conceivable, it is highly improbable that the decision hinged upon some personal matter between Wilson and Sisson.

Thus the evidence points toward the conclusion that Wilson underwrote the publication of the documents as a way of rationalizing his decision to intervene against the Bolsheviks despite his commitment to the principle of self-determination. The President had been intensely aware of that dilemma from the outset of the crisis, and it had caused him great torment and anguish. But he had ultimately intervened. Yet knowing Wilson, it seems extremely unlikely that the overt act resolved the personal and ideological agony. And so, perhaps as a last effort to ease that terrible pressure, the President acquiesced in Sisson's insistent pleas. If such was the case, then it was an appropriate curtain for the tragedy of intervention.

The historian and the citizen can choose from among several arguments concerning the wisdom of intervention. He can agree with Winston Churchill that the revolutionary baby should have been strangled at birth. He can feel with Raymond Robins that the first opening to the left should have been explored; that such a course might have prevented, or at least significantly mitigated, subsequent suffering endured by the entire world. Or he can fatalistically conclude that it all would have turned out just the same no matter what had been done differently between November 1917 and April 1920.

Whatever the final evaluation, however, it does seem both more accurate and more helpful to begin the process of reflection on the consequences of intervention with the awareness that the action was anti-Bolshevik in origin and intent.

Studies on the Left
(Fall 1963, Spring 1964)

A Second Look
at Mr. X

George Frost Kennan's appointment as United States Ambassador to the Soviet Union was a move of vital significance in the Cold War. For the choice of Kennan, self-acknowledged author of the policy of containment and publicly proclaimed "inside strategist" of the Cold War, reemphasized Washington's determination to press the original policy of containment—even though Kennan himself has hinted at the grave fallacy of his master plan. And while the Truman administration has yet to take note of its own expert's apparently changed views, the Republicans, under the guidance of John Foster Dulles, bid fair to push containment to its logical conclusion—preventive or provoked war. Clearly, these aspects of current American policy toward Russia point up the need to take a second look at Kennan.

The errors of fact, violations of logic, and cases of judgment by double standard that may be found in Kennan's published writings comprise a total far beyond the scope of a single paper. But the fundamental character of his work is apparent in the famous "X" article, first printed in *Foreign Affairs* in July, 1947, and later republished in Kennan's volume on *American Diplomacy, 1900–1950*. Ostensibly an article on the Soviet political structure, Kennan's "X" article was originally written as a policy document for Secretary of Defense James Forrestal—

and actually was but a condensation of the views Kennan had expressed as early as the first part of 1946. This background is important, for it reveals that Kennan's policy of containment was the product of long-term reflection on American-Russian relations; and Kennan was the leader of that small coterie of State Department personnel specifically trained in that field.

Despite the care that went into its preparation, the "X" article contains two signal weaknesses: Kennan's failure to probe the relationship between economic forces and foreign policy; and his attempt to analyze the history of the world since 1917 (and make recommendations for the present) without acknowledging, or addressing himself to, the fundamental challenge that the Bolshevik Revolution presented to the western world in general, and to the United States in particular. For the challenge of contemporary Russia is far more than that of a giant military machine: the Soviet Union is equally potent as the symbol of a fundamental critique of capitalist society that is currently the basis of action in many non-Russian areas of the world.

To evade or ignore this aspect of American-Russian relations is to explain the past inadequately and to formulate current policy without comprehending the basic forces that condition day-to-day actions and decisions. It would require one to account for the non-Russian centers of Communism, for example, *solely* on the basis of pre-1917 concepts of political treason or a quite inexplicable index of psychiatric maladjustment. And that pattern of causation (while apparently accepted by many in the western world) has little relevance to the rise of Russian influence in China.

Even within his own frame of reference, however, Kennan's review of American-Soviet relations is open to serious question. There was "little" that the United States "could have done," he observes in *American Diplomacy,* "to moderate" the Soviet's "burning hostility" toward the West. Begging the question of what foundation in fact that antagonism might have had (both during and after the Bolshevik Revolution), Kennan concludes that "it was hardly to be altered by anything" the United States could have done directly, and observes that the "best reaction to it on our part would have been at all times an attitude of great reserve, consistency, and dignity." (P. 81.)

That is certainly not a unique view of American-Soviet relations, but since Kennan is an expert on the question, his omission of several key aspects of history is difficult to understand. Surely Kennan is aware that Secretary of State Robert Lansing was avowedly and militantly opposed to the Bolshevik Revolution because of its economic and social goals; that the Wilson administration ignored several specific overtures from Lenin for collaboration against Germany and Japan; and that President Wilson openly "cast in his lot with the rest" and actively supported counter-revolutionary forces in an attempt to overthrow the Soviets.

Hard to comprehend, in short, is Kennan's decision to ignore the fact that from the early days of the November Revolution to the failure of the 1937 Brussels Conference on Japanese aggression in China, the Soviet Union persistently wooed the United States in search of an understanding that would serve to decrease the probability of a conflict that Kennan describes as "at best a war of defense" for the West. Since Kennan is apparently unaware that Tsarist Russia made three overtures of a similar nature to the United States between 1905 and 1912, his failure to place these Soviet advances in a broad framework is perhaps understandable; but even considered as purely post-1917 moves, they can hardly be explained as examples of "burning hostility." Indeed, they document a remarkable Marxist heresy by the very torchbearers of the faith. For economic and political collaboration with the United States designed to preserve Moscow would also preserve Washington—a fact that could not have been missed by the men in the Kremlin. Far from being forced to alter unmitigated antagonism, as Kennan implies, the United States had a standing opportunity to respond to positive advances.

Nor does Kennan deal candidly with American foreign policy as a whole during the interwar years. Far from isolationism, Washington's policy is perhaps best described as an attempt to exercise dominant power within a framework of "freedom without responsibility." Political and economic (and in some cases military) intervention in Latin America, Europe, and China is not isolationism. And the Roosevelt administration's disinterest in the terms of appeasement offered to Mussolini and Hitler as long as they did not touch American interests is striking evidence of the refusal to accept responsibility. These are but the most glaring examples of Kennan's failure to grapple with basic problems in their entirety. The result is clear: Kennan's recommendations lack validity. That these conclusions can be accepted as a basis for action is a matter of record, but to expect them to promote the "national interest" (a well-worn generality that Kennan declines to define) is neither logical, necessary, nor possible.

Kennan's statement of the policy of containment is major evidence in support of this judgment. For when he came to apply his "theoretical foundation" to the specific problem of policy-making, the result was a recommendation for action designed to effect either a definitive change in, or the actual destruction of, the Soviet Union. To be sure, his point of departure is an admission that the sincerity of Soviet leaders cannot be questioned—that they do desire the betterment of life in

Russia—but he immediately concludes that they have explained what Kennan takes to be lack of progress in that direction by the prior necessity to establish the security of the government.

Kennan's first problem, therefore, is to establish the validity of this thesis. For a review of the facts, however, he substitutes a statement that enables him to label the security argument as no more than a rationale by which the Soviet leaders maintain themselves in power—no more, in short, than a technique of control. "Tremendous emphasis," Kennan writes, "has been placed on the original Communist thesis of a basic antagonism between the capitalist and Socialist worlds." But, he continues, "it is clear, from many indications that this emphasis is not founded in reality. The real facts concerning it have been confused by the existence abroad of a genuine resentment provoked by Soviet philosophy and tactics and occasionally by the existence of great centers of military power, notably the Nazi regime in Germany and the Japanese Government of the late 1930's, which did indeed have aggressive designs against the Soviet Union." There is, Kennan then concludes, "ample evidence that the stress laid in Moscow on the menace confronting Soviet society . . . is founded not in the realities of foreign antagonism but in the necessity of explaining away the maintenance of dictatorial authority at home." (P. 113.)

These comments and interpretations require further examination. Two notable omissions are Kennan's failure to point out that capitalist leaders militantly opposed socialism (both verbally and more actively) long years before the existence of the Soviet state, and his like failure to note Soviet overtures to the United States from 1917 to 1937. He also neglects to mention the fact and character of allied intervention in Russia. Nor does the reader find any reference to the avowed policy aims of Herbert Hoover (the "abandonment of their present economic system" on the part of the Bolsheviks) and Charles Evans Hughes (who conditioned recognition on "fundamental changes" in the Soviet economic system). Likewise peculiar is the use of the word "occasionally" and the chronology "in the late 1930's" to characterize the threat to Russia from Germany and Japan.

"Occasionally" can hardly be applied to an armed challenge that concerned the world for the majority of the interwar years. And the phrase "in the late 1930's" does not take account of Japan's activities in the intervals from 1917 to 1922 and from 1931 to 1941—or Hitler's from 1934 forward. Kennan's argument that neither Japan's occupation of eastern Siberia and subsequent attacks along the border between Manchuria and Russia nor Hitler's expansion in Central Europe was a threat to Soviet security contrasts strangely with his claim that Moscow was a dire threat to America at a time when the United States had the only stockpile of atom bombs. Yet upon this questionable foundation Kennan proceeds to build his entire argument.

Kennan goes on to deal with two other factors that are central to an analysis of his policy recommendation. "The theory of the inevitability of the eventual fall of capitalism," he writes, "has the fortunate connotation that there is no hurry about it." (P. 116.) And again, "the Kremlin is under no ideological compulsion to accomplish its purposes in a hurry." (P. 118.) He points out, however, that the Soviet Government, "like almost any other government . . . can be placed in a position where it cannot afford to yield even though this might be dictated by its sense of realism." (P.119.)

For this reason, Kennan emphasizes, "it is a *sine qua non* of successful dealing with Russia that the foreign government in question should remain at all times cool and collected and that demands on Russian policy should be put forward in such a manner as to leave the way open for a compliance not too detrimental to Russian prestige." (P. 119.) This statement would appear to indicate that Kennan (despite his inaccurate and misleading presentation of past policies toward Soviet Russia) envisaged some careful effort to establish a basic security accommodation with Moscow. His actual conclusion, however, can hardly be described in that manner.

Rather does Kennan prescribe the use of "unanswerable force," a coupling of words that has no meaning save in a military sense. Nor is his formulation vague. The United States, he concludes, "has it in its power to increase enormously the strains under which Soviet policy must operate, to force upon the Kremlin a far greater degree of moderation and circumspection than it has had to observe in recent years, and in this way promote tendencies which must eventually find their outlet in either the break-up or the gradual mellowing of Soviet power." (Pp. 126–127.) And Kennan's choice of words further emphasizes his resort to force: had he meant "a result to be expected," he would have used the phrase *will eventually*. Instead he wrote *must eventually,* an expression of obligation under "physical or logical necessity." But men do not surrender nations or social systems to the dictates of logic, as Kennan himself admits.

Thus Kennan disregards both his own warning about "tactless and threatening gestures" and his concern "to leave the way open for a compliance not too detrimental to Russian prestige." For his policy calls for the application of a steadily rising military pressure to challenge existing Soviet leadership. (Pp. 119, 120.) To this the Soviet leaders can hardly be expected to reply other than by preparations for a short-range showdown. This will hardly bring a "mellowing" of internal controls in Russia. By the same token, Kennan's proposals destroy the "fortunate connotation" in Soviet theory that there is "no hurry." A more classic *non sequitur* could hardly be conceived—even as an exercise in mental gymnastics. But the responsibility for the future of American-Russian relations cannot be classed as intellectual amusement, for upon their character depends the immediate future of the world. And freedom is not nurtured by nations preparing for war.

There is considerable evidence that Kennan later came to realize the fallacy of his 1946 policy recommendations. In 1951, while on leave of absence from the Department of State, he was a bit less disingenuous—and considerably more moderate—in his statements. First, he cautioned that no war (a more candid substitute for his earlier phrase "unanswerable force") with Russia "could be more than relatively successful" (pp. 129–30); took care to point out that even a defeated Russia would not emerge in the image of America (p. 131); sharply redefined the character of the role that the United States could play—from "has it in its power to increase enormously the strains" to "our role can be at best a marginal one"; and finally warned that any attempt "at direct talking by one nation to another about the latter's political affairs is a questionable procedure." (Pp. 130, 53, 152.)

Later still, on the eve of his departure for Moscow, Kennan more openly indicated doubts about his earlier analysis. "I want to assume that everything I've thought up to now is wrong," he is reported to have observed, "and see whether I come out at the same place this time." He remarked, however, that any change in his earlier conclusions was "improbable"—an admission that raised serious questions as to Kennan's ability to free himself from the thought patterns of the "X" article. Kennan left no doubt, though, that he was worried by the consequences of containment, for he expressed a fear that it was "a lesson that Americans have learned rather too well." (*The New Yorker,* May 17, 1952, pp. 111, 112.) His concern is well founded, but nothing can alter the fact that it was Kennan himself who served as their tutor.

Central to Kennan's shift was his belated realization that the United States will never have enough power to force Russia to "unquestionably yield to it." Once he awoke to this basic error of his "X" article, Kennan quickly saw that his policy in action could well "increase [the Russians'] fear of being warred upon." (*The New Yorker,* pp. 112, 116.) Small wonder that he seemed to be giving expression to a fear that his policy of containment is one for which he does not relish ultimate responsibility.

But Kennan cannot escape that responsibility. If he has in fact abandoned containment, he owes the world a formal statement of his decision—for his was the conception and the early implementation of the policy. To date, it has not been abandoned by the United States. If its author now finds it lacking in validity and dangerous in its consequences, then his is the responsibility to throw his weight on the side of revision.

Yet Kennan's greatest failure lies in his inability to define that "something which goes deeper and looks further ahead" —without which containment, by his own admission, "can only remain sterile and negative." (*American Diplomacy,* p. 153.) That "something" is no less than the courage to acknowledge the broad challenge of the Bolshevik Revolution. One must conclude that so far, at any rate, Kennan is unaware of the challenge, and until he faces that issue candidly he cannot be expected to formulate an effective response to the challenge of Soviet power.

Monthly Review
(1952)

The Legend of

Isolationism

in the

1920's *

The widely accepted assumption that the United States was isolationist from 1920 through 1932 is no more than a legend. Sir Francis Bacon might have classed this myth of isolation as one of his Idols of the Market-Place. An "ill and unfit choice of words," he cautioned, "leads men away into innumerable and inane controversies and fancies." [1] And certainly the application of the terms *isolation* and *isolationism* to a period and a policy that were characterized by vigorous involvement in the affairs of the world with consciousness of purpose qualifies as an "ill and unfit choice of words." Thus the purpose of this essay: on the basis of an investigation of the record to suggest that, far from isolation, the foreign relations of the United States from 1920 through 1932 were marked by express and extended involvement with—and intervention in the affairs of—other nations of the world.

It is both more accurate and more helpful to consider the twenties as contiguous with the present instead of viewing those years as a quixotic interlude of low-down jazz and lower-grade gin, fluttering flappers and Faulkner's fiction, and bootlegging millionaires and millionaire bootleggers. For in foreign policy there is far less of a sharp break between 1923 and 1953 than

* This paper was read before the December, 1953, meeting of the Pacific Historical Association, held at Davis College, California.

generally is acknowledged. A closer examination of the so-called isolationists of the twenties reveals that many of them were in fact busily engaged in extending American power. Those individuals and groups have not dramatically changed their outlook on foreign affairs. Their policies and objectives may differ with those of others (including professors), but they have never sought to isolate the United States.

This interpretation runs counter to the folklore of American foreign relations. Harvard places isolationism "in the saddle." Columbia sees "Americans retiring within their own shell." Yale judges that policy "degenerated" into isolation—among other things.[2] Others, less picturesque but equally positive, refer to a "marked increase of isolationist sentiment" and to "those years of isolationism." Another group diagnoses the populace as having "ingrained isolationism," analyzes it as "sullen and selfish" in consequence, and characterizes it as doing "its best to forget international subjects." Related verdicts describe the Republican party as "predominantly isolationist" and as an organization that "fostered a policy of deliberate isolation." [3]

Most pointed of these specifications is a terse two-word summary of the diplomacy of the period: "Isolation Perfected." [4] Popularizers have transcribed this theme into a burlesque. Their articles and books convey the impression that the Secretaries of State were in semi-retirement and that the citizenry wished to do away with the Department itself.[5] Columnists and commentators have made the concept an eerie example of George Orwell's double-think. They label as isolationists the most vigorous interventionists.

The case would seem to be closed and judgment given if it were not for the ambivalence of some observers and the brief dissents filed by a few others. The scholar who used the phrase "those years of isolationism," for example, remarks elsewhere in the same book that "expansionism . . . really was long a major expression of isolationism." Another writes of the "return to an earlier policy of isolation," and on the next page notes a "shift in policy during the twenties amounting almost to a 'diplomatic revolution'." A recent biographer states that Henry Cabot Lodge "did not propose . . . an isolationist attitude," but then proceeds to characterize the Monroe Doctrine—upon which Lodge stood in his fight against the League of Nations treaty—as a philosophy of "isolation." And in the last volume of his trilogy, the late Professor Frederick L. Paxton summed up a long review of the many diplomatic activities of the years 1919–1923 with the remark that this was a foreign policy of "avoidance rather than of action." [6]

But a few scholars, toying with the Idol of the Market-Place, have made bold to rock the image. Yet Professor Richard Van Alstyne was doing more than playing the iconoclast when he observed that the "militant manifest destiny men were the isolationists of the the nineteenth century." For with this insight we can translate those who maintain that Lodge "led the movement to perpetuate the traditional policy of isolation." Perhaps William G. Carleton was even more forthright. In 1946 he pointed out that the fight over the League treaty was not between isolationists and internationalists, and added that many of the mislabeled isolationists were actually "nationalists and imperialists." Equally discerning was Charles Beard's comment in 1933 that the twenties were marked by a "return to the more aggressive ways . . . [used] to protect and advance the claims of American business enterprise." All these interpretations were based on facts that prompted another scholar to change his earlier conclusion and declare in 1953 that "the thought was all of keeping American freedom of action." [7]

These are perceptive comments. Additional help has recently been supplied by two other students of the period. One of these is Robert E. Osgood, who approached the problem in terms of *Ideals and Self-Interest in American Foreign Relations*.[8] Though primarily concerned with the argument that Americans should cease being naive, Osgood suggests that certain stereotypes are misleading. One might differ with his analysis of the struggle over the Treaty of Versailles, but not with his insistence that there were fundamental differences between Senators Lodge and William E. Borah—as well as between those two and President Woodrow Wilson. Osgood likewise raises questions about the reputed withdrawal of the American public. Over a thousand organizations for the study of international relations existed in 1926, to say nothing of the groups that sought constantly to make or modify foreign policy.

Osgood gives little attention to this latter aspect of foreign relations, a surprising omission on the part of a realist.[9] But the underlying assumption of his inquiry cannot be challenged. The foreign policy issue of the twenties was never isolationism. The controversy and competition were waged between those who entertained different concepts of the national interest and disagreed over the means to be employed to secure that objective. Secretary of State Charles Evans Hughes was merely more eloquent, not less explicit. "Foreign policies," he explained in 1923, "are not built upon abstractions. They are the result of practical conceptions of national interest arising from some immediate exigency or standing out vividly in historical perspective." [10]

Historian George L. Grassmuck used this old-fashioned premise of the politician as a tool with which to probe the *Sectional Biases in Congress on Foreign Policy*. Disciplining himself more rigorously in the search for primary facts than did Osgood, Grassmuck's findings prompted him to conclude that "the 'sheep and goats' technique" of historical research is eminently unproductive. From 1921 to 1933, for example, the Republicans in both houses of Congress were "more favorable to both Army and Navy measures than . . . Democrats." Eighty-five percent of the same Republicans supported international economic measures and agreements. As for the Middle West, that much condemned section did not reveal any "extraordinary indication of a . . . tendency to withdraw." Nor was there "an intense 'isolationism' on the part of [its] legislators with regard to membership in a world organization." [11] And what opposition there was seems to have been as much the consequence of dust bowls and depression as the product of disillusioned scholars in ivory towers.

These investigations and correlations have two implications. First, the United States was neither isolated nor did it pursue a policy of isolationism from 1920 to 1933. Second, if the policy of that era, so generally accepted as the product of traditional isolationist sentiment, proves non-isolationist, then the validity and usefulness of the concept when applied to earlier or later periods may seriously be challenged.

Indeed, it would seem more probable that the central theme of American foreign relations has been the expansion of the United States. Alexander Hamilton made astute use of the phrase "no entangling alliances" during the negotiation of Jay's Treaty in 1794, but his object was a *de facto* affiliation with the British Fleet—not isolation.[12] Nor was Thomas Jefferson seeking to withdraw when he made of Monticello a counselling center for those seeking to emulate the success of the American Revolution. A century later Senator Lodge sought to revise the Treaty of Versailles and the Covenant of the League of Nations with reservations that seemed no more than a restatement of Hamilton's remarks. Yet the maneuvers of Lodge were no more isolationist in character and purpose than Hamilton's earlier action. And while surely no latter-day Jefferson, Senator Borah was anything but an isolationist in his concept of the power of economics and ideas. Borah not only favored the recognition of the Soviet Union in order to influence the development of the Bolshevik Revolution and as a check against Japanese expansion in Asia, but also argued that American economic policies were intimately connected with foreign political crises. All those men were concerned with the extension of one or more aspects of American influence, power, and authority.

Approached in this manner, the record of American foreign policy in the twenties verifies the judgments of two remarkably dissimilar students: historian Richard W. Leopold and Senator Lodge. The professor warns that the era was "more complex than most glib generalizations . . . would suggest"; and the scholastic politician concludes that, excepting wars, there "never [was] a period when the United States [was] more active and its influence more felt internationally than between 1921 and 1924." [13] The admonition about perplexity was offered as helpful advice, not as an invitation to anti-intellectualism. For, as the remarks of the Senator implied, recognition that a problem is involved does not mean that it cannot be resolved.

Paradox and complexity can often be clarified by rearranging the data around a new focal point that is common to all aspects of the apparent contradiction. The confusion of certainty and ambiguity that characterizes most accounts of American foreign policy in the twenties stems from the fact that they are centered on the issue of membership in the League of Nations. Those Americans who wanted to join are called internationalists. Opponents of that move became isolationists. But the subsequent action of most of those who fought participation in the League belies this simple classification. And the later policies of many who favored adherence to the League casts serious doubts upon the assumption that they were willing to negotiate or arbitrate questions that they defined as involving the national interest. More pertinent is an examination of why certain groups and individuals favored or disapproved of the League, coupled with a review of the programs they supported after that question was decided.

Yet such a re-study of the League fight is in itself insufficient. Equally important is a close analysis of the American reaction to the Bolshevik Revolution. Both the League Covenant and the Treaty of Versailles were written on a table shaken by that upheaval. The argument over the ratification of the combined documents was waged in a context determined as much by Nikolai Lenin's *Appeal to the Toiling, Oppressed, and Exhausted Peoples of Europe* and the Soviet *Declaration to the Chinese People* as by George Washington's Farewell Address.[14]

Considered within the setting of the Bolshevik Revolution, the basic question was far greater than whether or not to enter the League. At issue was what response was to be made to the domestic and international division of labor that had accompanied the Industrial Revolution. Challenges from organized urban labor, dissatisfied farmers, frightened men of property, searching intellectual critics, and colonial peoples rudely interrupted almost every meeting of the Big Four in Paris and were echoed in many Senate debates over the treaty. And those who determined American policy through the decade of the twenties were consciously concerned with the same problem.

An inquiry into this controversy over the broad question of how to end the war reveals certain divisions within American society. These groupings were composed of individuals and organizations whose position on the League of Nations was coincident with and part of their response to the Bosheviks; or, in a wider sense, with their answer to that general unrest, described by Woodrow Wilson as a "feeling of revolt against the large vested interests which influenced the world both in the economic and the political sphere." [15] Once this breakdown has been made it is then possible to follow the ideas and actions of these various associations of influence and power through the years 1920 to 1933.

At the core of the American reaction to the League and the Bolshevik Revolution was the quandary between fidelity to ideals and the urge to power. Jefferson faced a less acute version of the same predicament in terms of whether to force citizenship on settlers west of the Mississippi who were reluctant to be absorbed in the Louisiana Purchase. A century later the anti-imperialists posed the same issue in the more sharply defined circumstances of the Spanish-American War. The League and the Bolsheviks raised the question in its most dramatic context and in unavoidable terms.

There were four broad responses to this reopening of the age-old dilemma. At one pole stood the pure idealists and pacifists, led by William Jennings Bryan. A tiny minority in themselves, they were joined, in terms of general consequences if not in action, by those Americans who were preoccupied with their own solutions to the problem. Many American businessmen, for example, were concerned primarily with the expansion of trade and were apathetic toward or impatient with the hullabaloo over the League.[16] Diametrically opposed to the idealists were the vigorous expansionists. All these exponents of the main chance did not insist upon an overt crusade to run the world, but they were united on Senator Lodge's proposition that the United States should dominate world politics. Association with other nations they accepted, but not equality of membership or mutuality of decision.

Caught in the middle were those Americans who declined to

support either extreme. A large number of these people clustered around Woodrow Wilson, and can be called the Wilsonites. Though aware of the dangers and temptations involved, Wilson declared his intention to extend American power for the purpose of strengthening the ideals. However noble that effort, it failed for two reasons. Wilson delegated power and initiative to men and organizations that did not share his objectives, and on his own part the president ultimately "cast in his lot" with the defenders of the status quo.[17]

Led by the Sons of the Wild Jackass, the remaining group usually followed Senator Borah in foreign relations. These men had few illusions about the importance of power in human affairs or concerning the authority of the United States in international politics. Prior to the world war they supported—either positively or passively—such vigorous expansionists as Theodore Roosevelt, who led their Progressive party. But the war and the Bolshevik Revolution jarred some of these Progressives into a closer examination of their assumptions. These reflections and new conclusions widened the breach with those of their old comrades who had moved toward a conservative position on domestic issues. Some of those earlier allies, like Senator Albert J. Beveridge, continued to agitate for an American century. Others, such as Bainbridge Colby, sided with Wilson in 1916 and went along with the president on foreign policy.

But a handful had become firm anti-expansionists by 1919.[18] No attempt was made by these men to deny the power of the United States. Nor did they think that the nation could become self-sufficient and impregnable in its strength. Borah, for example, insisted that America must stand with Russia if Japan and Germany were to be checked. And Johnson constantly pointed out that the question was not whether to withdraw, but at what time and under what circumstances to use the country's influence. What these men did maintain was that any effort to run the world by establishing an American system comparable to the British Empire was both futile and un-American.

In this they agreed with Henry Adams, who debated the same issue with his brother Brooks Adams, Theodore Roosevelt, and Henry Cabot Lodge in the years after 1898. "I incline now to anti-imperialism, and very strongly to anti-militarism," Henry warned. "If we try to rule politically, we take the chances against us." By the end of the first world war another generation of expansionists tended to agree with Henry Adams about ruling politically, but planned to build and maintain a similar pattern of control through the use of America's economic might. Replying to these later expansionists, Borah and other anti-expansionists of the nineteen-twenties argued that if Washington's influence was to be effective it would have to be used to support the movements of reform and colonial nationalism rather than deployed in an effort to dam up and dominate those forces.

For these reasons they opposed Wilson's reorganization of the international banking consortium, fearing that the financiers would either influence strongly or veto—as they did—American foreign policies. With Senator Albert B. Cummins of Iowa they voted against the Wilson-approved Webb-Pomerene Act, which repealed the anti-trust laws for export associations. In the same vein they tried to prevent passage of the Edge Act, an amendment to the Federal Reserve Act that authorized foreign banking corporations.[19] Led by Borah, they bitterly attacked the Versailles Treaty because, in their view, it committed the United States to oppose colonial movements for self-government and to support an unjust and indefensible status quo. From the same perspective they criticized and fought to end intervention in Russia and the suppression of civil liberties at home.[20]

Contrary to the standard criticism of their actions, however, these anti-expansionists were not just negative die-hards. Senator Cummins maintained from the first that American loans to the allies should be considered gifts. Borah spoke out on the same issue, hammered away against armed intervention in Latin America, played a key role in securing the appointment of Dwight Morrow as Ambassador to Mexico, and sought to align the United States with, instead of against, the Chinese Revolution. On these and other issues the anti-expansionists were not always of one mind, but as in the case of the Washington Conference Treaties the majority of them were far more positive in their actions than has been acknowledged.[21]

Within this framework the key to the defeat of the League treaty was the defection from the Wilsonites of a group who declined to accept the restrictions that Article X of the League Covenant threatened to impose upon the United States. A morally binding guarantee of the "territorial integrity and existing political integrity of all members of the League" was too much for these men. First they tried to modify that limitation. Failing there, they followed Elihu Root and William Howard Taft, both old time expansionists, to a new position behind Senator Lodge. Among those who abandoned Wilson on this issue were Herbert Hoover, Calvin Coolidge, Charles Evans Hughes, and Henry L. Stimson.

Not all these men were at ease with the vigorous expansionists. Stimson, for one, thought the Lodge reservations "harsh and unpleasant," and later adjusted other of his views.[22] Hoover and Hughes tried to revive their version of the League after the Republicans returned to power in 1920. But at the time all of them were more uneasy about what one writer has termed Wilson's "moral imperialism." [23] They were not eager to identify themselves with the memories of that blatant imperialism of the years 1895 to 1905, but neither did they like Article X. That proviso caught them from both sides, it illegalized changes initiated by the United States, and obligated America to restore a status quo to some aspects of which they were either indifferent or antagonistic. But least of all were they anxious to run the risk that the Wilsonian rhetoric of freedom and liberty might be taken seriously in an age of revolution. Either by choice or default they supported the idea of a community of interest among the industrialized powers of the world led by an American-British entente as against the colonial areas and the Soviet Union.

This postwar concept of the community of interest was the first generation intellectual off-spring of Herbert Croly's *Promise of American Life* and Herbert Hoover's *American Individualism.* Croly's opportunistic nationalism provided direction for Hoover's "greater mutuality of interest." The latter was to be expressed in an alliance between the government and the "great trade associations and the powerful corporations." [24] Pushed by the Croly-Hoover wing of the old Progressive party, the idea enjoyed great prestige during the twenties. Among its most ardent exponents were Samuel Gompers and Matthew Woll of the labor movement, Owen D. Young of management, and Bernard Baruch of finance.

What emerged was an American corporatism. The avowed goals were order, stability, and social peace. The means to those objectives were labor-management co-operation, arbitration, and the elimination of waste and inefficiency by closing out unrestrained competition. State intervention was to be firm, but moderated through the cultivation and legalization of trade associations which would, in turn, advise the national government and supply leaders for the federal bureaucracy. The ideal was union in place of diversity and conflict.[25]

Other than Hoover, the chief spokesmen of this new community of interest as applied to foreign affairs were Secretaries of State Hughes and Stimson. In the late months of 1931 Stimson was to shift his ground, but until that time he supported the principle. All three men agreed that American economic power should be used to build, strengthen, and maintain the co-operation they sought. As a condition for his entry into the cabinet, Hoover demanded—and received—a major voice in "all important economic policies of the administration." [26] With the energetic assistance of Julius Klein, lauded by the National Foreign Trade Council as the "international business go-getter of Uncle Sam," Hoover changed the Department of Commerce from an agency primarily concerned with interstate commerce to one that concentrated on foreign markets and loans, and control of important sources.[27] Hughes and Stimson handled the political aspects of establishing a "community of ideals, interests and purposes." [28]

These men were not imperialists in the traditional sense of that much abused term. All agreed with Klein that the object was to eliminate "the old imperialistic trappings of politico-economic exploitation." They sought instead the "internationalization of business." [29] Through the use of economic power they wanted to establish a common bond, forged of similar assumptions and purposes, with both the industrialized nations and the native business community in the colonial areas of the world. Their deployment of America's material strength is unquestioned. President Calvin Coolidge reviewed their success, and indicated the political implications thereof, on Memorial Day, 1928. "Our investments and trade relations are such," he summarized, "that it is almost impossible to conceive of any conflict anywhere on earth which would not affect us injuriously." [30]

Internationalization through the avoidance of conflict was the key objective. This did not mean a negative foreign policy. Positive action was the basic theme. The transposition of corporatist principles to the area of foreign relations produced a parallel policy. American leadership and intervention would build a world community regulated by agreement among the industrialized nations. The prevention of revolution and the preservation of the sanctity of private property were vital objectives. Hughes was very clear when he formulated the idea for Latin America. "We are seeking to establish a *Pax Americana* maintained not by arms but by mutual respect and good will and the tranquillizing processes of reason." There would be, he admitted, "interpositions of a temporary character"—the Secretary did not like the connotations of the world intervention—but only to facilitate the establishment of the United States as the "exemplar of justice." [31]

Extension to the world of this pattern developed in Latin America was more involved. There were five main difficulties, four in the realm of foreign relations and one in domestic affairs. The internal problem was to establish and intregrate a concert of decision between the government and private economic groups. Abroad the objectives were more sharply defined: circumscribe the impact of the Soviet Union, forestall and control potential resistance of colonial areas, pamper and cajole Germany and Japan into acceptance of the basic proposition, and secure from Great Britain practical recognition of the fact that Washington had become the center of Anglo-Saxon collaboration. Several examples will serve to illustrate the general outline of this diplomacy, and to indicate the friction between the office holders and the office dwellers.

Wilson's Administration left the incoming Republicans a plurality of tools designed for the purpose of extending American power. The Webb-Pomerene Act, the Edge Act, and the banking consortium were but three of the more obvious and important of these. Certain polishing and sharpening remained to be done, as exemplified by Hoover's generous interpretation of the Webb-Pomerene legislation, but this was a minor problem. Hoover and Hughes added to these implements with such laws as the one designed to give American customs officials diplomatic immunity so that they could do cost accounting surveys of foreign firms. This procedure was part of the plan to provide equal opportunity abroad, under which circumstances Secretary Hughes was confident that "American businessmen would take care of themselves." [32]

It was harder to deal with the British, who persisted in annoying indications that they considered themselves equal partners in the enterprise. Bainbridge Colby, Wilson's last Secretary of State, ran into the same trouble. Unless England came "to our way of thinking," Colby feared that "agreement [would] be impossible." A bit later Hughes told the British Ambassador that the time had come for London's expressions of cordial sentiment to be "translated into something definite." After many harangues about oil, access to mandated areas, and trade with Russia, it was with great relief that Stimson spoke of the United States and Great Britain "working together like two old shoes." [33]

Deep concern over revolutionary ferment produced great anxiety. Hughes quite agreed with Colby that the problem was to prevent revolutions without making martyrs of the leaders of colonial or other dissident movements. The despatches of the period are filled with such expressions as "very grave concern," "further depressed," and "deeply regret," in connection with revolutionary activity in China, Latin America, and Europe.[34] American foreign service personnel abroad were constantly reminded to report all indications of such unrest. This sensitivity reached a high point when one representative telegraphed as "an example of the failure to assure public safety . . . the throwing of a rock yesterday into the state hospital here." Quite in keeping with this pattern was Washington's conclusion that it would support "any provisional government which gave satisfactory evidence of an intention to re-establish constitutional order." [35]

Central to American diplomacy of the twenties was the issue of Germany and Japan. And it was in this area that the government ran into trouble with its partners, the large associations of capital. The snag was to convince the bankers of the validity of the long range view. Hoover, Hughes and Stimson all agreed that it was vital to integrate Germany and Japan into the American community. Thus Hughes opposed the French diplomacy of force on the Rhine, and for his own part initiated the Dawes Plan. But the delegation of so much authority to the financiers backfired in 1931. The depression scared the House of Morgan and it refused to extend further credits to Germany. Stimson "blew up." He angrily told the Morgan representative in Paris that this strengthened France and thereby undercut the American program. Interrupted in the midst of this argument by a trans-Atlantic phone call from Hoover, Stimson explained to the president that "if you want to help the cause you are speaking of you will not do it by calling me up, but by calling Tom Lamont." Stimson then turned back to Lamont's agent in Europe and, using "unregulated language," told the man to abandon his "narrow banking axioms." [36]

Similar difficulties faced the government in dealing with Japan and China. The main problem was to convince Japan, by persuasion, concession, and the delicate use of diplomatic force, to join the United States in an application of its Latin American policy to China. Washington argued that the era of the crude exploitation of, and the exercise of direct political sovereignty over, backward peoples was past. Instead, the interested powers should agree to develop and exercise a system of absentee authority while increasing the productive capacity and administrative efficiency of China. Japan seemed amenable to the proposal, and at the Washington Conference, Secretary Hughes went a great distance to convince Tokyo of American sincerity. Some writers, such as George Frost Kennan and Adolf A. Berle, claim that the United States did not go far enough.[37] This is something of a mystery. For in his efforts to establish "co-operation in the Far East," as Hughes termed it, the Secretary consciously gave Japan "an extraordinarily favorable position." [38]

Perhaps what Kennan and Berle have in mind is the attitude of Thomas Lamont. In contrast to their perspective on Europe, the bankers took an extremely long range view of Asia. Accepting the implications of the Four and Nine Power Treaties, Lamont began to finance Japan's penetration of the mainland. Hughes and Stimson were trapped. They continued to think in terms of American businessmen taking care of themselves if given an opportunity, and thus strengthening Washington's position in the world community. Hughes wrote Morgan that he hoped the consortium would become an "important instrumentality of our 'open door' policy." [39] But the American members of the banking group refused to antagonize their Japanese and British colleagues, and so vetoed Washington's hope to finance the Chinese Eastern Railway and its efforts to support the Federal Telegraph Company in China.

In this context it is easy to sympathize with Stimson's discomfort when the Japanese Army roared across Manchuria. As he constantly reiterated to the Japanese Ambassador in Washington, Tokyo had come far along the road "of bringing itself into alignment with the methods and opinion of the Western World." [40] Stimson not only wanted to, but did in fact give Japan every chance to continue along that path. So too did President Hoover, whose concern with revolution was so great that he was inclined to view Japanese sovereignty in Manchuria as the best solution. Key men in the State Department shared the president's conclusion.[41]

Stimson's insight was not so limited. He realized that his predecessor, Secretary of State Frank B. Kellogg, had been right: the community of interest that America should seek was with the Chinese. The Secretary acknowledged his error to Senator Borah, who had argued just such a thesis since 1917. Stimson's letter to Borah of February 23, 1932, did not say that America should abandon her isolationism, but rather that she had gone too far with the wrong friends. The long and painful process of America's great awakening had begun. But in the meantime President Hoover's insistence that no move should be made toward the Soviet Union, and that the non-recognition of Manchukuo should be considered as a formula looking toward conciliation, had opened the door to appeasement.

Science and Society
(Winter 1954)

The Frontier Thesis

and American

Foreign

Policy

One of the central themes of American historiography is that there is no American Empire. Most historians will admit, if pressed, that the United States once had an empire. They promptly insist that it was given away. But they also speak persistently of America as a World Power.[1] Whatever language is used to describe the situation, the record of American diplomacy is clear in one point. The United States has been a consciously and steadily expanding nation since 1890. This essay is an initial exploration of one of the dynamic causes behind that extension of varying degrees of American sovereignty throughout the world.

Three continuing and interacting processes produce foreign policy. First, the domestic and overseas activity of the citizenry, and of other countries, which forces a government to take action in the international area. Second, the nature of that official action. And third, the reactions that such policies provoke among its own people and on the part of the foreigners who are affected. The circle is thus closed and rolls on through time. In studying foreign policy it ultimately becomes necessary to break into this continuity and find out, if possible, what the people in question thought they were doing.

One way to do this is to reconstruct the reality with which given men were forced to deal, look at it through their eyes, interpret it with their ideas, and then conclude as to the consequences of such a world view. The argument here, based on such a methodology, is that a set of ideas, first promulgated in the 1890's, became the world view of subsequent generations of Americans and is an important clue to understanding America's imperial expansion in the twentieth century.[2]

One idea is Frederick Jackson Turner's concept that America's unique and true democracy was the product of an expanding frontier.[3] The other idea is the thesis of Brooks Adams that America's unique and true democracy could be preserved only by a foreign policy of expansion. Turner's idea was designed to explain an experience already ended and to warn of the dangers ahead. Adams' idea was calculated to preserve Turner's half-truth about the past for his own time and project it into the future. Both ideas did much to prevent any understanding of a wholly new reality to which they were applied, and to which they were at best inadequate and at worst irrelevant.[4] But taken together, the ideas of Turner and Adams supplied American empire builders with an overview and explanation of the world, and a reasonably specific program of action from 1893 to 1953.

Turner's influence began when he was declared the parent of the frontier thesis by a star chamber court—the American Historical Association.[5] His statement of the idea then became the central, if not the only, thesis of Everyman's History of the United States. His personal influence touched Woodrow Wilson and perhaps Theodore Roosevelt, while his generalization guided subsequent generations of intellectuals and business men who became educational leaders, wielders of corporate power, government bureaucrats, and crusaders for the Free World.[6]

Adams preferred direct ties with the policy-makers. He did not achieve Turner's fame among laymen, but he passed his ideas on to Theodore Roosevelt and others who guided American expansion at the turn of the century. Fifty years later he was discovered by two groups of intellectual leaders. Scholars awarded him intellectual biographies and estimates of his influence. Those more immediately concerned with public policy, like columnist Marquis Childs and foreign service officer George Frost Kennan, introduced him to the public and applied his ideas to later problems.

Turner and Adams first offered their ideas on the marketplace of opinion and influence between 1893 and 1900, the years of crisis at the end of three decades of rough and rapid progress. American society had undergone, in the space of a generation, an economic revolution in each of four critical areas: steam, steel, communications, and agriculture. The coincidence and convergence of these upheavals produced a major crisis.[7] Bewildered by its quadruple triumph, the United States momentarily panicked. Then, reassured by illusions of ideological purity and international omnipotence, it embarked upon a second industrial revolution. But in that frightening pause between culmination and renewal Turner and Adams looked out upon a harsh and disturbing reality.

The basic steel industry and transportation system of the country were completed. The rate of national economic growth was falling off. New technological advances had yet to be applied in wholesale fashion. Instead, it seemed that the giants of the economic community had turned aside from their conquest of nature to despoil their own kind. Trusts, holding companies, and corporations began to wolf down the individual business man in a feast of consolidation and concentration. Farming was ceasing to be a family affair. Development of the public domain was coming more and more to be controlled by large capital. The Census Director emphasized the sense of foreboding when he announced, in April, 1891, that "there can hardly be said to be a frontier."

This, to Turner and Adams, was the most dangerous omen

of all. Both men grew up believing in the traditional conservative philosophy that the key to American democracy was the dynamic competition between men and groups who had a stake in
society. They shared the conviction, or more probably the assumption, that this stake had been, for capitalist and farmer
alike, the readily available and extensive supply of land. Railroads, steel plants, and wheat production were all similar in
being based on control of landed resources and wealth. Now the
life blood of American democracy was gone.

The consequences seemed appalling. Men looked to be making capital out of each other. Real estate speculation rapidly collapsed, even in the South. Wheat prices declined steadily. But
the rate of interest seemed immune to the laws of economic grav-
ity. Men were no longer going west as hired hands and becoming land owners. Tenancy, not ownership, seemed the institution with a future. One hundred and eighty thousand people retreated eastward from Kansas. Those who stayed raised more
cain than corn. Even the cowboy went on strike in parts of Texas.

Workers were no happier. The relative rate of increase in
real wages slacked off, and then, from 1889 to 1898, wages lost
ground in an absolute sense. "Strike!" became the rallying cry.
Miners came out of the ground in Idaho, Colorado, and Virginia. Switchmen became pickets in Buffalo. Eugene V. Debs
led his American Railway Union to the relief of the industrial
peons of the Pullman Company. The Army of the United States
countermarched with fixed bayonets against American civilians
in Chicago. Debs saw in the polished steel of those bayonets the
vision of American socialism. But other men were too preoccupied with the mirage of a square meal. They roamed the country looking for jobs. Their wives stayed home to scavenge the
garbage cans. And in Pennsylvania the heroes of Homestead
could not buy shoes for their children.

In the molten flux of this crisis, on July 12, 1893, Frederick Jackson Turner undertook to explain what was happening to America.[8] His interpretation also contained an implicit recommendation for action. His famous paper on "The Significance of the Frontier in American History" was Turner's application of his philosophy of history to American problems. History, for Turner, was nothing if not utilitarian. *"Each age,"* he had emphasized two years earlier, *"writes the history of the past anew with reference to the conditions uppermost in its own time."* For Turner his was the "age of machinery, of the factory system, and also the age of socialistic inquiry." Present-minded concern with the crisis which coincided with his intellectual maturity conditioned Turner's entire frontier thesis.

Thus Turner consciously sought a dynamic explanation of America's more happy history in the eighteenth and nineteenth centuries. He had the answer by 1891. "The ever-retreating frontier of free land is the key to American development." Then, in 1893, he changed the formulation of that thesis from a negative to a positive construction, and in the process used a vigorous, active verb—expansion. "This perennial rebirth, this fluidity of American life, this expansion westward with its new opportunities, its continuous touch with the simplicity of primitive society, furnish the forces dominating American life." Expansion, he concluded, promoted individualism which "from the beginning promoted democracy."

Expansion, Individualism, and Democracy was the catechism offered by this young messiah of America's uniqueness and omnipotence. The frontier, he cried, was "a magic fountain of youth in which America continuously bathed and rejuvenated." Without it, "fissures begin to open between classes, fissures that may widen into chasms." But he was confident that these dangers could and would be avoided. "American energy

will continually demand a wider field for its exercise." Ultimately he lauded the pioneer as the "foreloper" of empire. And
to drive home the lesson he quoted Rudyard Kipling, the laure-
ate of British imperialism. Turner had explained the past and
implied a program for the present. Materialistic individualism
and democratic idealism could be married and maintained by a
foreign policy of expansion.

Turner gave Americans a nationalistic world view that
eased their doubts, settled their confusions, and justified their aggressiveness. The frontier thesis was a bicarbonate of soda for
emotional and intellectual indigestion. His thesis rolled through
the universities and into popular literature as a tidal wave. Expansion a la Turner was good for business and at the same time
extended white Protestant democracy. Patrician politicians like
Theodore Roosevelt and Woodrow Wilson could agree with
railway magnate Edward H. Harriman, financier J. P. Morgan,
and the missionaries on the validity of Turner's explanation of
America's greatness. Turner's thesis thus played an important
role in the history of American foreign relations. For his interpretation did much to Americanize and popularize the heretofore alien ideas of economic imperialism and the White Man's
Burden.

Meanwhile, in that same month of July, 1893, another student of the frontier came to the same conclusion reached by
Turner. Within a month he, too, read a paper which stated the
same thesis but in a different manner. But Brooks Adams was
tucked away in America's ancestral home in Quincy, Massachusetts. The public knew nothing of his work. Astringent and argumentative, he was forty-five and fed up with America's professional intellectuals. He read *his* paper to a peer, brother Henry
Adams. Together they shared it with a few of their fellow New
England noblemen, like Henry Cabot Lodge, John Hay, and

Theodore Roosevelt, who did what they could to translate the implications of its thesis into official American policy.

The paper that Brooks read to Henry was the manuscript copy of *The Law of Civilization and Decay*. It was a frontier thesis for the world. Adams, like Turner, sought meaning and significance for the present from his study of history. "The value of history lies not in the multitude of facts collected, but in their relation to each other." Unlike Turner, Brooks Adams took the world as his subject and studied it with the aid of psychology and economics. He concluded that the centers of world civilization followed the frontiers of economic wealth and opportunity westward around the globe. The route was unmistakable: from the Mediterranean Basin through Western Europe to Great Britian. And to him the crisis of the 1890's was the turmoil incident to its further movement across the Atlantic to New York.

Brooks Adams was confronted with the same gloomy report of the Census Director that had so disturbed Turner. The continental West was filled up. America no longer had a frontier. As with Turner, this was a body blow to his early and easy assumption of steady evolutionary progress. He did not duck the truth. The thesis, he wrote brother Henry, worked out "in such a ghastly way that it knocks the stuffing out of me." He counterpunched with a policy of aggressive expansion designed to make Asia an economic colony of the United States. Russia was the most dangerous opponent; but Japan also needed to be watched. The strategy was to play them off against each other. America would be left as mistress of the vast frontier of Asia. "I am an expansionist, an 'imperialist,' if you please," he told a Boston newspaper man, "and I presume I may be willing to go farther in this line than anyone else in Massachusetts, with, perhaps, a few exceptions." [9]

Thus did Turner and Adams reach the same conclusions in

their separate studies of the frontier. Adams said that civilization followed the frontier of economic wealth. Turner agreed. Adams called the frontier the zone between "barbarism and civilization." Turner used "savagery and civilization." Adams maintained that American industry's "liberal margin of profit" had been "due to expansion" across the continent. Turner argued that America's true democracy was the product of this same expanding frontier. Both men saw the end of the continental frontier as the cause and symbol of crisis. Both dreaded the revolution—be it socialistic or monopolistic—that seemed to threaten at every turn. Adams chimed in that dissolution and decay might also follow. And implicitly or explicitly both men agreed on the program to avert chaos. Further expansion was the Kentucky rifle with which to cut down the night riders of catastrophe—Socialists, Robber Barons, and Barbarians.

Turner's thesis became America's explanation of its success and the prescription for its own and others' troubles. His interpretation of the American experience reassured and then inspired the millions. This is not to say that Turner had no influence on those who sat at the desks of decision. He did. Possibly with Theodore Roosevelt; certainly with Woodrow Wilson, and the generations of businessmen and bureaucrats whose teachers assured them that an expanding frontier was the cause of America's democratic success. But primarily he was the apostle of a revival movement that restored the faith of the conquerors of North America and made them international crusaders.

A far-western newspaper editor, writing in the summer of 1955, provided one of the clearest statements of this function and influence:

The idea, our forefathers believed, was to "push the Indians back to the frontier." Then, with the Indians pushed back to

the wilderness, all would be well. . . . Well, remember Kai-
ser Bill? He rather replaced the Indians. . . . Then, while
World War I's doughboy was still wearing out pieces of his
uniform, it became obvious that the woods, out along the
frontier, were still full of Indians. The thing to do, we fig-
ured, was to push back the Indians.[10]

Novelists of the frontier have used Turner's insight as the
central theme of their works. Indeed, their protagonists often
seem more Turnerian than human. Consider, for example, an
impromptu speech delivered by one of Ernest Haycox's Oregon
pioneers:

We grew up in the American notion that we could start
from nothing and become rich or get elected president.
That's our religion, much as any we've got—that we could
turn a dream into beefsteak and prosperity and happiness,
leave our children more than we had, and so on. When we
got older we saw that it wasn't that sure a thing. But we
couldn't admit the dream was bad, for that would be saying
hope is an illusion. So we saw empty land out here and
we've come here to make a fresh start, hoping that what was
wrong back East won't be wrong here.[11]

Such examples suggest that the history of Turner's thesis may
well offer a classic illustration of the transformation of an idea
into an ideology.[12]

Adams, for his part, became something of a Marx for the influential elite. He lost much of his direct personal significance
after Theodore Roosevelt stepped down as President in 1909,
though he did continue to have the ear of Senator Henry Cabot
Lodge. But thirty years later Charles Austin Beard revealed that
Adams, as well as Turner, was one of the men who had

changed his mind. Beard even republished *The Law of Civiliza-tion and Decay* with a long introduction praising Adams as a penetrating and original thinker. A bit later Adams was discov-ered by a new group of policy-makers. State Department offi-cials, columnists and commentators, and other advisors to the powerful began to cite him in footnotes and—more often—to paraphrase his ideas as their own. One even reissued his for-eign policy recommendations of the 1890's as a guide for the United States in the Cold War.

Adams always exercised his more personalized influence within the mainstream of Turnerism. He caught Theodore Roo-sevelt after the last battles of *The Winning of the West.* Turner had meanwhile encouraged Roosevelt to continue his interpreta-tion of the westward movement as the civilizing conquest of the savage by the Anglo-Saxon democrat. He also may have sharp-ened Roosevelt's uneasiness about the close of the frontier. Roosevelt was "very much struck" by Turner's essay on the sig-nificance of the frontier. He thought it contained "some first class ideas" which came "at *the* right time." Turner's ideas were "so interesting and suggestive" that Roosevelt wrote a blind let-ter to open the correspondence.[13] But Roosevelt's great awaken-ing came in his seminars with Brooks Adams.

Fellow aristocrat though he was, Adams rudely frightened Roosevelt. The strenuous life connected with destroying the In-dian and winning the West had been fun. Not so with the bat-tle to break down the powerful arguments and demolish the dreary logic of *The Law of Civilization and Decay.* Perhaps Roosevelt never quite forgave Adams for having written and published the book. And once, probably in a moment of anger with him for having thrown human nature into the perpetual motion machinery of evolution, he went so far as to call Adams "half-crazy." But the best that Roosevelt could do with *The Law* was to admit that it would be hard work to repeal it and ask Adams for advice on strategy and tactics.

Adams thus became something of the chairman of an informal policy-planning staff for the executive department in the years from 1896 to 1908. His was not, of course, the only influence brought to bear on President Roosevelt, Secretary of State John Hay, and other leaders. Exporters of cotton, capital, and kerosene all demanded that the government open the door to consumers around the world. Protestants and Populists wanted to export their respective brands of Americanism to the emotional and intellectual markets of colonial areas. But Adams, even more than Alfred Thayer Mahan, offered an interpretation of such pressures and a program for using them to control Asia.

For the foreign policy section of his first presidential message, Roosevelt borrowed a magazine article written by Adams and paraphrased it for the Congress. The recommendation was an Adams classic: use economic and military power to expand the frontier of the United States westward to the interior of China. Quite in keeping with Adams' plan, Roosevelt backed Japan in its war against Russia. But the maneuver went awry. Russia threatened to retaliate with social revolution. Adams feared this possibility more than anything else. He was afraid that such a revolution would turn into a secular reformation that would halt American expansion. Roosevelt and Adams frantically did what they could to prop up the old regime and left the problem for their successors.

Woodrow Wilson was ultimately to try his hand at controlling such a revolution in Russia. But first he had to contend with Mexican and German challenges to American democracy. Throughout these years Turner was an unseen intellectual roomer in the White House. Wilson and Turner had been close friends as well as visiting professor and student at Johns Hopkins University in the 1880's. Long walks after classes gave them a chance to learn from each other. Wilson knew and loved the aristocratic South. Turner told him about the West, and explained how it had made America democratic. And they talked about "the power of leadership; of the untested power of the man of literary ability in the field of diplomacy."

Wilson relied extensively on Turner's frontier thesis in presenting his own interpretation of American history. "All I ever wrote on the subject came from him." A comment overgenerous, perhaps, but not misleading. Read Wilson on American expansion after 1896: "The spaces of their own continent were occupied and reduced to the uses of civilization; they had no frontiers. . . . These new frontiers in the Indies and in the Far Pacific came to them as if out of the very necessity of the new career before them."

Wilson did not miss or fail to act on the economic implications of the frontier thesis, but he was the very model of Turner's crusading democrat. Indeed, Wilson's religious fervor called him to this duty even before the First World War. Earlier Americans had taught the Mexicans the meaning of Manifest Destiny and Dollar Diplomacy. Later, in the midst of revolution, the Mexicans seemed to forget American ideas about constitutional government and property rights. Wilson stepped in and became an enthusiastic tutor in moral imperialism. Vigorous though this instruction was, the President's former pupil was a bit critical of his old professor. "I hadn't his patience with Mexico," admitted Turner.

He likewise felt that Wilson was a bit too slow to act against the Germans. But he recognized the need for a perfect moral posture before the world. He devoutly supported the war to make the world safe for democracy. Fourteen years earlier Turner had observed that America's duty was "to conserve democratic institutions and ideals." Small wonder that he was "warmly in favor" of Wilson's Fourteen Points and the League of Nations. Wilson called his own proposals the "only possible program for peace" which "must prevail." Even more than in the case of Theodore Roosevelt, the policies of Woodrow Wilson were classic Turnerism.

It has been suggested that so also were the early policies of President Franklin Delano Roosevelt. Professors Curtis Nettels, James C. Malin, and Richard Hofstadter advance strong arguments in support of this view.[14] Roosevelt's speech at the Commonwealth Club of San Francisco during the campaign of 1932 is the basis of this interpretation. "Our last frontier has long since been reached," Roosevelt announced. "There is no safety valve in the form of a Western prairie . . . equality of opportunity as we have known it no longer exists. . . . Our task now is not discovery or exploitation of natural resources, or necessarily producing more goods. It is the . . . less dramatic business of administering resources and plants already in hand, of seeking to reëstablish foreign markets for our surplus production . . . of distributing wealth and products more equitably."

The extent to which Roosevelt wrote and understood what he said is debatable, but immaterial to the discussion at hand. One group of his advisors certainly acted within this framework. The N.I.R.A., the A.A.A., and other similar legislative measures were clearly based on the idea that the frontier was gone. But this relationship does not mean that Turner was the intellectual father of the New Deal's regulatory legislation. The fact of the frontier's disappearance was not the burden of the Turner thesis, but rather of the Census Director's dissertation. Turner's frontier thesis made democracy a function of an expanding frontier. The idea that the national government should use its power to rationalize, plan, and control the corporate development of the country had been Americanized and promoted by Herbert Croly, not Frederick Jackson Turner. Croly's *Promise of American Life* would seem more the intellectual handbook of the New Deal than Turner's essay on the frontier.

But there was a Turnerism in Roosevelt's speech at the Commonwealth Club. It was the remark about "seeking to reëstablish foreign markets for our surplus production." No single phase of the New Deal was pushed harder than Secretary of State Cordell Hull's campaign to expand trade. The real Turnerians among the New Dealers were those who converted a thesis about landed expansion into one about industrial expansion. Thus the inner history of the New Deal, and later administrations, can fruitfully be studied as a three-way tug-of-war between the Croly planners, the Turner inflationists and expansionists, and the Adamites, a group which sought to synthesize the two ideas.[15] The planners lost much of their influence during the recession of 1937–1939. Recovery came only through expanded production for war. And it was during this period that Roosevelt and others began openly to apply Turner's thesis to the new economic situation. An expanding economy became the dogma of an industrial America.

Roosevelt had always been, at heart, a Turnerian in foreign policy. He was sure, save for a short interlude during the years between the wars, that America's frontier was the world.[16] This attitude does much to explain Charles Beard's attacks on Roosevelt. Beard was a brilliant student of history keenly aware of the consequences of imperial expansion. He also understood, and had written about, the influence of the expansionist ideas of Turner and Adams. His study of these men led him to develop a Beardian antithesis on foreign policy. *In a closed world the attempt to maintain an expanding national frontier, be it ideolog-*

ical, political, or economic, would lead to war and tyranny. Democracy would be negated.[17] Thus he approved much of the early domestic program of the New Deal while militantly opposing Roosevelt's foreign policy. Self-containment and development comprised Beard's program. His motivation, his logic, and his conclusions were disdainfully dismissed or angrily assaulted until, a dozen years later, the Soviet Union began to manufacture hydrogen bombs.

Roosevelt's Turnerism was meanwhile blended with the *Realpolitik* of Adams. Roosevelt made much of his desire to end nineteenth-century colonialism. The Good Neighbor Policy, developmental projects for the Near East, and the plan to elevate China to the rank of a great power were offered as demonstrations of this democratic purpose. Little was said of the somewhat patronizing attitude and the more materialistic objectives of this approach. While the left hand reformed, however, the strong right was to serve as the mailed fist. Thus at the Atlantic Conference the Four Freedoms were matched by an understanding with Great Britain to police the world after the war. Russia would be admitted to this Anglo-American coalition if circumstances made that necessary. They did. Russia had been rejuvenated by the very revolution so feared by Brooks Adams, and its new strength was essential if Hitler was to be defeated. This fact delimited America's frontier. And to further complicate the situation the Russians, in Marx and Lenin, had an Adams and a Turner all their own.

At this point, and no doubt unconsciously, Roosevelt took the worst from Turner and Adams. He seemed, from the spring of 1942 to the fall of 1944, to base his plans for the postwar era on the idea of a concert of power. Then, in October, 1944, he in effect reaffirmed the Open Door policy of John Hay. First he gave the impression of accepting Russian predominance in Eastern Europe. But at the same time he claimed "complete freedom of action" in the future.[18] The Russians either declined or were unable to acquiesce in such unilateral reassertion of the frontier thesis. For the leaders of the frontier communities of the world had heard of Marx as well as Turner. And if the doors of the world were to be thrown open in one direction, why not in the other? The temptations and the pressures inherent in that question did much to produce the Cold War.

At some hour in the early years of the Cold War someone rediscovered Brooks Adams. Who it was and when it was may remain one of those tantalizing secrets of history. But done it was. Perhaps it was Marquis Childs, a newspaper columnist whose intellectual friends included many New Deal bureaucrats. In late 1945 or 1946 Childs wrote a long, laudatory introduction for a new edition of *America's Economic Supremacy,* Adams' old handbook for empire builders. Childs left no doubt as to the reason for his action. "If Adams had written last year, for publication this year, he would have had to alter scarcely anything to relate his views to the world of today." [19]

Or perhaps it was George Frost Kennan, looking into the past for guidance after he became chief of the policy planning division of the Department of State. Kennan, in explaining and defending the policy of containment, mentioned Adams as one of the small number of Americans who had recognized the proper basis of foreign policy. Later, as in one of the few State Department policy discussions of which there is current public record, and in his estimate of the *Realities of American Foreign Policy,* Kennan's analysis and argument was in many respects remarkably similar to that of Adams. Only the as-yet-unopened files in the archives can reveal whether these correlations were initally patterns of causation.[20] But it is not unknown for an idea first picked up and used as a rationalization to become an engine of later action.

Turnerism, meanwhile, retained its vigor during these years. The Truman Doctrine seemed an almost classic statement of the thesis that the security and well-being of the United States depended upon the successful execution of America's unique mission to defend and extend the frontier of democracy throughout the world. Another of President Harry S. Truman's major speeches spelling out certain aspects of this obligation was indeed entitled *The American Frontier*.[21] But there were critics who insisted that the President was too conservative. Perhaps the leader of this group was John Foster Dulles, who was so dissatisfied with the limitations of Truman's formulation that he termed it positively "un-moral." And Dulles might well claim that his plan to liberate all people not ruled according to the precepts of individualistic democracy was the definitive statement of the thesis.

Yet as was the case when the United States liberated the Philippines in 1898, it was sometimes hard, in the years of the Cold War, to determine just what definition of freedom was being used by the Turnerians. A somewhat strange assortment of political theories and social institutions seemed to qualify as individualistic and democratic if they facilitated American expansion. This imperial standard of judgment stemmed in considerable part from the ideological nationalism of Turner's frontier and the nationalistic materialism of the Adams analysis of the world frontier. But these characteristics were synthesized in the concept of an expanding economy, which became the new American credo in the years after 1935, and particularly during the Cold War.

The argument that continually expanding industrial production was the basic remedy for the economic and social ills of industrial society was not, of course, originally advanced by either Turner or Adams. Nor is the idea itself irrelevant to the problem of keeping up with—and ahead of—the increasing minimum demands of a growing population. This essay is not concerned with such a historical and theoretical critique of the idea. But it is suggested that the manner in which American leadership accepted the proposition that an expanding economy provided the key to "building a successfully functioning political and economic system," in the words of Secretary of State Dean Acheson, was not unrelated to the milieu established by Turner and Adams.

Walter Prescott Webb has outlined the general nature of this intellectual association in his study of *The Great Frontier*.[22] It does seem necessary to recapitulate the evidence which illustrates the manner in which Americans refer to Latin America and other areas as their new frontiers. It is more fruitful to review the discussions incident to the formulation of American foreign policy since 1945. Much emphasis has rightly been placed on the extent to which these programs were conceived within a framework of increasing tension with the Soviet Union. But this is only part of the story. One of the most striking themes to emerge from the multiplicity of hearings on this legislation is the degree to which it was motivated by the effort to solve American and world problems through the medium of an expanding economy.

Dean Acheson outlined this approach very carefully in May, 1947, as background for the forthcoming Marshall Plan. Three years later, after becoming Secretary of State, he emphasized the same idea even more directly. He explicitly denied that the situation of the United States viz à viz the Soviet Union was in any sense as desperate as that faced by Great Britain in 1940. "I do not imply," he concluded, "that the only reason for continuing the European recovery program is the threat of further expansion by the Soviet Union. On the contrary, the free world, even if no threat of this kind existed, would face the same hard task of building a successfully functioning system." [23]

William C. Foster, an early administrator of the European Recovery Program, provided the neatest statement of the underlying assumption. "Our whole philosophy in the United States," he explained, "is that of an expanding economy and not a static economy to produce more, and not divide up what you have." W. Averell Harriman, who exercised general supervision over this program, shared this outlook. Nelson Rockefeller, another leader in the effort, tied the approach directly to the frontier thesis. "With the closing of our own frontier," he pointed out, "there is hope that other frontiers still exist in the world." So, too, did Harriman, when he was questioned on the relationship between American aid to European nations and the efforts of those countries to strengthen and maintain themselves in Africa, the Near East, and Asia. "It is, in a sense," he explained, "their frontier, as the West used to be with us." [24]

Harriman further maintained, completing the analogy, that the United States, in order to sustain its expanding economy, had to support such action and develop its own position in those areas. Point IV assistance was described and defended as "absolutely essential" within this framework. Secretary Acheson agreed.[25] And from one "heavily indebted to George Frost Kennan for much stimulation and guidance" came the most candid summary of all. America's interests in colonial territories "coincide with the interests of European metropolitan countries. . . . The best possible situation is a series of 'happy' colonial relationships. . . . We should not let our 'rabbit ears' . . . dominate decisions in which a substantial degree of the national interest is at stake and in which there are no clear moral 'rights' and 'wrongs.' " [26]

Such testimony offers considerable support for Webb's generalization that Americans viewed the frontier "not as a line to stop at, but as an *area* inviting entrance." [27] And this attitude, whether held by the public or its elite, would seem to have been generated in part by Turner's thesis that democracy was a function of an expanding frontier and Adams' argument that the frontier was also the source of world power.

But it began to appear, after 1952, that Turner and Adams had met their match in Einstein and Oppenheimer. The General Theory of Relativity seemed likely to antiquate the frontier thesis. For armed with hydrogen bombs the messiahs become gladiators whose weapons will destroy the stadium. Their battle would make the world a frontier for fossils. Even the Russian followers of Marx and Lenin gave signs of becoming aware that their version of the thesis needed to be revised to accord with this new reality.

Perhaps Charles Beard can now rest easy. He was a better historian than either Turner or Adams. Yet he never found his Roosevelt or Wilson. Beard was always a bit too sharp and tough-minded for America's professional and intellectual politicians. He would chuckle to know that his idea of self-containment was reintroduced to Americans by Winston Spencer Churchill. Churchill's intellectual migration from aggressive imperialism to reluctant coexistence chronicled the demise of the frontier thesis. And Beard might ultimately have an American spokesman. The followers of Turner and Adams remained numerous and influential in the councils of state, but they hesitated to take the awful responsibility for acting on their theses. They seemed dimly aware that the United States had finally caught up with History. Americans were no longer unique.

Henceforward they, too, would share the fate of all mankind. For the frontier was now on the rim of hell, and the inferno was radioactive.

Pacific Historical Review
(November 1955)

The Age of
Re-Forming
History

Powerful though it is, and perceptive as it may be, the Pulitzer Prize Committee raised more questions than it settled by awarding this year's honors in History to Richard Hofstadter's *Age of Reform*. The issue is not whether Hofstadter can write first-rate History. He has done so: recently in *The Development of Academic Freedom in the United States,* and earlier in *The American Political Tradition.* But he did not win the prize for either of those works. Instead, he received it for a volume which is not History, and which does not match their quality. Neither, for that matter, is it as well written as either of them. An examination of the nature, methodology and implications of *The Age of Reform* may offer insights into the outlook and standards of the ascendant group of American intellectuals.

The Age of Reform is the full statement of a theme that Hofstadter has been developing, in various articles and lectures, during the past five years. The liberal, he says, has become a conservative. Much of his argument, delivered in a stage whisper, amounts to an extensive criticism of radicals. None of this is original, but Hofstadter does present it in the most up-to-date intellectual fashion, and he has an audience that accepts his interpretation as a justification for its own ideology.

This audience is composed of the New Liberals, those first cousins of the species known as Flying Buttress Catholics. What-

ever their appearances to the contrary, both groups support the
Existing Institution. Hofstadter's work in the temper of *The
Age of Reform,* which includes his essays on Charles A. Beard,
Manifest Destiny, and the New Conservatism, appeals to this
New Liberalism because it explains and justifies what the liberal
has been doing—and what he has not done. Hofstadter's analysis offers the liberal all this world and heaven, too. For it implies that wisdom, the pot of gold, the moderately baggy tweeds
of acceptability and a favorable verdict from History itself are
all to be found along or at the end of the road of least resistance.

All this may be just what contemporary psychiatry pre-
scribes for achieving serenity in an age of rapid and extensive
change, but it is not History. It is, in fact, a transformation of
History into Ideology. Whether or not this has been carried out
consciously is not even a very interesting question, let alone a
relevant or a rewarding one. However reached, the conclusion
indicates that the predominant group of American intellectuals
is so wholly immersed in contemporary American society that
no member of it can deal with the past, present, or future save
in terms of the present.

Thus a more pertinent inquiry into Hofstadter's History concerns its methodology and implications. His approach has two
central features. None of these studies is based on extended research in the primary evidence. In place of research, Hofstadter
has come more and more to apply the concepts of social
psychology—and in particular the idea of the struggle for
status—to the research of other students and to a narrow
selection of published evidence.

There is no indication, for example, that he has subjected
Julius K. Pratt's study of the coming of the Spanish-American

War to rigorous internal criticism, an exercise which opens up sizable gaps in its thesis. Nor does he investigate the primary sources. Even when dealing with one man, as in the essay on Beard, he neglects key aspects of the story. Thus he ignores the importance, for understanding Beard's book on the Constitution, of Beard's antecedent and primary concern with developing, testing and using a theory of social causation. In both instances, therefore, Hofstadter substitutes a social psychological theory of Progressivism for the history in question.

These examples lead directly to the question of Hofstadter's technique of applying social psychological concepts and logic to the data he does use. Social psychology is itself a method of understanding and interpreting *primary* evidence. As such it is a useful tool for the Historian. Thus Hofstadter is not to be criticized for using it, but rather for so seriously limiting, *a priori* and regardless of his chosen system, its fruitfulness by his own research methods. And he also seems to overlook the vital fact that whatever else psychology reveals (and this is considerable, of course), it cannot tell us how the world appeared in the consciousness of the actors—what they thought they were doing —or the relationship between a given conception of the world, entertained by individuals and groups with power, and subsequent events.

It is all well and good for Hofstadter to tell us, for example, that the Populists and other Americans went to war against Spain out of frustration with their lot at home. But this is neither as accurate nor as helpful, when we get down to cases, as ferreting out such facts as that specific labor leaders and their unions agitated for war on the grounds that it would strengthen their hand against employers; that the silverites thought of war as a last chance to establish a stronger competitive position with the British Empire for the type of foreign trade that would benefit them; or that many influential business men and politicians did indeed favor war for immediate as well as general economic reasons.

For even assuming that the only function of History is to help avoid such aggressiveness in the future, it would still seem prophylactic to know that the general neurosis takes rather specific economic and functional forms. Of course, this might suggest the need for structural changes as opposed to group therapy; but that is one of the risks of studying anything—even History.

It is not much more fruitful, to cite another instance, to stress the role of the Populists in accounting for latter-day anti-Semitism without undertaking the research which would tell us, among other things, whether or not Populist rhetoric was based on a factual coincidence of a religious-cultural ethic and economic power among their opponents. Evidence of this kind certainly could not condone such attacks or the form they took, but it would help us to understand the hostility. And even by the logic of social psychology such understanding is a prerequisite for sublimation—to say nothing of resolution.

Hofstadter remarks in one place that the frustration-aggression pattern is a psychological commonplace, but he seems to overlook the fact that such outsized abstractions are not the stuff of History. It is possible, and often fruitful, to establish factually based categories and to draw broad conclusions from a viable historical inquiry. But it is not possible to write valid History by using social-science concepts or contemporary political discretion as substitutes for facts.

It is particularly illuminating, therefore, to review Hofstadter's use of the concept of status, in the sense of social recognition. The issue here is whether, and in what circumstances, status becomes an independent engine of causation. Hofstadter

appears to argue that such is the case when neither any significant segment or class, nor the society itself, is faced by a basic
economic problem. This is a persuasive thesis, especially in a decade when both the Democrats and the Republicans are using
the same slogan about Americans never having had it so good.
That it also has an intimate relationship to the New Liberalism
becomes apparent when it is employed, as by Arthur M. Schlesinger, Jr., in his recent article in *The Reporter,* to discount the
need for any structural changes in American society.

While this may be good politics (though even that may be
questioned), it most certainly is weak methodology. For status,
as C. Wright Mills has written, is "the shadow of money and
power." But while status is inseparably connected with power,
money is not necessarily the same thing as power. Power is not
measured in dollars but, as Robert Bierstedt points out, in terms
of the ability to invoke and apply ultimate sanctions. And in
American society, at any rate, that capability is a function of the
position and control one enjoys in, or in relationship to, the productive system. Whether or not Hofstadter is a follower of
Mills, it is significant that both men fail to observe this distinction in their latest books.

For his part, Mills treats the high military as one of the
three independent, albeit associated, variables in American society. His argument, drastically condensed, holds that the current definition of reality in military terms stems from the military's exercise of that power. But the military did not originally
define reality in military terms. That was the outcome of a long
argument, back in the period between 1937 and 1941, among
the corporate economic leaders of the country. Roosevelt and his
political, administrative and military supporters could not get
their program under way in an effective manner until the bal-

ance within the corporate area shifted in their favor. Mills is not
the only student who slights this part of the story, however, for
the same weakness pervades the existing historiography of
American entry into the war.

Hofstadter's efforts to characterize and explain the reform
movement, and certain contemporary conservatives, in terms of
their status-hunger, is very similar to Mills's argument about the
role of the military. So, too, are its shortcomings. Those who appear to Hofstadter either to be hankering after naught but status, or to have engineered nothing but a status revolution, are in
fact (whatever their temporary monetary standing) concerned
with effective power. They are quite aware, if only in a negative
sense, that money is not to be confused with the power to establish for themselves a participating role in deciding their future.
They are not unconcerned with status, but it is secondary to
them.

Hofstadter's analysis tends to direct attention away from this
truth towards a preoccupation with superficial goals. And this,
in turn, makes it only easier for the existing centers of power to
continue their manipulation of his audience. Perhaps this confusion can be understood as a result of the New Liberalism having
mistaken a pseudo-status conferred upon it by the High and the
Mighty with the authentic influence and esteem it might attain
by dealing with the realities instead of the appearances.

In place of this, Hofstadter employs the ideas, concepts and
hypotheses of social psychology as though they were cookie patterns. The metaphor is apt, for not only does his dough of reality lack essential ingredients; he also uses only that portion of it
which falls within the confines of his moulds. But social psychology offers models *of* reality, not moulds *for* it. Hence it is a
fundamental mistake to restructure reality according to the
model. And for this reason Hofstadter's recent History makes

sense at all only when he uses ideal evidence, or when he ignores that part of reality for which there is no place in his
model.

This does much to explain the greater value of *The American Political Tradition* as compared with his work on Beard,
Manifest Destiny and *The Age of Reform.* For in that case Hofstadter was working with first-rate materials; as, for example,
with the research and interpretations supplied by Richard Current on Calhoun, Kenneth Stampp on Lincoln, and Frank Freidel on Franklin Delano Roosevelt. And in that instance, furthermore, Hofstadter himself was not so engrossed in the
manipulation of social psychological concepts. It may be too
much to say that Hofstadter's later social psychological History
works only when he constructs ideal types that function in his
model, but it is not too much to say that he has seldom of late
dealt with people as people.

And that is both the function and the test of the Historian.
Hofstadter's protagonists are not actual personalities, groups, or
classes; they are abstracted ideal types. Thus they cannot, in his
pages, either re-create their world or communicate to us their
view of that world or their insights. Instead, they prance about
as the hirelings of a master martinet. It is a magnificent performance, let there be no misunderstnding about that, but the individuals appear only as model enlisted men in Hofstadter's drill
team.

This demonstration may indeed mark, as *The New York
Times* and the Pulitzer Committee suggest, a turning point in
History and political theory. If so, it would seem to symbolize
the transformation of an ideal into ideology. For History as a
reasoned facsimile of the past has always been the intellectual's
ideal, whereas implicit in Hofstadter's methodology is the view

of History as a body of information to be manipulated. And that literally makes a myth of History. A disturbing thought, that; for Rome once felt so sure of itself that it took up the sport of disregarding reality.

The Nation
(June 30, 1956)

A Note on
Charles Austin Beard's
Search for
a General Theory
of Causation

The emphasis recently placed on the relativism of Charles Austin Beard's historiography tends to obscure another facet of his intellectual history. The clue to this second theme in his work lies in Max Lerner's observation that Beard was "as much a political thinker using historical techniques as he was a historian using political insights." [1] Lerner's evaluation is substantially correct for the first portion of Beard's career. This early period may be dated from his first book, *The Industrial Revolution* (New York, 1901), through his two volumes on foreign policy, *The Idea of National Interest,* with G. H. E. Smith (New York, 1934), and *The Open Door at Home* (New York, 1934). Beard then initiated, during the late years of this first phase of his work, a conscious effort to modify his methodological theory and practice. But he never formulated or employed a new approach to history with the same rigor that characterized his first system of thought. Several considerations would seem to account for this latter-day difficulty. He did not wholly discard his earlier outlook. He understood but imperfectly the second approach. And the new ideas were in themselves incomplete and unsystematized. Yet, in making this effort to broaden his early outlook, Beard was a pioneer who helped break new and fertile soil in American historiography.

"A treatise on causation in politics," judged Beard in 1908, "would be the most welcome contribution which a scholar of scientific training and temper could make." [2] Beard's early labor was essentially a search for such a general theory of causation. It was a quest for what he later called "predictive realism." [3] Even the most off-hand survey of his work during these years reveals a central concern with correspondence, correlation, and causation. He uncovered the what and the when for the purpose of finding out the how and the why. He readily admitted, of course, that the final statement of a general theory of causation would be made by someone with the "attributes ascribed by the theologians to God." [4] Beard never claimed such qualifications. But he did stress the value and need of a synthesis, and did what he could to develop such an analytical tool. Call it tragic or pathetic, according to one's personal metaphysic, Beard studied history in the years from 1901 to 1934 as research for a general theory.

Beard presented a summary outline of his general theory in *The Economic Basis of Politics,* delivered first as lectures in 1916 and published in 1922. He had previously published *An Economic Interpretation of the Constitution* (first ed., 1913) and *Economic Origins of Jeffersonian Democracy* (New York, 1915) as fragments of his research for the theory. Then, in *The Rise of American Civilization* (New York, 1927), *The American Party Battle* (New York, 1928), and *The Idea of National Interest,* he applied the theory to the whole span of American history. He also employed it as a tool for reviewing books; as, for example, in his analyses of Brooks and Henry Adams (1920), Frederick Jackson Turner (1921), and Vladimir Ilich Lenin (1933). [5] And ultimately he used it as a basis upon which to formulate domestic and foreign policies for the future: "A 'Five Year Plan' for America" (1931), [6] and *The Open Door at Home.*

In these same years, however, Beard began to modify his

general theory. He announced and explored the shift in four essays on historiography: "Written History as an Act of Faith"
(*American Historical Review*, XXXIX, January, 1934), "That
Noble Dream" (*AHR*, XLI, October, 1935), *The Discussion of
Human Affairs*, and, with Alfred Vagts, "Currents of Thought
in Historiography" (*AHR*, XLII, April, 1937). His writings
offer considerable, though incomplete, evidence on the reasons
behind this shift. He seems to have grown tired and impatient
with the difficulties of the theory—or concluded temporarily
that they could not be solved. This was coupled with a discour-
aging realization that the chance-proof prediction of particulars
was an illusory goal. Both these considerations are related to his
discovery of the German theorists who worked in the wake of
Wilhelm Dilthey. This part of the story, which remains largely
untold, may be the most significant phase of Beard's historiographical history.[7]

Important parts of the explanation, to be sure, may be found
elsewhere. Perhaps Beard was caught, ironically enough, in the
validity of his theory, unable to accept, because of his own historical background, the very program that his theory pointed to
as a solution for contemporary problems.[8] Current issues, such as
President Franklin Delano Roosevelt's developing foreign policy, certainly distracted him to an increasing extent. And perhaps a personal crisis, of which the outsider knows nothing,
served as the incident to shift his whole approach to history.
Whatever the final assessment, it is clear that Beard's historiography after 1934 was different from what it had been in the
years before.

Much criticism of Beard confuses these two periods of his
work. This is understandable. He did not wipe clean the slate in
the late 1920's and the early 1930's. His later writing is confused. But it may help to clarify the situation if Beard's confu-

sion is separated from that of his critics. Beard had two kinds of trouble with the Germans. They were themselves unable to resolve the dilemma which arose in the course of their own redefinition of history. And he misread or misunderstood their valiant efforts.[9] An important clue to his failure to comprehend the Germans may be found in the carry-over, as he read them, of his earlier ideas about a general theory. Perhaps, too, he chose consciously to reject certain of their arguments, concluding that they did not offer satisfactory alternatives to elements of his own theory. Thus, because it came first and served as a background for this later activity, it may be helpful to review briefly Beard's development and employment of a general theory of causation in the years before 1934.

The main elements of Beard's general theory would seem to have been, in turn, the *Weltanschauung* of his youth and the writings of Karl Marx, James Madison, and Brooks Adams. Beard matured in the harsh work-a-day world of industrial America in the late 1880's and 1890's. He capped that experience with several exciting years in the midst of socialist agitation in Germany and the ferment of the labor movement in England. His life in the family home, his field trips from De Pauw to the stockyards of Chicago, his reconnaissance of the battle between German conservatives and socialists, and his labors in behalf of Fabianism in England all seemed to verify one central theme. Property was the stuff of politics.

Beard's male ancestors were landowning businessmen who thought and acted in terms of those responsibilities, opportunities, and precepts. He was reared in the same tradition, even to the point of being backed, as a high school graduate, in a newspaper venture of his own. He never quite accustomed himself to the stir he provoked by pointing up the relationship between property and history. "People ask me why I emphasize economic questions so much," he once remarked with some wonder. "They should have been present in the family parlor, where my father and his friends gathered to discuss public affairs." [10]

Beard saw little in Chicago, Berlin, and London to change his early understanding of the world. His experience seemed only to verify his awareness that men and groups of different positions in the economic life of society looked at the world from conflicting points of view, and competed among themselves for influence and power. Beard may have moved away from the views of his father's particular group, but he did not retreat from this fundamental way of making sense out of the past which he studied or the present in which he lived. He may have changed his point of view in, but not about, the struggle. And it is easy to overemphasize the extent to which he shifted his opinion of given programs or policies. Beard never attacked private property as such, even in the heyday of the Progressive movement or the New Deal. He is reported to have remarked, at one point in his early years, that he was "almost a socialist." [11] But the leap from "almost a socialist" to a socialist is perhaps the longest in politics. Beard never made that jump. Both his critics and his defenders tend to overlook this essential fact.

Thus it is not surprising either that Beard was attracted by Marx's efforts to generalize about the relationship between the productive forces of society or that he never became a Marxian.[12] It is misleading to argue, or imply, as do many of his critics, that Beard merely seized James Madison as a hostage against those who attacked him as a Marxian after the publication of *An Economic Interpretation of the Constitution*. Beard never claimed he read Madison's *Federalist No. 10* while a college freshman and henceforth closed his mind to all other ideas.

All he ever said or implied, and this at but one stage of his career, was that he came to consider Madison's theory of factions the most generally satisfying thesis about the engines of the "great transformations in society." [13]

Of course Beard "discovered Madison a good deal later than he discovered Karl Marx." Beard first read Marx as a student at De Pauw, again while in England, and once more during the Great Depression. But this chronology does not prove that his theory of causation was produced by "a grafting of Marx on Madison." [14] Joan Robinson has remarked, in her usual witty and penetrating manner, that "Marxism is the opium of the Marxists." [15] The manner in which Beard is persistently treated as a Marxian, either explicitly, implicitly, or by innuendo, suggests that there is a corollary to her axiom: Anti-Marxism is the opium of the non-Marxists.

Those who call Beard a Marxian would seem to make the fundamental error of equating economic determinism with Marxism. Economic determinism is an open-ended system of causal analysis. Marxism, as generally understood and as used by the critics of Beard, is a closed system of utopian prophecy. Beard tried to clarify the difference between these two systems by pointing out that the ancients, from Aristotle to James Harrington, had emphasized economic differences as a source of dynamic conflict and change. He might have done better to quote Marx or Lenin on the question. Both men readily admitted that earlier thinkers stressed the relationship between economics and politics.

Lenin spelled out the difference that existed in his mind between an economic determinist and a Marxian in one classic sentence in his essay *The State and Revolution*. "A Marxist is one who *extends* the acceptance of the class struggle to the acceptance of the *dictatorship of the proletariat*." Whether Lenin might more accurately have written Communist for Marxist is by no means an irrelevant question. It would seem, indeed, to be a very crucial one. But here the key point is that Beard never extended his acceptance of the class struggle to an acceptance of the dictatorship of the proletariat. The only inevitability that Beard ever accepted was the certainty of conflict and change.

Beard was keenly aware of the central problem of economic determinism. Postulating a connection between economics and politics raises the question of defining and analyzing the nature of the relationship. The difficulty is overcome with relative ease in cases where the record makes it possible to trace economic motives from rational calculations of profit through to the formulation of public policy and political action. Beard correctly insisted that this specific pattern could be established in more instances than many of his critics cared to admit. But it may be doubted, despite several suggestions that have been made to this effect, that he generalized these precise examples into a general theory based on the economic motive.[16]

Beard quite understood that economic determinism runs into its most difficult theoretical problem when the circumstances are generalized beyond the realm of individualized and specified rational calculations of profit. Here is a situation in which the calculus operates at the much broader level of maximizing achievement. Achievement, as Beard appreciated, includes such considerations as attaining prestige and status, and holding the line against loss and outside challenges, in addition to increasing economic gain. He also knew, from reading their correspondence (as well as their polemics), that Marx and Engels fretted over the relationship between economics and other phases of human development. References to the "reflection" of economics into ideas, to the "superstructure" of ideas, or to the "correspondence" of economics and ideas, do not answer this central ques-

tion. But just because Beard concerned himself, in some instances, with economic motives does not mean that he artifi-
cially restricted economic determinism to that level of analysis. This is to take an argument advanced to account for one
specific relationship and, for purposes of general evaluation,
make it into a general theory. Such practice would seem to reveal more about the critic than about the subject.

Beard himself turned, at this point, from Marx to Madison
because he concluded that Madison's system of factions handled
the relationship between economics and politics in a more subtle, supple, and satisfying manner. Beard's commitment to *The
Federalist No. 10* suggests that Madison's careful analysis is
worthy of serious attention in an age when social scientists labor
mightily to construct complex and logical models of the social
system. Such a review is useful on two counts. It may serve to
clarify Madison's work, which is significant in its own right as a
theory of causation. And it is more illuminating to discuss
Beard's early production in terms of his efforts to test and apply
Madison's basic theory than it is to criticize Beard as no more
than a Progressive who used scholarship as a weapon in politics.
The following analysis of Madison's system is designed to serve
both purposes.

The most striking, and in a sense misleading, feature of the
No. 10 is the small part of it actually given over to the problem
of causation. Madison devoted by far the greatest portion of his
paper to a defense of the Constitution as a device for moderat-
ing the very consequences of his law of causation. "Among the
numerous advantages promised by a well-constructed Union,"
he explained, "none deserves to be more accurately developed
than its tendency to break and control the violence of
faction." [17] But his general theory was no less complete for the
brevity of its statement. He had worked it out in great detail,

and with much thought, in preparation for the Constitutional Convention in Philadelphia. This enabled him to state it precisely and vigorously in the opening section of the *No. 10*.

A faction, Madison begins, is "a number of citizens, whether amounting to a majority or minority of the whole, who are united and actuated by some common impulse or passion, or of interest, adverse to the rights of other citizens, or to the permanent and aggregate interests of the community." Four aspects of this definition need emphasis. (1) Madison immediately denies the homogeneity of society. (2) He subdivides it into an unnumbered plurality of groups. To each of these smaller units he attributes the characteristics of the "in-group," both as to its own internal system and its attitude toward "out-groups," as defined by contemporary sociologists and psychologists. (3) He likewise specifies the role of belief or ideology as a motivational engine functioning in series or parallel with material interests. (4) And finally, the term *aggregate* is one lately coming back into favor among the most rigorous and advanced economic theorists as descriptive of the important over-all consideration in any economic calculus.

Madison next developed his theory of personal and group motivation. Being human, man's "opinions and his passions will have a reciprocal influence on each other; and the former will be objects to which the latter will attach themselves." Here Madison wasted no effort trying to destroy the idea, or the reality, of self-interest as the mainspring of motivation. Instead he stated and argued, in twenty-odd words, the thesis that self-interest is subjective rather than objective. An individual's idea of self-interest is formed by the pressures of his ego, his libido, ideas and ideals, and by rational calculations of material gain.

Madison goes beyond this ancient truth so elaborately and eloquently re-revealed by modern scholarship. As an animal, however human, man is born unequal in his passions and his reason. The many combinations of varying degrees of self-love and reason lead to "different and unequal faculties of acquiring property, from which the possession of different degrees and kinds of property immediately results; and from the influence of these on the sentiments and views of the respective proprietors, ensues a division of the society into different interests and parties." In itself this is a most sophisticated equation composed of three variables interacting through time.

Madison's superb command of the language may have erected, at this point, a barrier against later students of his work. For he has stated, in very few words, a subtle system of causation. It starts with passion and ability, progresses to rewards, which, in turn, affect passion and ability. Let it be followed with care. (1) In any given individual, man's passions, for ideas as well as sexual objects and material goods, and his self-love are found in varying combinations. (2) Likewise, the faculty of reasoning power and the ability to carry out a given conclusion are also present in different degrees. (3) By virtue of these two variables, it follows that the extent to which a man is able to acquire valuable property in the form of intellectually valid conclusions and material wealth is also unequal. (4) To this acquired property, be it intellectual or material, his own self-love immediately becomes attached. (5) But, and to Madison's entire system this is all-important, this property also exerts a reciprocal influence on the individual's initial concept of his self-interest. This property, concludes Madison, "would certainly bias his judgment, and, not improbably, corrupt his integrity."

Madison concludes by placing his system in time and in the real world. Initial inequalities of temperament and intellect are brought to bear upon the aggregate of society's resources and lead to inequalities of material property. This unequal division of the existing aggregate takes two forms. First, there is the broadest split between those who are creditors and those who are debtors. Secondly, within the creditor class there are different kinds as well as degrees of wealth. Madison here anticipated the functional school of sociologists by specifying a "landed interest, a manufacturing interest, a mercantilist interest, a moneyed interest," and many other "lesser interests."

Such unequal division of society's aggregate material wealth is the "most common and durable source of factions." Thus at the given moment of a specific birth the new man begins his competition for a share of this aggregate property on the basis of a double inequality. His native endowment is unequal and the existing aggregate is already divided on an unequal basis. This was, in summary, Madison's general theory, which Beard found more attractive than Marx's schema and which he set out to test through research in American history.

Three problems arise in dealing with Beard's efforts to validate and use Madison's theory of politics. First, there is the question of Beard's misunderstanding or distortion of the system. Second, it is important to place *An Economic Interpretation of the Constitution* and *Economic Origins of Jeffersonian Democracy* in their proper relation to Beard's work with the theory. And third, Beard's subsequent use of the system needs to be examined. Only then will it be possible to gain some understanding of the way in which Beard later tried to integrate the ideas of various German thinkers and the theory of Brooks Adams into the Madisonian system.

Morton G. White and Douglass Adair charge most directly that Beard misread or distorted Madison. White argues that Madison's theory, far from being economic determinism, is based on a "biological rooting of class differences in human nature." [18] Adair insists that Beard ignored Madison's list of noneconomic factions. He also claims that Beard is guilty of a "misstatement" in failing to deal with Madison's reference to man's "reason and his self-love, his opinions and his passions," as well as to the influence of material interests.[19] Both critics would seem to overlook important considerations in drawing up their indictments.

White is correct on one point. Madison does posit men as being born unequal. But White does not mention that Madison immediately modifies this biological determinism by noting the influence of property "on the sentiments and views of the respective proprietors." Madison insists that a man's property "would certainly bias his judgment, and, not improbably, corrupt his integrity." White also neglects Madison's awareness that biological inequality is modified by the fact that men are not born into a state of nature but into the inequality of a going society.

A good case could be made that biological inequalities would be the key factor in a continuing state of nature. This would seem, indeed, the only circumstance in which biology could function in a deterministic manner. But Madison was not theorizing about a state of nature. He was writing about a very real world. And beginning at least as early as John Adams, many Americans have stressed the fact that the economic circumstances of birth powerfully modify the biological inequalities of conception.[20] Nor is it by any means certain that the biological inequalities which survive the friction of existing class differences play a determining part in later competition and achievement.[21] The property complex of birth includes, furthermore, the amount and availability of undistributed property as well as the allotment of the titled claims. And the importance of biology would seem to vary, in considerable part at any rate, with the amount of unclaimed property.[22]

Madison's emphasis on the influence of property on passion

and reason indicates his keen awareness of these considerations. The property complex into which one is born immediately modifies the significance of the biological endowments of birth. Or, in Madison's language: "From the protection of different and inequal facilities of acquiring property, the possession of different kinds of property immediately results." But property inequalities could not result immediately from biological inequalities, no matter how favorable the government's policy toward biological inequalities, unless the official protection served to guarantee property differences at the instant of birth. Madison does not appear, upon a close reading, to be a biological determinist in quite the sense that White argues.

Adair's charge that Beard misrepresents Madison would seem also to be a bit wide of the mark. Adair's basic assertion is all inclusive: "when Beard paraphrases from *Federalist* 10 . . . his method is to quote one passage of that essay incompletely; to change subtly, but decisively, a key element in Madison's theory into Marxian terms; and then to buttress this misstatement of Madison's 'economic determinism' with a footnote which is almost a verbatim transcription of a paragraph by Engels." [23] The fact that Beard cited a source that his critics traced to Engels is clearly irrelevant to the question of whether Madison was distorted and may be ignored in considering Adair's central thesis.

Adair specifies that Beard omitted Madison's catalogue of noneconomic factions and discounted Madison's point that opinions can cause factional conflict. These particulars are literally correct. But Adair, in making the charge against Beard, neglects to quote Madison on two key points. He does not mention Madison's careful notation that property exerts a reciprocal influence on opinion. And here again, the circumstances of birth have much to do with later opinions. Nor does Adair quote Madison's concluding judgment on the manifold causes of faction. The catalogue of noneconomic factions ends with this unequivocal summary: "But the most common and durable source of factions has been the various and unequal distribution of property." Perhaps Madison, after all, is the best authority on the extent of Madison's economic determinism.

Having shifted his attention from Marx to Madison, Beard proceeded to subject Madison's theory to a series of two inquiries. The first was an elementary correspondence test. With this he sought primarily to check Madison's thesis that, despite many noneconomic causes of factions, the "most common and durable source of factions has been the various and unequal distribution of property." He did the bulk of his research in the archives of the Treasury Department. And the resulting book became first notorious and then famous under the title *An Economic Interpretation of the Constitution.* Beard's second project was more complex. He undertook an examination of Madison's contention that property influences opinion. His research materials for this study included political speeches, pamphlets, and treatises, as well as the raw facts of economic history. Though in many ways more stimulating than the first volume, the *Economic Origins of Jeffersonian Democracy* did not win the attention awarded the book on the Constitution. Largely on the basis of these two monographs, however, Beard went on to state publicly his broad acceptance of the general theory that economics is the basis of politics.

Any review of the relationship between Beard's search for a general theory and his reputation-making book on the Constitution may well begin with Professor Richard Hofstadter's recent analysis of the volume.[24] Hofstadter offers a different explanation for Beard's original interest in the economic standing of the Constitution-makers. "The answer," he writes, "must be found

in the fact that Beard was not simply a scholar; he was, and remained his life long, a publicist with an urgent interest in the
intellectual and political milieu in which he lived." Thus Beard
was caught up in the Progressive movement's concern with "the
motives and activities of the rich and established classes." And
Progressive reality "was the bribe, the rebate, the bought fran-
chise, the sale of adulterated food." [25] If this reading is correct,
Hofstadter sees Beard primarily concerned with economic motives rather than with any hypothesis about interests and ideas.
The bias of Progressive thought accounts for the contrast between Beard's meticulous work on the economic background of
the Constitution-writers and his rough outline of their political
ideas.

Hofstadter's perceptive social-psychological analysis would
seem to be a projection of his "psychic crisis" interpretation of
the 1890's.[26] Such a stimulating hypothesis can not, of course,
be counted out as wrong. His retrocast of the Progressive climate of opinion is especially illuminating. Yet two reservations
may be introduced. Both concern the methodological dangers
inherent in his approach. Hofstadter begins by placing Beard in
the generalized Progressive movement. This technique is useful
provided the actor, in this instance Beard, is not lost in the abstracted system of the group. But Hofstadter does mislay Beard's
individuality. He has to fall back on the only device he has left.
He reads the generalized character of the movement back into
Beard. This creates a fictional protagonist in place of a historical
character. Such procedure is useful for broad generalization, and
perhaps for purposes of prediction, but certainly less so for understanding a specific individual.

The second weakness of Hofstadter's interpretation stems
from the propensity, when using psychology at historical dis-
tances, to doubt all statements by the actor about his own moti-

vation and purpose. Such scientifically founded skepticism is likely to become unjustified disregard in the course of the research. Testimony is not always proof, but neither is it always irrelevant. And Hofstadter would appear to neglect the latter consideration in discounting so heavily Beard's explanation of his study of the Constitution.

Hofstadter's analysis of Beard's research *Weltanschauung* is helpful if taken with these reservations. Certainly Beard was conscious of the Progressive thesis on property, profits, and politics. But it may be recalled that he learned the basic principle involved, but with a different nuance, in the parlor of his own home. Beard no doubt anticipated, as Hofstadter suggests, the potential influence of his study. Yet involvement in reform politics does not hinge on a commitment to the profit motive thesis. There is still reason to believe that Beard had more in mind. A second look at the book seems to verify Beard's avowed purpose of testing a portion of Madison's general theory. Beard immediately announced that the work was "frankly fragmentary" and "designed to suggest new lines of historical research." And within a few pages he specified his particular method: "the inquiry which follows is based upon the political science of James Madison." [27]

Such use of the phrase "based upon" has no meaning save in the sense of being "guided by." This would seem clearly to indicate Beard's interest in evaluating Madison's theory. The more so, since he next proceeded to clarify which proposition he chose to test. Essentially it was very simple. He proposed a direct check on the correspondence between the economic standing of a given group of citizens and the political opinions and actions of the same group. An identity would create, he argued, "a reasonable presumption in favor" of Madison's conclusion that "the most common and durable source of factions has been the various and unequal distribution of property." That is all Beard claimed for the book. "To carry the theory of the economic interpretation of the Constitution out into its ultimate details," he carefully noted, "would require a monumental commentary." [28]

Hofstadter sees an ambiguity in Beard's refusal also to deal in similar detail with the political ideas of the group in question. There are two comments, beyond an exposition of Beard's own answer, which seem relevant to a discussion of this emphasis in Beard's research. First, the Constitutional Convention was the focus of a crisis situation. The men in attendance agreed on basic issues. Their compromises in Constitution Hall were tactical in nature, not strategic. The strategic compromise came later, when the decision was made to accept the Bill of Rights. Second, the political ideas of the Constitution-makers had been explored in considerable detail. Beard could reasonably assume that his readers were acquainted with that side of the story.

Hofstadter also comments on Beard's occasional references to the fact that certain of the document-writers were personally involved in the "outcome of their labors at Philadelphia." And he would seem, in the final judgment, to interpret such remarks as evidence for Lerner's argument that Beard was concerned with a theory of economic motives rather than with a general theory of economic determinism. But in view of the basic structure of the book on the Constitution, which follows Beard's announced object of running a simple, if detailed, correspondence test, Hofstadter's argument can not be accepted without considering the companion study of Jeffersonian Democracy.

Nor does the fact that specified, particular men acted from economic motives contradict, deny, or destroy a broader theory of economic determinism. Certainly not for Marx. Marx many times said that he was not primarily concerned with moralizing about motives. But he never denied that businessmen did, upon occasion, act from economic motives. And Madison, working within the general concept that property influences opinion, also left room for motives. "No man is allowed to be a judge in his own cause because his interest would certainly bias his judgment, and, not improbably, corrupt his integrity." All Beard said in the book on the Constitution was that a given body of men did, in a specific crisis, act in keeping with their interests. Upon this evidence he concluded that his correspondence test had, in fact, "a reasonable presumption in favor" of Madison's insistence that property was the most common and durable cause of faction.[29]

The thesis that Beard's volume was in essence the work of a Progressive in scholarship sheds even less light on the *Economic Origins of Jeffersonian Democracy*. This book was published but two years later. And it was in progress for at least two years before its release in September, 1915. It may seriously be doubted that Beard wrenched himself out of the Progressive milieu in the interval. His resignation from Columbia was still to come. That act certainly fitted the Progressive ethic—as did his statement of termination. Yet his study of the Jeffersonians is cut to the same theoretical pattern as the volume on the Constitution. The fathers of Progressivism come off no better than the authors of the Constitution. Beard concluded that the Republicans, too, went into politics on the basis of their economics. This opens up something of a gap in the argument that Beard's book on the Constitution was at bottom a Progressive indictment of wealthy conservatives on the ground that they were economically motivated. For such an interpretation offers no explanation of Beard's similar conclusion about the motivation of the Jeffersonians.

The study of the Jeffersonians goes beyond the technique of

the correspondence test to an analysis of ideas. Beard does establish, of course, a correspondence between opinion and property as the basis for subsequent research. In this he found that factions began to arise within the property-holding class soon after its various elements had collaborated to establish a creditor's government. This division was based on the kinds of property within the wealth-owning group. This correlation set the stage for further inquiry.

Beard's chapters on the political economy of John Adams, John Taylor, and Thomas Jefferson are clearly designed to examine two other aspects of Madison's theory: first, the degree to which noneconomic causes account for factions; and second, the time at which the reciprocal influence of property on opinion begins to act. Beard's analysis of the ideas of these three men is some of his best work. It might more often be remembered by those who criticize so freely his volume *The American Spirit.*

Beard strikes to the core of the problem in the essay on Adams. Adams, like Madison, in the beginning goes beyond economic facts to account for the origin of faction. But, as Beard emphasizes, Adams immediately qualifies this by remarking upon the influence of property on native endowment. *"Generally* those who are rich and descended from families in public life," Adams points out, "will have the best education in arts and sciences, and therefore the gentlemen will ordinarily, notwithstanding some exceptions to the rule, be the richer, and born of more noted families." [30] This proposition reinforced Madison's general theory, and Beard interpreted it in such fashion. By thus establishing Madison's system in time and society, through considering men as born into an existing correspondence between ideas and interests, Beard felt he had done much to verify Madison's system. "The grand conclusion," he wrote in

The Economic Basis of Politics, "seems to be exactly that advanced by our own James Madison in the Tenth Number of the Federalist." [31]

Beard went on to interpret the whole span of American history within this framework. Or, more exactly, that seems to have been his thought and intention. But he did not apply rigorously the very theory of causation which he had worked so hard to validate. He was at the outset confronted by a Gargantuan job of research. His recognition of the immensity of the labor involved may have been, indeed, a realization that helped ultimately to turn him away from his original concern with "predictive realism." [32] His poignant remarks about not being able to encompass history-as-actuality need to be read in the context of his comment, in 1913, that the "ultimate details" of an economic interpretation would require a "monumental commentary." The following comment on *The Rise of American Civilization* and *The Idea of National Interest* is made with such limitations in mind. Even so, the books are certainly among the best Beard ever wrote.

Beard had several difficulties when he began to interpret the sweep of American experience with his general theory. The first was a product of his tendency to think primarily in terms of the crisis situation. This would seem understandable because his two inquiries into the validity of the theory were based on research into such circumstances. But it made him overconscious of Madison's first class of economic inequality, that between creditors and debtors. He was further inclined, on the basis of his early research, to stereotype that division as commercial and agrarian. This, too, tended artifically to freeze the flexibility of Madison's system.

Another factor bears on Beard's later problems. Both his early studies were made at a time when the aggregate property was fixed. In a crisis situation in which aggregate property remained static, such as the large property holders' drive to overthrow the Articles of Confederation in 1787 and the landed interests' bid to capture the national government in 1800, the broad division into creditor and debtor, or commercial and agrarian, remained generally valid when applied to specific kinds of creditors. Beard handled the breakup of the Constitutional coalition quite well on this basis.

A crisis version of Madison's system continued to work satisfactorily when dealing with similar episodes, such as the Civil War and the turn of the trade balance, in later American history. Thus Beard saw the Civil War as the "Second American Revolution" and stressed the shift from continental to overseas economic expansion. But a crisis version of Madison's system did not serve to interpret satisfactorily the decades of accumulative change: periods when the aggregate property was increasing or decreasing, and when different kinds of property led to the rise of factions within the creditor and debtor groups. Had Beard worked more closely within Madison's system, he would have avoided criticism of the kind made by Professor Arthur P. Whitaker in his study *The United States and the Independence of Latin America.* Whitaker analyzed, with exceedingly fruitful results, the functional factions within the commercial and agrarian classes.[33]

Beard had further difficulties when he began to apply Madison's theory to American history after 1880. Then he had to contend with a highly complex industrial system. Here Beard knew fewer facts and understood far less about the system itself than he did when dealing with the pre-Civil War period. Nor did he take time to do the necessary research. He never prepared a monograph on industrial America that compared in quality or scope with his studies of the Federalists and the Jeffersonians. But he was perceptive enough to recognize his weakness.

Perhaps Beard's awareness of this limitation is implicit in the last chapters of *The Rise of American Civilization*. There his succession of bold generalizations begins to give way to a well-written recitation of events. He openly acknowledged his troubles a year later when he published *The American Party Battle*. He still praised and used Madison, but he also entered several reservations. Most of them pertained to the problem of getting the facts. "It takes a great deal of research and discernment to find the roots of 'different sentiments and views' in any particular political situation," he commented with obvious disappointment, "especially as it is hard to get all the pertinent data in the case." [34] Yet despite these weaknesses in using Madison's general theory, *The Rise of American Civilization* and *The Idea of National Interest* stand among the very few first-rate generalized reviews of American history. They may suggest, in fact, that historians need not cringe when their contemporaries among the social scientists speak of the need for a general theory.

Beard's turn to the German theorists who were laboring to develop a new historiography is beyond the scope of this essay. Yet it may be suggested that his shift was neither sudden nor complete. He cited German scholars as early as 1913, in the book on the Constitution. Their influence reappeared in his discussion of Madison in *The American Party Battle*. He credited Max Weber and Friedrich Meinecke for portions of the conceptual framework of *The Idea of National Interest*. And he gleaned other key ideas from Karl Mannheim, Karl Huessi, and Albert Schweitzer.[35] But it seems dubious to conclude that Beard gave up his interest in a general theory in the course of his journey among the Herrenvolk. He did abandon, in the early 1930's, his search for predictive realism. But he quickly took up the challenge of a general theory that would promote an understanding of historical change and contemporary events. Then, to accomplish this, he put the Germans in harness with Brooks Adams for the purpose of bringing Madison's theory up to date. The result was the 1945 revision of the 1916 lectures, *The Economic Basis of Politics.*

Beard announced the end of his effort to achieve predictive realism through scientific history in his statement on "Written History as an Act of Faith." He openly joined those who were "rightly suspicious of this procedure." [36] And he appeared to accept, as a new basis for interpretation, the extremely relativistic code of "to each his own." Soon thereafter he consigned the efforts of Henry Adams, Oswald Spengler, and other like-minded prophets "to the realm of curiosities." [37] Personal, professional, and philosophical critics saw these remarks as Beard's white flag of surrender.

Yet Beard was trying to formulate something entirely different from the absolute relativism with which he has been charged. Beard abandoned predictive realism but he did not forsake the idea of valid generalizations. He did not give up his view that "relationships in history" could be ordered in "a certain coherence." Nor did he ever retreat wholly from his emphasis on the importance of economics. "An examination of the history of the forms of government action impinging on economy shows," he insisted, "that few if any of them originate outside the sphere of economic interests." [38]

This left Beard with the old problem of the connection between economics and politics, and with his difficulties with relativism. He temporarily neglected the dilemma of relativism while he concentrated on the relationship between economics and ideas. This problem became acute, as he pointed out in 1928, when "two persons in the same economic situation and cherishing the same 'sentiments' may differ as to the best plan of action to advance their interests. Their motives may be purely economic and their prejudices identical, but their reasoning divergent." [39]

Beard seemed, for a time, to view technology as the missing link. Men solved their production problems with solutions conditioned by the job. But engineering concepts also organized men as well as materials. These newly structured men then acted socially within the framework of their economic organization. "New economic facts," i.e., the production problem to be solved, "produce new political facts," i.e., the social action of the men organized by the job. [40]

This line of thought led Beard into the sociology of knowledge. Here Huessi and Mannheim helped him avoid the absurdity of absolute relativism. Everyone has a frame of reference, concluded Beard, but the number available "are relatively few in number and their respective natures may be fairly well defined." He never hedged his debt to the Germans for their work in this area, calling it the "most important contribution of contemporary historiography to thinking about human affairs." [41] Beard then used Schweitzer's methodology and schema of *Weltanschauungen* in an effort to define and understand the "American spirit." [42] But he was unable, after establishing the concept in the first chapter, to pull the personal and group world views into one national *Weltanschauung* for the United States.

Beard's incomplete mastery of the Germans stemmed in considerable measure from his preoccupation with things more American. He gave the Germans less than full attention because he was tumbling along in the roughhouse debate over American foreign policy and the increasing centralization of economic and political power, and because he was excited about his rediscovery of Brooks Adams. Beard seems first to have responded to Adams in 1920. At that time he described as "troublesome" the introduction which Brooks provided for the publication of Henry's essays on methodology and scientific history.[43] But there is no trace of Brooks, or of his ideas, in Beard's published writings from 1920 to 1938.

The shock of the Great Depression seems to account, directly or indirectly, for Beard's return to Adams. Those were the years, to be sure, when Beard was abandoning the goal of predictive realism. Yet the depression cast new light on Madison's general theory. For Madison had called the shot on that major crisis from the distance of a hundred years. He had written, in 1829–1830, that economic and political tension would reach a critical point in a century, when the nation's aggregate wealth was again static, largely in the hands of a few citizens, and intensively developed.[44]

Beard had the same trouble with Henry Adams. In 1920, when he was still strong on Madison's theory, Beard thought Henry's effort to create a science of history was a "barbed shaft into the center of the target." By 1936, when in full flight from predictive realism, Beard consigned Henry's work to the "realm of curiosities." But in 1937 it was difficult to forget Henry's prediction that a major turn in world history would occur about 1944. Henry looked even then to be something more than a disillusioned dilettante. By 1943 Beard had come full circle. Henry's ideas ranked "high among the most comprehensive, penetrating, and profound utterances ever made, at least in the United States, on the office of the historian and the nature of history." [45]

Thus in the very years that Beard most decisively discounted the search for a general theory he was forced to admit that

James Madison and Henry Adams advanced good briefs for the opposition. Beard soon thereafter discovered that behind the fame of Henry stood the mind of Brooks. It is difficult to establish precise dates for these events which renewed Beard's interest in a general theory. But it seems reasonable to hypothesize that they occurred between 1936 and 1939. For one thing, Beard had the idea of a restricted number of frames of reference by 1935. And in 1936 he summarized the other concepts he gained from the Germans. Yet his comments before a Senate subcommittee, at the end of January, 1937, on the proposal to license corporations at the federal level suggests that he was both familiar with and attracted by Brooks Adams' thesis on the steady and irreversible centralization of power.

Beard began his testimony by mocking the "futile antitrust battle of dust and wind" that had been going on for fifty years. Then he demanded that the federal government intervene to squash, once and for all, the "irresponsible and reckless . . . corporate jugglery" that threatened to ruin the country. This was quite in keeping, both in character and tone, with Brooks Adams' arraignment of Economic Man and his proposals for salvation.[46] Perhaps this testimony of January, 1937, sets too early a date, but there can be little question that Beard had rediscovered Brooks Adams by 1938. For, either late in that year or early in 1939, Beard wrote Malcolm Cowley that "Brooks Adams' two books are thumping [good]." [47]

Adams attracted Beard for several reasons. Perhaps the most important was that Brooks, with Henry, had evolved a general theory that appeared to stand the test of later events. "With striking emphasis," Beard pointed out in 1946, "history-as-actuality since 1900 has verified many of their predictions." [48] Adams also used concepts very similar to those that Beard found among the Germans. He had done much to synthesize the two approaches, moreover, linking his Imaginative, Military, and Economic men to the material world in which they appeared and thrived. Thus Adams offered Beard a general theory that not only predicted within high probability limits but went far toward establishing a comprehensive connection between economics, psychology, politics, and ideas.

Beard could no more have resisted the appeal of Brooks Adams than he could have sailed away from America as an emigrant. Every major piece of historical writing that Beard published after 1940 bore the impact of Brooks Adams' two major volumes: *The Law of Civilization and Decay* and *The Theory of Social Revolution*. Beard first mentioned Brooks directly in *America in Midpassage*. Then, beginning in *The American Spirit*, Brooks received more and more attention. Beard took over almost verbatim his interpretation of John Quincy Adams. In later pages he discussed at some length Brooks's thesis on the causes and patterns of human activity [49]

A year later, in 1943, Beard republished, with a revealing and stimulating introductory essay, *The Law of Civilization and Decay*. And many of Beard's comments in *The Republic*, also published in 1943, are clearly related to the Adams thesis. Perhaps most striking of all is the space allotted to Adams in Beard's one-volume summary of American history, *A Basic History of the United States*. Beard gave approximately four pages of this small volume to a man he had ignored in the massive *Rise of American Civilization*.[50]

Nor can Beard's last two volumes on foreign policy be dissociated from his work with Adams.[51] The underlying theme of these volumes is Beard's fear that the inability to deal effectively with major domestic problems inclined political leaders to seek other explanations and solutions for their failure. Beard's concern with this tendency was apparent, of course, prior to his rediscovery of Adams. But the recession of 1937–1938 and Roosevelt's Quarantine Speech coincided with his intensive study of Adams. He began at this time to emphasize even more dramatically and militantly the ethics of centralized power.[52] The temper and tone of these last two books was unique among all Beard's work. Beard was a patriot of the highest quality and this explains much of his intensity. But it does not appear unreasonable to associate these volumes with Beard's growing familiarity with the ideas of Brooks Adams. Adams argued persuasively that Economic Man was incapable of stablizing his own creation. Outsiders had to take command. If this new leadership did not appear, or if it failed to accept or measure up to its responsibilities, the centralized corporate system would stagnate or destroy itself in war. The similarity between this thesis and Beard's last book is, at any rate, suggestive enough to be pointed out.

Beard had been at first shy of the cyclic theme in the early work of Adams. He could no more accept an Adams cycle than a Darwinian or Marxian utopia. He solved this by emphasizing Brooks's final conclusion that the future could develop along any of three lines: a reversion to barbarism, stagnation, or a new resolution followed by further development. But Beard was denied the time to assimilate and use the Adams thesis. He was an actor in the very play he sought to understand. He could not spend himself warning of the dangers in the current scene and at the same time work out the plot for the next act. Thus his hurried revision of *The Economic Basis of Politics* was confused and self-contradictory. He attempted to transpose Adams into Madison. The translation was too rushed, too literal, and based on too little thought to be successful.

But once again Beard was trying to formulate and state a general theory. The struggle to comprehend, to know and understand, was ever the battle closest to Beard's heart. In this he stood a head taller than his contemporaries. They were content to write well of the particular. Beard aimed to speak significantly of the general. How well he knew exactly what he had in mind. "When I come to the end, my mind will still be beating its wings against the bars of thought's prison." [53] Indeed it was. And for that reason Beard will remain both a challenge and a measuring rod for American historians and their historiography.

The American Historical Review (1956)

Schlesinger:

Right Crisis—

Wrong

Order

The Crisis of The Old Order:

1919–1933

Volume I of

The Age of Roosevelt

Introductory installments of multi volume biographies cast in the "life-and-times" format may be compared with operatic overtures: only the best can stand alone. Either the background merits intensive and extended development on its own, or the themes and central arguments could be stated more clearly and to greater usefulness in the form of a short, rigorous essay. Hence it is only to salute Professor Schlesinger's intelligence and talent to conclude that he almost realizes the ideal. But the gap remains: the highly distilled essence of this volume would provide a far more powerful introduction to the study of the Roosevelt Era which is yet to come.

Thus the reader will find paragraphs of keen analysis, sections of exciting and living description, and passages of moving evocation of attitudes and moods. The most brilliant portion is Schlesinger's dissection of Roosevelt's character and temperament, and his outlook on Man and the world (pp. 386–87,

409–10). This analysis not only provokes an abiding, bowel-stirring uneasiness about the American conception and practice of *noblesse oblige;* it leaves one in sadness that Schlesinger should have to mouth the banality about its being "subjective, of course." Schlesinger has given us *the* Roosevelt, once and for all: let us admit this and go on from there.

Almost as much may be said of some portions of Schlesinger's reconstruction of the depression. By no means all of it is art, let alone superior description. But parts of it are so powerful that the reader is apt to mistake the smoke from his cigarette for the frosty breath of a novice hobo squatting on the fringes of a jungle in Iowa. For those who have the memories to twitch, the passages prompt us to drop the book and pace the picture window to exorcise the anxiety. And, in some respects at least, not even the phonograph records and the newsreels of the event capture what Schlesinger gives us of Roosevelt's inauguration.

But we could have all this in a hundred pages; perhaps less, for there are more than occasional lapses where Schlesinger's flow of language insulates us from the feel, as well as from the substance of the story. As for the rest of it, either it has been done better by other leading entrepreneurs of the booming Roosevelt Industry, or it must be done far more thoroughly and rigorously before it can be summarized accurately, let alone with wit, insight, flavor and verve. And it is this latter weakness which undercuts the basic thesis advanced by Schlesinger in this volume, and which might subvert the full study.

The central clue to Schlesinger's inability to resolve the dilemma of the introductory volume *vs.* the sharply formulated essay lies in his treatment of the 1920s in general, and of Herbert Hoover in particular. Not that he neglects the period. Indeed, he worries it unmercifully. But while Schlesinger may master Roosevelt, he has already lost his one fall match with Hoover. For he simply fails to be done with Hoover; either as a tragic hero or as a pathetic failure, or by dispatching him to the Gehenna of New Liberalism or to the Old Conservatives' Valhalla. Hence the reader comes away from the book with the distinct sense that Schlesinger is more concerned and fretful over the twenties *per se* than he is interested in reviewing the decade as the prelude to the Roosevelt Era. This, too, measures Schlesinger's underlying comprehension of Twentieth-Century America. But it also provides the key to the basic contradiction in his central thesis.

For if, as Schlesinger correctly asserts, the roots of the Age of Roosevelt go back to Populism, and more especially to the Square Deal of Theodore Roosevelt's New Nationalism, then the real Crisis of the Old Order occurred in the panic and the depression of the 1890s. And this, in turn, means that the crash and depression of 1929 *et. seq.* was not the Crisis of the Old Order at all, but rather the last adolescent paroxysm of the New Order as it lurched into the maturity of full-blown corporatism. What Schlesinger has done, in short, is to stretch one phase— or stage—of American history far beyond its actual limit. The result is a skewed perspective on, and a faulty understanding of, the men, ideas and programs of the years 1890–1933 (and later).

Schlesinger's harsh picture and judgment of the bankers offers a convenient point at which to initiate a consideration of these results. He seeks to cinch and dramatize his thesis of the Crisis of the Old Order by emphasizing the failure and the helplessness of the bankers (pp. 457–59, 474–81). Now a banking crisis existed, and no one need fear that this criticism is based on the absurd assumption that the depression never occurred, or the argument that it was essentially moderate in scope and depth.

The key point is quite different: the banking crisis can be equated with the Crisis of the Old Order only by assuming or defining finance capitalism to be the final institutional form of the Old Order. But this is precisely what finance (or investment) capitalism was not: financial capitalism was the institutional technique devised and employed between 1890 and 1910 to effect the transition from the old individualistic capitalism to the new corporate capitalism.

Once this essential difference is understood, it becomes possible to outline the two central developments of the period from 1890 to 1926–27; and hence to grasp the fact that the crisis of 1926 *et. seq.* was a crisis of the new corporate capitalism. One line of events concerns the intellectual and political reactions to the fundamental shift from individual to corporate capitalism. The other pattern deals with what happened within the economy itself. Since the basic changes of the economy provoked the responses, it is more fruitful to consider them first.

Schlesinger ignores the central economic pattern of the years 1890–1933. This was the corporation's reassertion, along about 1926–27, of its economic independence of the investment, or financial, capitalist. The fact that the corporation was faced with the problem of doing this goes back to the crisis of the 1890s. That crisis had two sides. The negative aspect was the collapse of the old individualistic capitalist. But that deflation left the young corporation without the funds required to exploit the opportunity, and so sustain the system itself. The urgency of the situation is documented by the extent and tone of the social and political crisis. The Old Order had been dying since the Panic of 1873, and without capital for corporate rationalization and expansion the system itself would have collapsed.

The capital was supplied by external savings garnered and controlled by the investment bankers. The corporation hired this money and paid for it by signing over control of the key decisions. A few corporations realized the consequences before the act, and chose to skimp along on smaller profits until they could save enough to control their own expansion. Others had such a sure-fire product that they could, with less effort, likewise circumvent the bankers. Ford is an example of both considerations in one corporation.

But the corporation held the trump card, for it, and not the bankers, was the productive element in the economy. Hence it was only a matter of time until the corporation accumulated enough savings to buy itself back, so to speak, from the investment banker. In this process, of course, World War I was a windfall for the corporation. For the government itself stepped in as a supplier of outside savings for expansion, and this greatly accelerated the rate at which the corporation reasserted its power over the bankers.

The boom markets of the early twenties, foreign as well as domestic, enabled the corporation to finish the job. But this success only confronted the corporation with full responsibility for continued expansion. This difficulty was compounded by the fact that foreign loans, which underwrote part of the post-war market expansion, had reached the saturation point in most areas, and in some cases had already begun to default. This had two results: it accelerated the collapse of the bankers, which was already assured by the corporation's reassertion of economic sovereignty; but it also accentuated the difficulties of the corporation because it had come to rely on the markets originally financed by the bankers and by the government. Schlesinger is quite correct in pointing out the failure to underwrite continued domestic markets by cutting prices and raising wages. But he makes a signal error in seeing this mid-twenties collapse of the investment banker as the central crisis. For the basic structural crisis concerned the corporation itself.

Corporation correspondence and literature after 1926 is filled with a growing concern over markets. Three solutions received more and more attention. A small group concentrated on the virtues of establishing plants abroad, planning to bring the profits home through the international money exchange. Another group, remembering the benefits of government action during the war, began to badger the government to step in with foreign loans. Still others looked to Russia as the great market to resolve the problem. These last two approaches converged during the last months of Hoover's term in the successful demand for the government to begin underwriting exports to the Soviet Union.

By then it was too late: the corporation needed much more much faster. But the crisis concerned the new corporate order, not an older order; and in overlooking this Schlesinger misses the real clue to dealing effectively with Hoover himself. The same consideration weakens his outline of the system of ideas being forged by Roosevelt and his advisors.

Schlesinger's thesis holds that Roosevelt found himself, in the flux of the crisis, and "with the campaign scarcely underway, . . . in the center of a triangle of advice: at one corner, integration and social planning; at another, retrenchment, budget balancing, and *laissez faire;* at a third, trust busting and government regulation." This is a convenient summary, and as sound, as far as it goes, as his view that these proposals came down to 1932 as the descendants of TR's New Nationalism, Wilson's New Freedom, and a senile infatuation of the old individualistic capitalist for Adam Smith's "lazy fairy." He goes even further, in one or two places, and toys briefly with the proposition that the New Nationalism and the New Freedom had merged in the heat and pressures of World War I. But he drops this part of his analysis, and as a result his treatment of the twenties is seriously weakened.

One of the principal reasons for this is the dilemma inherent in trying to save the system by integration and social planning. For the corporate giants can be controlled only by using organized labor, and this strengthens an engine which drives the system toward syndicalism or socialism. But if, from this fear, the corporate rulers are allowed to control the basic features of integration and planning, then the system drifts into what Reinhold Niebuhr (to whom Schlesinger dedicates his volume) once called "The New Feudalism." A spirit of *noblesse oblige* may moderate the lesser evils of such an order, but it cannot make it either democratic or new.

Wilson and his advisors sought to resolve the problem by building a cross-class alliance which would give them the power and the authority of the national government. This, so they thought, would be sufficient to bust the trusts and regulate the short-sighted selfishness of the corporation. Two difficulties intervened. Trust busting and regulation always come after the fact; and even if successfully pursued legally only serve to destroy or restrict one institutional entrepreneur without putting much in its place.

As with the New Nationalism, therefore, the New Freedom lowered its eyes at the para-legal reorganization of the trust or corporation, and turned to supporting overseas economic expansion as the next best remedy. But this afforded no solution because the little fellow could not compete in the international league of the old pros. Even the domestic giants had difficulties.

By 1920, therefore, the two corners of Schlesinger's triangle, labeled integration-planning, and trust-busting regulation, had for all practical and consequential purposes merged into one. And this, of course, was the program which Herbert Hoover outlined in *American Individualism* and endeavored to implement as Secretary of Commerce and as President. It is fundamentally wrong, therefore, to view Hoover either as an astute man trying to save the Old Order, or as an isolationist. He was trying desperately to rationalize the New Order, and correct its dangerous myopia, before it suffered the fate of individualistic capitalism.

As for foreign affairs, it is very misleading to label as an isolationist a man who defined the key problem of America foreign policy in the following terms:

> The hope of our commerce lies in the establishment of American firms abroad, distributing American goods under American direction; in the building of direct American financing and, above all, in the installation of American technology in Russian industries . . . [so that] Americans can undertake the leadership in the reconstruction of Russia when the proper moment arrives.

Hoover wanted a corporate economy in dynamic equilibrium: directed at home by a triumvirate composed of trade associations, capitalistic labor unions, and intellectual corporate bureaucrats in Washington; and drawing outside investment funds from the surplus returns on foreign investment, while balancing the import of raw materials with the export of industrial goods. And to state it bluntly, not a single New Dealer mentioned by Schlesinger had at that time anything to approach Hoover's overall conception. They could spot its weaknesses, as in agriculture, and propose correctives of a sort, but not one of them offered an equally coherent formulation of the idea—*let alone a radical alternative.*

If this is not enough to explain Schlesinger's difficulty with Hoover, the political aspects of the story are quite sufficient to finish the job. Schlesinger holds that "modern science and technology render political centralization inevitable; one must either accept power or reshuffle it," and concludes that "the best hope for individual freedom lies in the chinks and fissures created by the reshuffling process."

Explicitly and implicitly, Schlesinger maintains that all great problems are unsolvable. Hoover hangs hard to the proposition that man either resolves this particular problem or gives up the idea of democracy. This makes him a truly tragic figure, aware that either democracy is structured institutionally, or society devolves toward totalitarianism relieved only by continued overseas expansion or a more rapid circulation of elites. But continued expansion begets war, and relief by arms subverts the substance of democracy into the rhetoric of freedom. And an elitist version of the old game of musical chairs does the same thing.

On the one hand, therefore, Hoover drew back from a willy-nilly expansion of government in domestic affairs, or its similar expansion abroad, fearing fascism as the consequence. But he recognized, on the other hand, the revolutionary probabilities of a reactionary return to the Old Order of individualistic capitalism. Thus the double malaise: he was concerned to "make assurance doubly sure" in view of the terrible alternatives, and then he was paralyzed by his fear that Roosevelt's emphasis on action would reap one or the other of the consequences.

And in one short phrase, Schlesinger substantiates Hoover's anxiety over Roosevelt's approach to the crisis. Reviewing the attempted assassination in Florida, Schlesinger concludes the story with the observation that "Roosevelt, it was clear, really lacked physical fear." But the absence of fear is not courage, for courage is defined by a sharp consciousness of the danger over-ruled by a sense of responsibility. The courageous man can live with fear because he understands that it is not the central problem. The coward also knows this, but for many reasons surrenders anyway. Only the man who lacks fear can tell others that the only thing they have to fear is fear itself, and maintain that the central danger is a lack of action.

Now the proposition that all we have to fear is fear itself is an inspiring half-truth, to be sure, and one which did yeoman service for a short spell. But it is nevertheless a half-truth. And a particularly dangerous one in the bargain. Hoover understood this, and hence his deep concern. In his administration, of course, Roosevelt never came face to face with either danger so feared by Hoover; and this will enable Schlesinger to avoid a straightforward confrontation of the problem. But no study of the Age of Roosevelt can stand as definitive unless it is cast in these terms.

For we do have more, very much more, to fear than simply fear itself. Among other things, for example, there is the axiom that all the great problems are unsolvable. They may be, but once we admit it then the only Grail that remains is power itself. Contrary to Lord Acton, there is no need to get much of it under those circumstances, for we shall already have corrupted ourselves.

The Nation
(March 23, 1957)

The American Century:

1941–1957

For an American, at any rate, it was hard to believe—
even in 1957, after more than a decade of dreary and foolish
pronunciamentos of the Cold War. Not even the angriest author
of the rebellious Twenties, or the most crusading playwright of
the Thirties, would have risked writing such a line into his plot.

Yet there it was, in the black and white austere certainty of
The New York Times on the morning of August 13, 1957: the
Department of State had decreed that the projected visit of for-
ty-seven American students to Communist China "would be
subversive of United States foreign policy."

One could search for years and not find a more fitting footnote to the insight of those who once said that the Russians had
conquered America without a shot. And it was precisely this
sort of incident which prompted an Arab diplomat to remark,
last month, that "it is the West which is destroying the West."

Only sixteen years ago, supported by a chorus of enthusiastic
liberal and conservative intellectuals, Henry R. Luce announced
the maturity of The American Century. It was High Noon, he
judged, and hence time "to accept whole-heartedly our duty and
our opportunity as the most powerful and vital nation in the
world and in consequence to exert upon the world the full impact of our influence, for such purposes as we see fit and by such
means as we see fit."

Shared by big corporation executives, labor leaders and politicians of every ideological bent, this estimate of America's power and role in world affairs dominated policy-making decisions long after the Russians had tested their first nuclear weapons.

Secretary of State George C. Marshall summarized the order of the day in his curt comment of May, 1948, that "the problems presented to those who desire peace are not questions of structure." This persuasive sense of certainty confined whatever discussions that did arise to the issues of the means to be used, or the limits to which America should go in exerting its will and its way. What passed for a debate about the policy of containment, for example, revolved not around the validity of the policy, but about whether or not it went far enough fast enough. In a similar manner, Generals Douglas MacArthur and Omar Bradley disagreed not over the strategic question of how to establish peace, but over the tactical problem of which war should be fought at what time. And even as late as the election campaigns of the 1950s, the argument about the policy of liberation never got down to the central issue of whether or not the idea itself was viable.

By 1957, however, there is considerably less rhetoric in the style of doing things "as we saw fit," and a good deal more in the vein of calls for "give-and-take-negotiation." Though less dramatic than the Summit Conference of 1955, or the shock of surprise when Russia launched the first earth satellite, the incident of the student visit to China is even more revealing of this crisis in The American Century. Had the leaders of The American Century been imperialists of the old school (as, indeed, they seemed to be during the years of Secretary of State Dean Acheson's mercantilist policy of "total diplomacy"), they would have whisked the errant children off to the nearest American base with the swish of a jet-assisted take-off. Had they been poised and adroit administrators of an American Way of Life for the World (as indeed they seemed to be when managing a counter-revolution in Guatemala), they would at least have encouraged the visit, and more probably have subsidized it. But in first defining the proposal in terms approximating treason, only to acquiesce in the trip itself, they give stark evidence of their anxiety and indecision.

Such has not always been the case. Two generations ago, advocates of The American Century "went to bed and went to sleep and slept soundly." Even Franklin Delano Roosevelt initially thought about foreign affairs on the basis of this conception of America and the world. Thus he characterized the Spanish-American War as "the offer of a helping hand," a phrase which called up cousin Theodore's concept of America's *noblesse oblige* toward the rest of the world. He provided an even more explicit example of his thinking as part of his effort to sustain President Woodrow Wilson's crusade for the League of Nations. There was nothing to fear, Roosevelt assured his fellow Americans, because the United States would always control the votes of the Latin American countries. And in August, 1941, several months before America officially entered the war (but after Russia had), his conversations with Winston Churchill revealed the sanguine view that the United States, with some help from England, would police the world for an indefinite period after the war as a sort of bulldozing operation for the projected United Nations Organization.

In the course of the war, Roosevelt modified these casual assumptions about America's benevolent supremacy. On the one hand, he began to realize the extent to which the New Deal had failed to solve the problem of unemployment in a peace-time economy, and the degree to which the power structure of the country had been rationalized rather than altered—let alone revolutionized. His adventures among the "War Lords of Washington" prompted him to shift from traditional attacks of Big Business to much broader warnings about the danger of fascism in America. In the conduct of foreign affairs, meanwhile, the fierce resistance of the Axis powers and the rise of the Soviet Union acquainted him with some of the inherent difficulties of policing the world, however just and liberal the laws. By 1944 he was more ambivalent in foreign affairs, veering back and forth between the concept (and practice) of a concert of power with Russia and the idea (and practice) of asserting America's freedom of action throughout the world.

Those who succeeded Roosevelt have sought to resolve the dilemma by coming down hard on the side of an American Century. Not all of them have seen the world in the stark outlines etched by the 200-proof essence of this idea, any more than all of them have been creed-bound conservatives; but the great majority of them defined "internationalism," which has become their rallying cry and battle hymn (as well as their key propaganda symbol), in terms of a system organized and led by the United States in opposition to the Soviet Union, and exerting varying degrees of its power on other nations which sought to gain or retain a significant area of independent action. They disagreed among themselves over the means to be employed (though much less than it appeared, even at first), not the assumptions or the objectives of the program. Brushing aside the vigorous but limited and divided opposition to their outlook, these advocates and practitioners of The American Century rapidly established a pattern and a momentum of decision.

Their program was a hodge-podge misappropriated from the past. For domestic purposes, they prescribed an eclectic mixture of the Square Deal, the New Freedom, the New Era and the New Deal. As manifested in the conservative liberalism of the Fair Deal and the liberal conservativism of the New Republicanism, it combined corporate politics with economic subsidies for small business men, and the rhetoric of Jacksonian Democracy with the economics of an industrial corporatism. The small-business man has been sustained in his mythology by cutting him in on the Cold War boom as a sub-contractor to the giants, or by integrating him into the complex of service industries. Small farmers have been handled by an ingenious application of the old aphorism that flattery will get you nowhere. They are wooed to exhaustion by the politicians and the pundits, but the harvest of their fields is used to stuff the empty holds of maritime relics.

In reality, as defined by their function and relationships in the productive process, and by the misuse of their labor, these Americans are being subsumed in the general degradation of the middle class. Many of them who understood this process, and most of them who merely sensed it, turned in their weakness and anger to such men as Senator Joseph McCarthy. So, too, did others who aspired to the high roads of corporate power, but found themselves mired in the poverty of self-made wealth. The failure of this movement was one of the most ironic aspects of the Cold War. For by choosing anti-communism as their issue, these men defeated themselves. That was not an issue, but only an article of faith in the ideology of The American Century. In keeping with the logic of ancient scholasticism, the debate became a row about the number of Communists that could hide in the Department of State. A great many of the innocent faithful were destroyed, and the Truth was institutionalized in various oaths and rituals, but the cult itself was subsumed in the established church.

Rounding out the profile of domestic affairs, deeply

conservative corporation directors such as Averell Harriman campaigned with the rhetoric of left-wing liberals, while liberal intellectuals such as Adlai Stevenson reassured the corporation directors that "every new frontier in American progress has been, and will always be, opened up by the joint enterprise of business and government." In this fashion, the muddied politics of a corporate economy has deposited a sediment of evasion, half-truths, frustration and fear across the fabric of American democracy. Given this soil, McCarthyism was as natural as a thistle—and just as fruitful.

Domestic affairs are always writ large in foreign policy, and the bipartisans for an American Century provided additional proof of that axiom. Under their guidance, American power in the form of a monopoly of the atomic bomb, and an economy more powerful than that of the rest of the world combined, has been deployed vigorously and extensively to thwart the evil designs of the Soviet Union, and to structure the world for the positive application of American leadership. Within this framework, the public was assured, other countries would prosper according to the genius of the American political economy. Thus the internationalization of America's Permanent Revolution would subvert world communism. Theodore Roosevelt's civilizing mission would be fulfilled by American exports, the Strategic Air Command and the reforms of the Fair Deal. The democracy of all this has never been questioned. "What we must do now," explained Secretary of State James Byrnes in July, 1945, "is not to make the world safe for democracy but make the world safe for the United States."

In a perfect union of convenience and necessity, liberals have embraced conservatives before the altar of The American Century. Democrat Harry S. Truman enunciated a doctrine which sounded like a paraphrase of the Republican Roosevelt's corollary to the Monroe Doctrine (which had been conceived as a bipartisan option on the Western Hemisphere, and which Woodrow Wilson later proposed extending to the world). Republican John Foster Dulles completed the process of homogenization by delivering speeches and conducting foreign affairs in the crusading tradition of Democrat Woodrow Wilson. The rest of the world was assured that it had nothing to fear: its tomorrows would be even better versions of America's yesterdays. As Truman explained, the future itself is America's new frontier: "All we need to do is to undertake the proper development of vast areas and virtually unlimited resources in many parts of the world." Skeptics who fretted over the morality or the economics of the program were answered by Secretary of State Dean Acheson. Overseas aid and investment would solve the hard practical problem of building a functioning system at home. As for morality, nothing could be more just: "We are willing to help people who believe the way we do, to continue to live the way they want to live."

But within the last five years, it has become apparent that something is awry. Granting that it is a "tough assignment," as *The New York Times* pointed out, "to be policeman, banker, and baby-sitter" to the world, there are questions which remained unasked—let alone unanswered—by this explanation. Not only have the Russians achieved the bomb, but unimpeachable sources reveal that America is "losing touch with the peoples of the world." Most revealing of all, perhaps, is the way earlier analyses and arguments have been revised.

George Frost Kennan asserted in 1946 that America had it in its power "to force upon the Kremlin a far greater degree of moderation and circumspection than it has had to observe in recent years, and in this way to promote tendencies which must eventually find their outlet in either the breakup or the gradual mellowing of Soviet power." By 1956 he was willing to concede "to the Russians the privilege of their privacy and differences"; and concluded that any significant changes in Russia would come about, not as the result of America's ability "to force" them, but in the process of the natural slowing down of revolutions.

More recent progress reports suggest the need for revising other policies. South Korea's economy, noted C. L. Sulzberger of *The New York Times,* is "an impossible mess" with inflation "rampant and usury rife"; Syngman Rhee is "unabashedly anxious to start a new hot war." Sulzberger also warned that Turkey's economy, supposedly America's showplace in the Middle East, is stagnating on the brink of collapse. Latin Americans spoke for themselves, often employing humor to convey their estimate of Washington's outlook and policies (see U.S. and Latin America, by Betty Kirk, *The Nation,* October 5). One story, in particular, typifies a growing reaction in that region. It likened a nation which always followed Washington's wishes to a man "married to a rich woman who gives him a night out every week—on her money." But perhaps the crisis has been laid wide open by the American newspaper which, in printing the story, apparently thought it had countered the thrust with the flippant rejoinder: "Is that bad?"

However characterized and symbolized, the depth and scope of the crisis is apparent. Even Senator A. J. Ellender of Louisiana withdrew from the battle for white supremacy long enough to issue a call for "a new foreign policy." As with a number of other leaders, the Senator seemed unaware that it is well-nigh impossible to effect a fundamental improvement in foreign policy without rectifying a few errors at home. But many Americans are beginning to sense for themselves that a prosperity paid for in the coin of chicanery and collusion, inflation and inequities, aimlessness and alienation, is very apt to become an air-conditioned nightmare, even if it does not lead in their lifetimes to nuclear war. That rhetorical bluff about an "agonizing reappraisal," once employed as a maneuver to yank an ally back into line, has become a necessity for American society itself.

As one policy-maker plaintively admitted, "It was much more simple in the old days. Then, the Russians denounced everything we did. And we hollered right back. Now, it is hard to know just what to say." Or do, he might have added, for American leaders are still groping to come to terms with the fact that their central assumptions have turned out to be "unfounded." James Reston, one of the nation's most perceptive and responsible observers, suggests that America needs "a few good old-fashioned, cantankerous, argumentative, hell-raising, channel-crossing, fault-finding grumblers. Preferably with ideas." But as Reston no doubt understands, The American Century was not designed to mass-produce non-conformists with ideas.

For that reason, among others, it is difficult to overcome the inertia of bipartisanship. As the party of the outs, the Democrats might have been expected to take the initiative. They have not. "Seldom in contemporary history," concluded Reston in 1955, "has an opposition party been so slow or so ineffective in its criticism of major policies as the Democrats in the last two years. . . ." Later events have done little to modify that judgment, or to suggest that the Republicans have been doing their own homework.

Reston's criticism was short-sighted, however, in that it neglected the fact that new ideas stem from a new insight or a new angle of vision. They are not developed by the reactionary calculus of political opportunism, by the fuzzy logic of avoidance, or by giving old reforms a coat of new rhetoric. Neither is the direct, frontal assault apt to supply answers; perhaps, indeed, it is the most unsatisfactory of all methods. In one form or another, it distills a means appropriate in one instance into a doctrinaire policy for all cases; and this, in turn, either creates more problems than are solved, or leads to the conclusion that it is impossible to solve the big problems. And neither resignation nor frustration is conducive to a creative foreign policy. These are not, however, the only alternatives; for while it is true that trouble is the lot of man, it does not follow that any given difficulty is insurmountable. It is more helpful to realize that the big problems are more often solved by the positive application and development of an idea which usually seems unrelated to the issue at hand.

Thus, in the crisis of The American Century, it is more rewarding to turn from a scramble for panaceas to a re-evaluation of America's ideas about itself and the world. This shift in approach makes it possible to understand that it was not a laxness in the American weapons program which has produced the crisis. The crisis developed and matured during a period when America enjoyed a significant relative weapons advantage. The crucial factor was the way Americans interpreted this as an *absolute* superiority, and the manner in which they sought to use their supposed supremacy.

Thomas J. Hamilton of the *Times* provided a concise summary of the thinking that guided American policy-makers during those years: in 1946, he recalled, "and in fact until 1949, the United States . . . had the means of forcing the Soviet Union to its knees with a preventive war." Secretaries of State

Acheson and Dulles translated that assumption into a bipartisan program of "total diplomacy" designed to win the victory without the war. But the improvement in the power position of the Soviet Union destroyed the logic of Acheson's old argument that America could not negotiate until it established "positions of strength." By now it is apparent that America, assuming that it enjoyed a position of strength in the absolute sense, refused to negotiate during the years when it did hold a relative advantage.

"For too many years," as Senator Mike Mansfield belatedly realized, "the United States has been all too prone to underestimate the capabilities of the Soviet Union, and now the chickens are coming home to roost." *The assumption that the United States has the power to force the Soviet Union to capitulate to American terms is the fundamental weakness in America's conception of itself and the world.* This is the cause of the crisis. The lag in weapons is but a dramatic symptom. Crash programs designed to relieve such symptoms serve only to compound the basic weakness. Strategic errors are not corrected by tactical brilliance.

Whether it chooses to prepare in haste for a nuclear showdown with Russia, or to enter the Age of Coexistence, America will find it essential to re-examine and revise its central assumptions. If it accepts the inevitability of war, it cannot hope to strengthen itself and hold the allegiance of its allies without a new outlook. The same change is necessary if it is to compete effectively under the conditions of peace. Any effort to explain the crisis in partisan terms would be a grievous disservice to America and the world. The program was bipartisan—the responsibility is bipartisan.

It is essential, in short, to abandon the bipartisan imperialism of Thomas Jefferson and Theodore Roosevelt. America is neither the last best hope of the world nor the agent of civilization destined to destroy the barbarians. We have much to offer, but also much to learn. And the basic lesson is that we have misconceived leadership among equals as the exercise of predominance over others. Such an outlook is neither idealism nor realism; it is either self-righteousness or sophistry. Either is an indulgence which democracy cannot afford.

The Nation
(November 2, 1957)

Charles Austin Beard:

The Intellectual as

Tory-Radical

I

Late one night in 1929, aboard a train clickety-clacketing
northward along the Atlantic coast from the Carolinas, Charles
Beard gave away a vital insight into his intellectual and public
career. He was cornered in the smoker, defending himself
against, and explaining himself to, some professional historians
who challenged his emphasis on economics in history. One can
imagine him: his patience gone, his blue eyes sparking like
high-voltage electricity, and a scalpel's edge on his voice.

"I never said that economic motives explain everything!" he
roared. "Of course, ideas are important. And so are ethical concepts. What I have always said and all I have said is that,
among the various motives impelling men to action, the struggle for food, clothing, and shelter has been more important
throughout history than any other. And that is true, isn't it—
Isn't it?" [1]

Here, in one piercing paragraph, is the essence of Beard's intellectual personality. He was a radical in rooting to the heart
of the matter and insisting that man's economic struggle was
the "most important" part of history. But his conservative's caution was equally apparent. He refused to stereotype the relationship between the economic struggle and other phases of man's

activity, or the future nature of the struggle itself. He declined, in short, to grant the inevitability of any pattern of development. Spengler's *Decline of the West* left him as unconvinced and as unsatisfied as Darwin's middle-class utopia or Marx's prophecy of a communal Eden. Beard accepted only the certainty of change and conflict.

This suggests that Beard may most aptly be described as the intellectual as Tory-Radical. He had little, if any, confidence in revolutionary efforts to wrench mankind out of its historical continuity. For this reason some radicals have said that he was short-sighted and worse, that he lacked the nerve of failure. But he did believe that people could improve their lives by controlling more rationally and more equitably the economic system under which they lived. And for this the conservatives have called him subversive.[2]

The right-wingers are far closer to the truth. Beard contributed much to the currently neglected intellectual foundations of an American radicalism. He insisted that economic conflict and development is unending, and that it must constantly be analyzed, whatever the institutional organization of society. The American Left may be aware of this truth. It has failed, by and large, to act upon it since the days of its ideological romance with the New Deal's *noblesse oblige.* Beard also maintained that rulers who say one thing and do another, whatever the legal framework within which they act, undermine democracy. This morality is as important to those of the Left who close their ethical eyes while defending Franklin Delano Roosevelt's *conduct* of foreign affairs from 1938 to 1941 as it is to those who do likewise when discussing Soviet purges.

Thus Charles Beard's great legacy to American radicalism was not programmatic. Rather was it his persistent assertion, with great personal courage, that economics and morality are, respectively, the cornerstone and the keystone of the good life. Economic maladjustment will undermine morality; but the lack of ethical integrity will corrupt the best economic system. Beard never wholly neglected either of these propositions at any time during his career. Nor did he separate his intellectual and political activity. But he did tend to stress economic factors from his early maturity through the first years of the Great Depression. Thereafter he emphasized the ethics of power. Thus it may be helpful to review Beard's career within this framework: first his development and employment of a theory of social change; then his efforts to warn of the disastrous consequences of amoral politics.

II

Throughout both periods, of course, Beard's actions were in keeping with his analyses and morality. He considered the ivory tower as a refuge for the intellectual and moral coward—or scoundrel. The unity of theory and practice was to Beard a bit of Indiana common sense, not an alien philosophy to be disparaged or damned. In the earlier years, for example, he committed himself to educational and pragmatic efforts designed to increase his fellow citizens' understanding of causal forces, and to instruct them in the use and control of such forces to build a better society. Thus his vigorous work within the British working-class movement, his efforts to improve and extend American education, and his extremely practical proposals for rationalizing existing political institutions. During these years he worked primarily with other men, whether informally or in organized groups. But when he saw what seemed to him the rise of an essential immorality in American politics, Beard withdrew from group agitation to stand alone, unencumbered by conflicting loyalties, and to unmask in his writing the self-deceptions and public fabrications which he saw.

In a sense, of course, Beard stood so straight and so tall that he always stood alone. But he was not the lone wolf that some have pictured him. Only once before his attack on Roosevelt's foreign policy did he stand so much apart. That was in a similar situation, when, on October 8, 1917, he resigned from Columbia in defense of the principle of academic freedom. From the perspective of 1956 that act looms even larger than it did at the time.

"I am sure," he declared, "that when the people understand the true state of affairs in our universities they will speedily enact legislation which will strip boards of trustees of their absolute power over the intellectual life of the institutions under their management." [3] For it will not do to blame the people. The trouble was, and is, that Beard overestimated the extent to which his colleagues were concerned with discovering "the true state of affairs"—let alone communicating that knowledge to the people and acting on it themselves.

But Beard was a different kind of academic man. His troubles were always caused by his efforts to establish and publicize "the true state of affairs." His resignation from Columbia, for example, was the first major consequence of his dedication to the task of developing and using a theory of social change. He left Columbia as the final act in a series of events which began with the publication, in 1913, of *An Economic Interpretation of the Constitution*. Thus *The New York Times* (October 10, 1917) discussed Beard's resignation in a representative fashion —burying the issue of academic freedom in a diatribe against that book. And in this instance the *Times* is a source of accurate information, for the top levels of Columbia's administration had been fighting Beard ever since the publication of the volume. Their attacks on academic freedom were but a specific demonstration of their general antagonism to Beard's ideals and objectives.

A later generation of conservatives, realizing that the search for a general theory of social change is not in itself proof of radicalism, have acted less hysterically, though not necessarily less effectively. A theory of social change can be used to oppose radical innovations and reforms as well as to encourage them. Most recent research along this line has been motivated and financed, in fact, by those who have such a negative purpose. But Beard's early opponents thought that his case study of the origins of the Constitution established his desire for radical change, and so struck back vigorously and viciously. Beard never wholly committed himself, however, to using a theory of change in any one manner. He wanted to save what was best, yet improve it along with all the rest. Hence the ambiguity of his career.

III

Basically, though, Beard was more of a radical than he sometimes found it easy to admit to himself. For the commitment to search for a theory of social change undercuts the assumption of uniqueness upon which the theory and practice of the majority of American liberals and conservatives have been based. Such a denial that the United States is unique confronts those who understand it with a private and a general problem. It lays bare the uncomfortable truth, so personally pleasant to camouflage, that the evasion of basic issues ultimately becomes a terribly expensive flight from reality. And it thereby forces one either to continue such escape knowingly or else to grapple directly with the question of how to limit individual liberty without also de-stroying freedom.

Beard understood this. Prior to 1929 he was able to deny American uniqueness in theory while enjoying it in practice. But the Great Depression put an end to this idyll. And from that time forward Beard can only be understood in terms of a man wrestling with this central dilemma. These considerations also explain the changing nature of the criticism of Beard. His early opponents fought him because of his specific intellectual and political acts. His later critics, aware that he confronts them with the basic issue, assault the entire body of his work.

Save perhaps for a brief period early in the depression, Beard never came to grips directly with the theoretical and practical problems arising from the curtailment of individual liberty which was implicit in the idea of America living with and within itself. But Beard's own thesis that politics follows economics forced him, after the depression, to project two alter-nate paths for America's immediate future: rapid involvement in another general war, or self-containment within existing con-tinental boundaries or, at most, the Western Hemisphere. This is not a happy choice for a man (or a society) who matured in the tradition of "anything is possible," and the shock of its harshness may do much to account for Beard's seeming shift to relativism during the early '30s. Yet Beard always returned to the central question of whether it necessarily follows that free-dom is lost when liberty is curtailed. He never worked out a simple, programmatic solution for this problem. But he never denied, and only briefly evaded, the issue, and his basic answer was negative.

Beard's concentration on these key issues of causation and freedom does much to account for his interest in, and debt to, Karl Marx and James Madison. Those men labored all their lives over the same questions. But those who hope for a precise bookkeeping-style analysis of Beard's debt to these men will wait in vain. Beard was an on-going intellectual, concerned primarily with understanding and improving the world. He had little interest in, and even less time for, analyzing and defending himself.

Combined with his early experience in Chicago during the 1890s, Beard got from Marx a deep consciousness of change and an abiding sense of the importance to that change of the latent, long-run consequences of decisions made on the basis of short-term analyses. This emphasis on long-term generalized patterns helps to explain, for example, Beard's tendency to overlook immediate functional conflicts between economic groups. Beard's over-all interpretations, like those of Marx, are extremely difficult to destroy, whereas specific aspects of their analyses can be seriously modified or disproved.

Such weaknesses can not be inflated into proof of intellectual failure. It is possible, as several scholars have recently done, to demonstrate that some details of Beard's analysis of the origins of the Constitution are wrong.[4] Thus, as a case in point, his stress on the role and importance of the men who held obligations of the Continental Congresses can be interpreted to deny Beard's entire interpretation. But such concentration on functional analysis can lead the critics even further from the mark. For there is a very considerable difference between saying that Beard was mistaken about bondholders and going on to argue that economic alignments were not the central dynamic of the movement for the Constitution. Critics who attempt the second assertion would seem to be forgetting that a historical generalization is not an answer to every specific question.

Beard's intellectual relationship to Madison is also easy to confuse or misconstrue. Some scholars have taken Beard's some-

History as a Way of Learning

time assertion that he was a Madisonian at face value. More of
them have claimed that he merely used Madison as camouflage
for Marx. Both judgments seem a bit wide of the mark. It is
more probable that Beard viewed Marx and Madison as comple-
mentary thinkers. An analysis of his famous essay on *The Economic Basis of Politics* (1922) supports this view. The over-all
prognosis of Marx and Madison is very similar, as attested by
Madison's famous forecast, in 1829, that the United States
would suffer a serious economic and social crisis a century later.
Beard also realized that Madison's system of factions was nothing less than an unsystematized anticipation of the functional
school of sociological analysis. And, in some instances, Beard
followed Madison's model in his own work.

At times Beard failed to use these ideas of Marx and Madison as well as he might have. He was always in a hurry, for one
thing, and seldom took the time to dig out the facts on every
faction. Sometimes his insights as to which groups were the
most important were correct, and the finished essay was brilliant. In other cases, however, his research hypothesis was awry,
and the error was compounded in the completed work. It was
not that Beard ignored or monkeyed with the evidence, for he
was fanatically honest. But he tended, in his concern and haste
to find clues for the present, to work *with* his hypothesis instead of *from* it. But for Beard specific mistakes were of far less
concern than the validity of his general analysis of American
history. For he considered himself not so much an ivory-tower
historian as a functioning student of history.

IV

What did Beard mean when he called himself a student of history,
not a historian? The crucial difference between them lies in the

former's emphasis on his study as a means, whereas the latter considers his work as an end in itself. True, the historian's work may be the means to a personally satisfying life, but such an argument either misses or begs the issue. So, too, does the claim that all historians are also students of history. A difference of degree does lead to a difference of kind. Beard studied history to equip himself to comprehend and change his own society: to understand the direction and tempo of its movement, and to pinpoint the places at which to apply his energy and influence in an effort to modify both aspects of its development.

Analyzed from this perspective, it becomes very difficult to demolish his two central interpretations, *The Rise of American Civilization* (1927) and *The Idea of National Interest* (1934). For what Beard did in these books was to confront his readers with the hard fact that it was specific Americans who made American history, and that for the most part they had acted on the basis of a materialistic calculus. He ripped aside the appearances and the rationalizations to reveal the realities. No wonder he was attacked, for his lesson was quite outside any connection with existing politics. It was radical in the deepest sense of the term. And so it remains.

Though obviously pointing the moral of responsibility, and spelling it out in case after case, Beard's writing prior to the Great Depression was not characterized by any overriding sense of urgency. Neither were his actions. A man anticipating and dreading imminent and catastrophic crisis does not center his efforts on educational and political reform. Save for the academic freedom episode, the tenor of Beard's writings and actions was that of a concerned and responsible man who assumed that there was plenty of time to go slowly. It seems probable that this outlook was a product of Beard's American experience reinforcing his awareness that Marx's sense of time was quite foreshortened.

But the depression brought Beard up short. Here was deep
and general crisis. And there is little doubt that his intellectual
and personal outlook responded immediately. The tone of his
" 'Five Year Plan' for America," written in 1931, was markedly
different from that of his volume on *Public Service in America*
(1919), or the concluding pages of *The American Party Battle*
(1928). The earlier work is characterized by the assumption
that there is plenty of time. His essay on a five year plan is urgent, and probes far deeper in an effort to suggest new and significant changes.

Beard did not, however, launch any frontal attack on private property. His proposal was no more, in essence, than an
intelligent and rather extensive development of the idea of a
corporate society, previously advanced in America by such men
as Herbert Croly and Herbert Hoover. This concept of a corporate society is based on the proposition that every individual
holds membership in two of the three basic units of all industrialized societies. All people are citizens, hence are part of the
government. And, in addition, they belong either to capital or
labor. Thus the state, in theory at least, is at once the common
ground where both parties adjust their differences, and an independent power capable of enforcing judgments on both groups.

But corporatism is not a radical concept, for it is tied intimately to the principle of private property. And this weakens
both its theoretical and its practical value. For unless the power
to control investments, so vital to balanced economic growth, is
exercised on the basis of a public choice between alternate programs and policies, one half of the economic life of society remains in the hands of a tiny minority.

Thus Beard's radical insights into the malfunctioning of the
existing system were never matched by an equally fundamental
program for its renovation. His predilection for such a corporate

solution does explain, however, his support for much of the New Deal's domestic legislation. Beard and Roosevelt did see eye to eye on one point: they saw through the myth of rugged individualism. But when it came to the question of what to put in its place they turned first to a vague sort of corporatism, and then back to the dream of restoring competition. Neither of them looked forward to socialism.

V

The same disparity between radical analysis and conservative preference and program bedeviled Beard on foreign policy. There are few short analyses, for example, which match the quality of Beard's treatment of foreign affairs in *The Rise of American Civilization.* It is even more difficult to name a volume that is more rewarding in insights and suggestions than *The Idea of National Interest.* Beard stressed three points in these analyses of foreign policy: (1) it is intimately connected with domestic affairs, (2) empires are not built in fits of absent-mindedness, and (3) expansion does not in and of itself solve problems, and often complicates and deepens them.

These conclusions forced Beard to deal with several related problems. Both as a student of history and as an acting citizen it was vital for him to comprehend the system of ideas which first rationalize, and in turn further motivate, imperial expansion. In conjunction with his intrinsic intellectual ferment, and the shock of the depression, this need makes sense out of his sudden concentration on the work of German historians who were working on the general problem of *Weltanschauungen,* or conceptions of the world. This study was of key importance to Beard, for if he could come to grips with the general view of the world that was held by the expansionists, then he could attack it more directly and effectively.

He never carried through on this phase of his intellectual pursuits. It is, indeed, the weakest of all his performances. The reason that Beard never gave full attention to these studies, and rather shortly dropped them, lies in his growing concern over the drift of Roosevelt's foreign policy. Thus, after 1937, Beard gave less and less attention to the narrowly academic aspects of his work. It was not that his mind slowed down, but rather that his heart speeded up. Beard cared too deeply about America to bother with the formal rigmarole of the professional intellectual. And his love for his homeland brought him, deep in emotional turmoil, face to face with the multiple contradictions between his radical analyses, his strong concern for his fellow man, and his personal and philosophic commitment to private property. It would appear, on a close reading of his last books, that he sought a way out of this difficulty by emphasizing the primacy of moral integrity in public life.

One can only sympathize with Beard as he confronted his cruel dilemma. He realized, to start with, that the depression threatened the entire fabric of American society. This led him to cut through the cant of the claims of recovery and propose some serious modifications in the American economic system. He was quite aware, of course, that it was too late to "save capitalism" in the sense that the phrase was used by the New Dealers. Beard's fear was that the old order, though dying, would dominate the future. And he grew ever more disturbed as he realized that the New Deal was not economically successful. Nor could the failure be blamed only on the businessmen, for the New Dealers had few ideas about—let alone for—the future.

Then worse yet: he came to feel that the people in power were submerging the basic domestic problem in a foreign crisis, and defending this shift of emphasis by defining the new issue as the central danger. Here Beard confronted himself, for he too had to give an answer to this question of which was the crucial issue. It has been said, and often, that Beard failed this test. But the judgment is not that simple. Several things need to be kept in mind when appraising Beard's reaction. There was no radical program backed by organizational strength. Beard's position has often been misunderstood or misrepresented. And finally, the implicit import of Beard's criticism of Roosevelt is usually evaded.

It is possible to argue that an American socialism, structured around political and civil liberties and centralizing none but the economic power necessary to plan and administer balanced economic growth, leaving other property untouched, would have won Beard's support. Beard can hardly be blamed for the lack of such a choice. Indeed, a psychological analysis might well point to the conclusion that the New Deal intellectuals' attack on Beard is really indicative of their own sense of failure.

It will not do, furthermore, to argue that Beard would have opposed such a program because it carried the strong probability of entering the war. For Beard did not oppose the war that was fought. He did oppose the way that Roosevelt led this country into war, and the New Deal's strong inclination to think it was America's job to reform the world. This vital difference demands considerable emphasis because it is central to an understanding of Beard's thought and his importance. Beard made three central points in his attack on Roosevelt: the domestic crisis was being "solved" in a manner that only postponed and deepened it; this "solution" was being carried out in a manner —deceptively—that undercut democratic morality and practice; and the assumption by the United States of the right, or obligation, to police the world would compound both crises.

It is extremely difficult to deny the force of these arguments. Recovery and prosperity at the price of an extremely poor strategic position in World War II, a police action in Korea, and an atomic diplomacy based on cultivating the cold war *have* deepened the basic crises of the '30s. Nor were any of these developments inevitable. The consequences of Roosevelt's deceptive methods are perhaps less obvious, but perhaps even more dangerous. The practice of protecting the people from the truth in order to save them from themselves damages the fiber of a society. And, as Beard knew, no society can survive its own hypocrisy.

Thus Beard lived by the creed of grappling directly, honestly, and democratically with any problem, be it economic, social, or moral. And he fought hypocrisy and political chicanery with all the militance he could muster, a worthy example for American radicals.

American Radicals: Some Problems and Personalities,
ed. Harvey Goldberg
(New York: Monthly Review Press, 1957)

The Age of Mercantilism:
An Interpretation of
the American
Political
Economy,
1763 to
1828

Based upon the suggestion by Curtis P. Nettels that one of the consequences of British mercantilism was the creation "of a new mercantilist state on this side of the Atlantic," and upon recent re-evaluations of mercantilism by William D. Grampp, Gunnar Myrdal, Jacob Viner, Charles Wilson, and others, this essay advances the hypothesis that the central characteristic of American history from 1763 to 1828 was in fact the development and maturation of an American mercantilism.[1] Let it be emphasized that the interpretation is offered as a hypothesis and no more—as an idea to be examined and tested, then accepted, modified, or rejected on the basis of its relevance and validity. There is no intention, furthermore, even to imply that the approach as here stated offers final answers to all the vexing problems connected with understanding early American society. It is merely proposed that a re-examination of the era from this angle may lead to new insights, and hence contribute to a broader interpretation of the period.[2]

At the outset, for example, the use of the concept of mercantilism restores to its properly central place the fact that Americans thought of themselves as an empire at the very beginning of their national existence—as part of their assertive self-consciousness which culminated in the American Revolution. Though it may seem surprising, especially when contrasted with the image of isolationism which has been accepted so long, in reality this early predominance of a pattern of empire thought is neither very strange nor very difficult to explain. Having matured in an age of empires as part of an empire, the colonists naturally saw themselves in the same light once they joined issue with the mother country.

Revolutionary leaders were confident of their ability "not only to take territory by the sword, but to hold and govern it under a colonial status." [3] Long before the break with England, for example, Benjamin Franklin was a leader of those who entertained a "burning interest in westward expansion." At the threshold of the revolution he visualized an American Empire including Canada, the Spanish Floridas, the West Indies, and perhaps even Ireland.[4] George Washington, John Adams, John Livingston, and Thomas Lee were among those who shared such conceptions of an American Empire.[5] By the end of the war, such men as Silas Deane looked forward to the time when "Great Britain, America and Russia united will command not barely Europe, but the whole world united." [6] And in 1789, after remarking that "it is well known that empire has been travelling from east to west," Congregational minister and geographer Jedidiah Morse concluded that "probably her last and broadest seat will be America . . . the largest empire that ever existed." [7]

While the vigor, even cockiness, of such statements may be explained by the consciousness of having whipped the champion, the underlying emphasis on expansion and empire was an integral part of the general outlook of mercantilism, a conception of the world shared by most of the revolutionary generation. Though they revolted against British mercantilism, there is considerable evidence to suggest that early American leaders did not, as so often is assumed, rebel against the idea and practice of mercantilism itself. In stressing the role of natural-rights philosophy in the thinking of the leaders of the revolution, the traditional view of the American Revolution has slighted this key point.

An acceptance of natural law is not incompatible with mercantilism, as is indicated by John Locke's vigorous espousal of both systems. Much of the talk in America about natural rights, moreover, concerned what Thomas Paine called the "natural right" to one's own empire.[8] And though they were willing to use Adam Smith's polemic in behalf of laissez faire as a weapon against British mercantilism (and against their domestic opponents), most Americans adhered firmly in their own practice to the principle that the state had to intervene in economic affairs. America's romance with Smith's laissez faire came later and was of relatively short duration. Hence it would appear that a better understanding of early American history depends in considerable measure upon a grasp of the nature and practice of American mercantilism as it developed between 1763 and 1825.

Traditionally thought of as little more than a narrow and selfish point of view held by the trading interest, mercantilism was in fact a broad definition and explanation of the world shared by most of Western Europe in the seventeenth and eighteenth centuries.[9] In this sense it was the basic outlook of those who labored to build a dynamic balanced economy of agriculture and business organized on a capitalistic basis within a nationalistic framework. Depending upon their specific function and power at any given stage in the process, mercantilists argued among themselves over the best means to achieve and maintain such a system—and differed in their estimates of whether or not it had been established—but they agreed on the objective and upon the need to use the state as a tool.

Whether agrarian or urban, therefore, mercantilists were essentially nationalists who strove for self-sufficiency through increased domestic production and a favorable balance (and terms) of trade. Their emphasis on production and the control of export markets and sources of raw materials, rather than on consumption and economic interdependence, led them to fear surpluses as a sign of crisis and failure. Thus they dropped the old feudal restrictions on exports and replaced them with taxes on imports. Their greatest fear was a surplus of goods. In this respect, furthermore, mercantilism was reinforced—albeit in a backhanded and even unintentional way—by the broad ethical outlook of Puritanism (which frowned on luxury), even though mercantilism itself was a secular and almost amoral system. Likewise, the concept of a chosen people, so strong in Puritanism, also strengthened the secular and economic nationalism of mercantilism. Thus mercantilists constantly labored to build a tightly organized and protected national market and to increase their share of the world market. The key points in their program were integration at home and expansion abroad.

In the exuberant confidence of their victory over Britain, Americans tended to assume that each new state could survive and thrive as a mercantile empire unto itself. That attitude was not too surprising, for each of the new states appeared to enjoy the raw materials, labor supply, and trading facilities for a balanced economy. That estimate of the situation was supported and reinforced by the conviction, itself part of traditional theory that a state could remain democratic in political and social life only if it were small and integrated, and by the experiences of the colonies in dealing with Great Britain's imperial policy after 1763. Yet the political outlook and faith contradicted certain basic tenets of mercantilism, which Americans also entertained, or assumed.

The first attempt to reconcile the conflict produced the Articles of Confederation. That instrument of government stressed the independence of the states as self-contained units of mercantilism and democratic republicanism, yet also established a central government for the purposes of war and, as in the case of Canada, future expansion. But specific postwar developments, such as the serious recession, the expansionist conflicts between the states, and the difficulties in dealing with other countries in economic affairs, combined to disillusion many Americans with their experiment in particularistic mercantilism.

Broadly speaking, the resulting movement toward a stronger central government grew out of internal and international economic difficulties analyzed and explained with the ideas of mercantilism. By 1785, for example, most of the states, including the agrarian ones, were switching from tariffs for revenue to tariffs for international retaliation and protection. Merchants demanded American navigation acts, artisans agitated for protection of their labor, and agricultural interests wanted help in balancing their political economy.[10] Various groups of Americans who concerned themselves directly with the problem of strengthening the central government—and there were many who were preoccupied with local and immediate difficulties or opportunities—offered several proposals for handling the problem. Centered in New England, the smallest group favored establishing an aristocratic society at home and rejoining the British Empire as a contractual junior partner. Such men were not willing to return to colonial status, but they did favor economic and social reintegration. Most Americans opposed that solution, favoring instead either the delegation of more power to the central government under the Articles of Confederation or the substitution of an entirely new instrument of government.

A letter from James Madison to Thomas Jefferson in the spring of 1786 not only indicates that the agrarian as well as the urban interests favored one or the other of those last two approaches, but dramatizes the fundamental mercantilism of the entire movement. "A continuance of the present anarchy of our commerce," Madison explained, "will be a continuance of the unfavorable balance on it, which by draining us of our metals . . . [will bring our ruin]. In fact, most of our political evils may be traced up to our commercial ones, and most of our moral may to our political." [11]

Against this background, the Constitution appears as an instrument of centralized national government framed in the classic manner by men thinking within the framework of mercantilism and blessed with the physical and human resources for a balanced economy. It provided the foundation for a national system of economics and politics and organized American strength for the struggle with other mercantile empires and for the conquest of less powerful peoples. The latter considerations were essential, for the Founding Fathers resolved the contradiction between the stress on expansion in mercantilism and the emphasis on a small state in existing democratic political theory by developing a theory of their own which held that democratic republicanism could be sustained by just such expansion. James Madison, often called the Father of the Constitution, provided the most striking formulation of this proposition, but Thomas Jefferson, John Adams, and other early leaders either shared or adopted it in one form or another within a reasonably short time.

Taking his cue from David Hume, the Englishman who attacked Montesquieu's argument that democracy was a system that could work only in small states, Madison asserted that a large state offered a much better foundation for republicanism.[12] Institutional checks and balances could help, and were therefore necessary, but they were not enough in and of themselves. "Extend the sphere," he argued, "and you take in a greater variety of parties and interests; you make it less probable that a majority of the whole will have a common motive to invade the rights of other citizens; or if such a common motive exists, it will be more difficult for all who feel it to discover their own strength, and to act in unison with each other. . . ." [13]

While it is possible to conclude from Madison's remarks that he had in mind a static conception of such a large state, three considerations would appear to weaken that reading of his thesis. First, Madison used the verb "extend" in its active, unlimited sense. Second, he was stating a general theory, not making an argument in behalf of a given territorial settlement. And third, he advocated and vigorously supported the continued expansion of the United States. It seems more probable, therefore, that Madison was proposing, *as a guide to policy and action in his own time,* the same kind of an argument that Frederick Jackson Turner formulated a century later, when he advanced his frontier thesis which explained America's democracy and prosperity as the result of such expansion.

Madison's theory became the key to an American mercantilism. Merchants and manufacturers who wanted their own empire found it convincing and convenient. And Jefferson's thesis that democracy and prosperity depended upon a society of landholding freemen was a drastically simplified version of the same idea. Edward Everett of Massachusetts captured the essence of the interpretation in his judgment that expansion was the *"principle* of our institutions." [14] Additional support for this interpretation is offered by Madison's later prophecy (in 1828–29) that a major crisis would occur in about a century, when the continent was filled up and an industrial system had deprived most people of any truly productive property. In the event, Madison's fears proved true sooner than he anticipated. For in the crisis of the 1890's, when Americans *thought* that the frontier was gone, they advanced and accepted the argument that new expansion was the best—if not the only—way to sustain their freedom and prosperity.[15]

Madison's original statement of the expansionist thesis was important for two reasons. First, it provided the theoretical basis for an American mercantilism combining commercial and territorial expansion with political democracy. Second, by thus reemphasizing the idea of empire, and proposing expansion as the key to national welfare, Madison opened the way for a discussion of the basic questions facing American mercantilism. Those issues concerned domestic enonomic affairs, the kind of expansion that was necessary and desirable, and the means to accomplish such gains while the nation was young and weak.

Washington's Farewell Address formulated a bipartisan answer to the problem of basic strategy. The solution was to build a commercial empire (which included markets for agricultural surpluses) by avoiding political involvement in the European system, meanwhile retaining complete freedom of action to secure and develop a continental empire in the Western Hemisphere. Washington's proposition was classically simple: play from the strength provided by America's basic economic wealth and geographic location in order to survive immediate weakness and emerge as *the* world power. "If we remain one people, under an efficient government," he promised, "the period is not far off when we may defy material injury from external annoyance . . . when we may choose peace or war, as our interest, guided by justice, shall counsel." Sharing that objective, and quite in agreement with the strategy, Thomas Jefferson summed it all up a bit later in one famous axiom: "entangling alliances with none." And with the enunciation of the Monroe Doctrine, freedom of action became the avowed and central bipartisan theme of American foreign policy.

As a condition of that persuasive agreement, however, several serious conflicts had to be resolved. Perhaps they can be discussed most clearly by defining and considering them within the framework of the gradual defeat and amalgamation of the pro-British and pro-French minorities by a growing consensus in favor of an American mercantilism. Such an approach has the additional value of making it possible to organize the analysis around familiar personalities as symbols of certain ideas, functional groups, and special interests. Let it be posited, therefore, that the following men are key figures in the evolution of an American mercantilism: Timothy Pickering, John Adams, and John Quincy Adams of Massachusetts; Alexander Hamilton of New York; and James Madison, Thomas Jefferson, and John Taylor of Virginia.

In many respects, at any rate, Pickering and Taylor represented the nether fringes of American mercantilism. Pickering trod the trail from reluctant revolutionary to threatening secessionist in the name of a domestic merchant aristocracy functioning as a quasi-independent contractual member of the British Empire. His ideal was a central government charged with the responsibility (and armed with the power and authority) to establish and sustain a politically and socially stratified society and to provide the economic assistance (especially funded credit) that was necessary for the rationalized operations of overseas correspondents of British mercantilism and for domestic speculative ventures. Though Pickering and his supporters fit the traditional stereotype of mercantilists, they were in fact and function no more than the agents of British mercantilism. They were very successful agents, to be sure, but they did not view or define America in terms of its own mercantilism. Rather did they visualize it as a self-governing commonwealth of the British Empire. Hence it was only very late and with great reluctance, if at all, that they supported the measures necessary for a mercantilist state in America.

At the other extreme, John Taylor developed his program as a variation on a theme first stated by the French physiocrats. He emphasized the primacy of agriculture as narrowly as Pickering stressed the virtue and necessity of the merchant-trader-speculator. Taylor's tirades against funded debts and bank stock, and his soliloquies in praise of the noble farmer, seem alike in their total opposition to the principles of mercantilism. But in other respects his ideas were not so untainted by mercantilism as his rhetoric indicated. As with most other planters, for example, his theory of labor coincided at all essential points with the view held by British mercantilists.[16] So, too, did his conception of the role of western lands in the economy of the seaboard "mother country."

With respect to foreign trade, moreover, Taylor was trapped by the weakness of the physiocrats in that area of economics.[17] Ostensibly free traders, the physiocrats did not favor the navy essential to such a program. Taylor and other American imbibers of the physiocratic elixir awoke to discover that their vision did not correspond to reality. Taylor himself was not very adaptive, and ended his career in attacks on Jefferson and other agrarians who did develop an American mercantilism. But Taylor's position does dramatize the dilemma faced by the agrarians.[18] The contradiction between theory and actuality confronted them with a rather apparent choice: either they could content themselves with slow economic stagnation or they could build an American maritime system, accept dependence upon a foreign naval power, or support an American industry. In that choice lies a key aspect of the rise of a mature American mercantilism; for it developed most consciously and was ultimately practiced most rigorously by the southern agrarians who are often assumed to have been most rabidly antimercantilist. If nothing else, the weakness of their ideal program drove them into mercantilism.

It is particularly important to keep that fact in mind when considering Hamilton, about whom the discussion of American mercantilism has billowed for so long. Joseph Charles was essentially correct in his view that "the standard works on Hamilton evade the main issues which his career raises," and his judgment remains relevant despite the plethora of centennial essays and biographies.[19] The entire question of Hamilton's mercantilism has to be decided with reference to three points: the meaning and significance of the *Report on Manufactures,* his role in the Jay Treaty episode, and his plans to join in the further expansion of the British Empire in the Western Hemisphere. However difficult it may be to pin him down with an alternate characterization, Hamilton simply cannot be considered the fountainhead of American mercantilism unless those aspects of his career can be interpreted within the framework of mercantilist thought and action.

Since the *Report on Manufactures* is often accepted as proof, as well as evidence, of Hamilton's mercantilism, it is convenient to give first consideration to that document. In doing so, it seems wise to recall the chronology of his three state papers on economic affairs. Hamilton was commissioned as Secretary of the Treasury on September 11, 1789; and there followed the manifesto on public credit in January 1790, the report on a central bank in December 1790, and the paper on manufacturing in December 1791. Even the most cursory review of those dates catches the two-year delay between the reports on credit and manufacturers. That interval becomes even more striking when viewed in the context of other events.

It was Madison rather than Hamilton, for example, who gave more attention to protective duties on manufactures during the Constitutional Convention. That is still more illuminating since associations for the promotion of American manufactures had appeared in New York, Boston, Providence, and Baltimore as early as 1785; and resolutions for domestic goods had followed the next year from such additional and widely separated localities as Hartford, Germantown, Richmond, and Halifax (South Carolina). By 1789, furthermore, not only had the anti-Federalists picked up political support from such groups in New England, New York, and Pennsylvania, but the special session of Congress received numerous requests and petitions from various manufacturing societies.[20]

Having passed an emergency revenue bill in the form of tariff legislation, the Congress then *ordered* Hamilton, on January 15, 1790, to prepare a specific report on manufactures. That makes his delay even more noticeable, whatever allowances may be granted for his other duties and the thoroughness of his research. As late as October 1791, moreover, the administration saw no need to increase the tariff of 1789. In matters of chronology, urgency, and emphasis, therefore, it seems clear that Hamilton gave priority to funding the debt and establishing the bank. Those operations represented precisely the needs and objectives of the merchants who were semiautonomous correspondents of British mercantilism, and who were fundamentally opposed to a strong American industry. Their economic, political, and social position would be threatened by a vigorous program of industrialization; for at the very least they would have to make drastic changes in their outlook and actions. Since Hamilton's personal and political position was based on his rapport with that group, it seems relevant to consider whether Hamilton's mercantilism was as thoroughgoing as historians have assumed it was.

In Hamilton's behalf, it can be argued with considerable validity that domestic industry had to have a sound credit system as a cornerstone. But that approach only raises the question of why Hamilton did not present his funding and bank programs as the means to achieve an independent balanced economy. Since he did not, the most relevant explanation would seem to be that Hamilton was in fact a mercantilist who was hamstrung by his political dependence upon the Federalists around Pickering. His association with Tench Coxe would serve to strengthen that analysis.[21] The same argument could then be used to explain why Hamilton delayed his paper on manufactures for almost two years after the Congress had asked for it in January 1790.

The weakest point in that interpretation concerns Hamilton's response to Madison's resolution of January 3, 1794, that "the interests of the United States would be promoted by further restrictions and higher duties in certain cases on the manufactures and navigation of foreign nations employed in the commerce of the United States." Working through William Smith of South Carolina, Hamilton killed Madison's entire program which was designed to promote commercial and industrial independence. Instead, Hamilton's committee in the House reported in favor of more borrowing and further domestic taxes. For that matter, neither Hamilton nor the Federalist party acted to increase protection after 1792.[22]

The explanation of Hamilton's action which does the most to sustain his reputation as an American mercantilist is not as generous to his standing as a reformed monarchist. For given the broad and vigorous agitation from manufacturing societies for greater protection, Madison's resolutions offered Hamilton a striking opportunity to widen the base of the Federalist party. That would have strengthened his hand against the pro-British group within the party and have enabled him to give substance to the *Report on Manufactures*. If it be said that Hamilton favored domestic excise taxes in preference to domestic manufacturing, then his mercantilism appears even more questionable. A stronger argument could be made by reference to Hamilton's known reservations about democracy, which would account for his refusal to court the manufacturers as a counterweight to the merchants around Pickering.

It may be, however, that Hamilton's vigorous opposition to Madison's resolutions of 1794 derived in considerable part from the fact that Madison's program was aimed at Great Britain. Not only was that true in the immediate, particular sense, but it also was the case in that Madison's proposals pointed toward general economic independence. That approach to the question of Hamilton's mercantilism has the virtue of having considerable relevance to his role in Jay's Treaty. An American mercantilist could explain and defend Hamilton's basic attitude and maneuvers behind Jay's back by one or both of two arguments. First, England had to be courted while the United States built a navy. Second, Hamilton stressed the political side of mercantilism.

Neither of those explanations is very convincing: Hamilton always favored the army over the navy, and political mercantilism is such a contradiction in terms that it begs the entire issue. That interpretation becomes even less convincing when asked to account for the fact that at the end of his career Hamilton turned not toward manufacturing but in the direction of becoming a partner in Britain's imperial adventures in Latin America. Indeed, Hamilton's foreign policy does less to settle the question of his mercantilism than to recall the report in 1793 that "the English considered Hamilton, [Rufus] King, and [William] Smith, of South Carolina, as main supports of British interest in America. Hamilton, not Hammond, was their effective minister." [23] Perhaps the most to be said of Hamilton's mercantilism is that it was latent and limited, for his actions belied his rhetoric.

As in many other contexts, it is Madison who emerges as the central figure in the development of an American mercantilism. While there are many illustrations, perhaps his resolutions of January 1794 provide the most illuminating evidence. Once again Charles points the way: "The program with which Madison began the first strategic moves against the Federalists was not one which could be called anti-Federalist, particularist, or States' rights." [24] His plan was to combine landed expansion to the west with support for domestic manufacturing and an independent American commercial policy. Considered at the practical political level, it represented a bid to the growing numbers of dissident Federalists who opposed a one-way relationship with Britain. Some of those men eyed a bull market for domestic manufactures. Others thought of an expansionist foreign policy with the established states cast in the role of "mother country." Madison saw such groups as allies for the anti-Federalists, as well as the building blocks of an American mercantilism.

Madison's conception of an American mercantilism was possibly too comprehensive as well as too premature politically to be adopted by Congress in 1794, though it was extensively debated before being sidetracked by Hamilton and Smith. But it did serve as a keen analysis and program for the growing consensus among anti-Federalists. That drive toward economic independence manifested itself in the Non-Intercourse Bill introduced in the summer of 1794, a move which was defeated only by the vote of Vice-President John Adams. Equally significant is the fact that it was backed by congressmen from Pennsylvania and Delaware as well as by those from southern states. Madison's mercantilism picked up new allies very rapidly, and two subsequent events served as catalysts in the process. Considered in the order of their importance, they were Jay's Treaty and the last stage in the defection of John Adams from High Federalism.

Following so closely upon the narrow defeat of the Non-Intercourse Bill, Jay's Treaty added injury to frustration. The great majority of Americans reacted bitterly and vigorously. Already weakened by deep fissures, the Federalist party cracked open under the ensuing attack. It cost them key leaders in such states as New Hampshire and Pennsylvania and alienated unknown numbers of voters south of the Potomac. As one who had cast the deciding vote against the Non-Intercourse Bill only with great reluctance, John Adams provided temporary leadership for such Federalist dissidents.

Adams strengthened his position even more by refusing to go quietly along to war with France at the bidding of the High Federalists. The differences between Hamilton and Adams were numerous, but perhaps none is so important to an appreciation of the maturing American mercantilism as the contrast between Hamilton's passion for a large army and Adams' emphasis on an American navy. Hamilton's military policy was that of the British nabob in North America, while that of Adams represented American mercantilism. Against that background, and in the context of his deciding vote on the Non-Intercourse Bill of 1794, it is possible to appreciate the full impact of Jay's Treaty on Adams. He made peace with France and forced Pickering out of the cabinet.

Little wonder, then, that Jefferson was willing to give way

in favor of Adams. But thanks to Madison, who had been organizing a party as well as projecting a theory and a program, Jefferson became President. Once in power, Jefferson and his supporters were prodded by necessity and spurred by their own
visions of empire toward the full development of an American
mercantilism. There are several explanations for this phenomenon. Among the most important, one might list the following:
the foreign-trade dilemma inherent in physiocratic theory
(which was intensified by the wars stemming from the French
Revolution); the creative leadership provided by such men as
Madison and Albert Gallatin (who made his own *Report on
Manufactures* in 1810); the political necessities and expediences
of unifying and sustaining a national party; and the maturing
thought of Jefferson himself. But wherever one chooses to place
the emphasis, the fact remains that the Jeffersonians in action
were far more mercantilistic than the Federalists had been—
even in theory and rhetoric.

As early as 1791, for that matter, Jefferson began to shift
away from the physiocratic dogma of free trade. And by 1793
he concluded his *Report on Commercial Policy* with a series of
retaliatory proposals that were as mercantilistic as any he criticized. Perhaps even more significant was his early ambivalence
toward manufacturing, which he never condemned outright
once and for all. Jefferson disliked cities and the factory system
for what he judged their negative impact on politics and morals,
and for the conditions and style of life they imposed upon
human beings, but he never discounted the importance of home
manufacturing and commerce. He could not afford to, either as
the leader of agrarians beginning to produce surpluses for sale,
or as one who sought and accepted support from the increasing
number of urban groups of all classes who preferred an empire
of their own to rejoining the British system. Even if Jefferson

had not caught the intellectual flaw in physiocratic trade theory, its practical consequences were something he could not avoid. In substance, therefore, the Jeffersonians based their strength and their policies on the mercantilistic program of a balanced economy at home and a foreign policy of expansion.

Their strategy was to exploit the policy of neutrality initiated by Washington and continued by John Adams. To do so, Jefferson ultimately resorted to the intensely mercantilistic policies of the embargo and nonimportation against Britain and France. It was with obvious pride that he remarked, in 1809, that those policies "hastened the day when an equilibrium between the occupations of agriculture, manufactures, and commerce, shall simplify our foreign concerns to the exchange only of that surplus which we cannot consume [in return] for those articles of reasonable comfort or convenience which we cannot produce." [25] Not even Madison ever provided a more classic statement of American mercantilism.

Quite in line with Jefferson's recommendations of the 1790's, and his actions between 1800 and 1809, his successors acted vigorously against such weaker opponents as the Barbary Pirates who threatened American trade. On a more general level, Jefferson's argument that American democracy depended upon a surplus of land was but another, even more overtly formulated, version of Madison's theory that extending the sphere was the key to controlling factions. Hence he and his followers initiated and encouraged such expansion wherever they could, as in Florida and to the west; and it was precisely Jefferson's general expansionist outlook which overrode his concern that the Louisiana Purchase was unconstitutional.

The Louisiana Purchase opened the way to apply the tenets of American mercantilism to the entire hemisphere. It also encouraged an explicit American formulation of the expansionist philosophy of history that was implicit in mercantilism. Americans began to call openly and militantly for further expansion whenever and wherever they encountered domestic or foreign difficulties. Indians and Spaniards had to be pushed out of the way or destroyed. Interference with exports had to be stopped, by war if necessary. Canada offered the solution to other domestic economic problems, and should be taken forthwith.

After 1807, when economic troubles appeared at home, that expansionist outlook and program focused on Great Britain as the chief offender against the American Empire. Growing out of an alliance of business and agrarian interests which favored war to relieve immediate difficulties and forestall future crises, the War of 1812 was a classic mercantilist conflict for trade and colonies.[26] The Jeffersonians' earlier economic and maritime warfare, which almost secured the immediate objectives, and which had appeared capable of clearing the way for a general advance, was just as mercantilistic in nature. Though in many ways it failed to attain its avowed objectives, the War of 1812 was in no sense a strategic defeat for American mercantilism. If only in turning Americans to the west and the south, it focused the general spirit of expansion in a new and powerful manner. Perhaps even more significant, the stalemate strengthened the idea of an American System as opposed to the rest of the world. It was in the wake of the War of 1812, after all, that the vapors of Manifest Destiny gathered themselves for an explosion westward to the Pacific.

John Quincy Adams formulated his own concept of Manifest Destiny as early as 1796, when he assured President Washington that the American System would "infallibly triumph over the European system. . . . "[27] Fifteen years later he defined America as "a nation, coextensive with the North American Continent, destined by God and nature to be the most populous and most powerful people ever combined under one social compact." [28] He pushed overseas economic expansion just as vigorously. Even his harshest critics, the High Federalists of New England who wanted to re-enter the British Empire in some form or another, recognized his mercantilism. They called him one of the species of "amphibious politicians, who live on both land and water. . . ." [29]

Both before and after he served as Secretary of State under President James Monroe, Adams devoted his energies to building such an American Empire. His rational program for a dynamic balanced economy at home was too demanding for his countrymen. They grew ever more enamored of a philosophy that assured them that expansion was the way to ease their dilemmas and realize their dreams. Hence they paid little heed to his proposals for domestic development or to his warning that America should go "not abroad in search of monsters to destroy." But to the extent that Adams wanted an empire big enough to sustain such a balanced economy, and to the degree that he partook of the expansionist elixir, he won support and influence. And, indeed, his very presence in the cabinet of Monroe was a symbol of the maturity of American mercantilism. Having broken with the old pro-British party to vote for the Louisiana Purchase and the measures of economic warfare against Europe, Adams became the leader of those business interests which supported territorial as well as commercial expansion.

In timing, authorship, and content, the Monroe Doctrine was the classic statement of mature American mercantilism. Seizing the opportunity presented by the decay of the Spanish Empire, Monroe and Adams moved quickly, decisively, and independently to give substance to Henry Clay's fervent exhortation to "become real and true Americans and place ourselves at the head of the American System." [30] Adams caught the tone and meaning of the doctrine in his famous remark that it was time for America to stop bobbing along as a cock-boat in the wake of the British Empire. Acting in that spirit, he spurned Secretary George Canning's not-so-subtle suggestion that America join England in a joint guarantee of Latin American independence and a pledge against their own expansion in the region. Canning claimed high honors for having brought in the New World to redress the balance of the Old, but one would like to think that Adams enjoyed a hearty chuckle over such ability to put a rhetorical gloss on a policy defeat. For what Canning had done was to block the old empires only to be confronted by the challenge of a mature American mercantilism.

In the negative sense, the Monroe Doctrine was designed to check further European colonization in the Western Hemisphere. But Americans were quite aware of the positive implications of the strategy: it left the United States as the most powerful nation on the scene. America's ultimate territorial and commercial expansion in the New World would be limited only by its energies and its preferences—just as Washington had argued.[31] The negative side of the Monroe Doctrine is the least significant feature about it: the crucial point is that it was, in the minds of its authors, in its language, and in its reception by Americans, the manifesto of an American Empire.

The Monroe Doctrine was the capstone of a system destined to succumb to its own success. For in broad historical perspective, the classic function of mercantilism was to build a system strong enough to survive the application of the principles of Adam Smith. Without an American mercantilism there could have been no Age of Jacksonian Laissez Moi Faire. Perhaps, indeed, the greatest tribute to the leaders of American mercantilism lies in the fact that their handiwork withstood the trauma of a civil war and the sustained shock of unrestrained and irrational exploitation for some seventy years—until it became necessary in the Crisis of the 1890's to undertake the building of a new corporate system.

The William and Mary Quarterly
(October 1958)

The Large Corporation
and American
Foreign
Policy

The large corporation is generally acknowledged to have wielded an extensive influence in American domestic affairs since 1890. While it has never dominated American society in the literal sense, clearly it has been and is an *imperium in imperio;* for throughout the century it has proposed and disposed in competition and collaboration with the government. Such power and authority also enabled the large corporation—if it so chose—to play an equally important role in the day-by-day and long-term relations between the United States and the rest of the world. It did so choose and, directly and indirectly, at home as well as overseas, it has exercised that potential in foreign affairs. There is considerable evidence to suggest, indeed, that the central features of the large corporation's conception of the world—its definition and explanation of reality—had by 1950 come to delineate crucial aspects of American foreign policy.

The extent to which that correlation exists, and hence the relevance of fundamental questions which it raises, can most effectively be gauged by examining various facets of the relationship between the large corporation and foreign policy. These may be outlined as follows:

1. Though the concept of the large corporation as used herein includes financial as well as industrial institutions, the

study is not concerned directly with the long and learned discussion about the precise number of such firms and the decimal percentages of their concentrated power. Those calculations and related investigations make it clear that the large corporation, in its fundamental role as the organizer of a disorganized nineteenth-century capitalism, in its supplementary function as architect of a vast network of subcontracting, marketing, and servicing connections, and through its influence and participation in local and national government, has exerted a predominant influence in the American political economy since the crisis of the 1890's.

2. The large corporation exercises several kinds of influence on foreign policy: direct and indirect, and economic and intellectual. In each of those ways, moreover, the large corporation's power can be used either to initiate, delay, or veto foreign policy proposals. Some of its most important influence has been of a negative character, as when it postponed, emasculated, or killed other programs.

Viewed collectively as an institution, for example, the large corporation is the dynamic and crucial private element in the American economic system. Its economic decisions and actions affect political and social developments as well as economic affairs. And since it is central to the economy *per se,* government investment and spending are also undertaken to an extensive degree through the large corporation. A specific corporation, on the other hand, can and does function as a special economic interest in the conduct of foreign affairs. A good example of such action, which also illustrates the negative side of corporation influence, is offered by the corporations which resisted President Franklin Delano Roosevelt's efforts to send more aid to the Allies prior to Pearl Harbor.

All of those economic and other influences appear as facts to intellectuals and politicians attempting to formulate a coherent overview of American society or an appropriate foreign policy. Finally, the leaders of the large corporation function as intellectuals (a category which includes some academics but is not defined thereby) in their work of knowing, systematizing, interpreting, and acting upon the reality about them. Their conception of the world takes on dramatic importance when they enter the government.

3. The rise of the large corporation in the 1890's confronted the labor movement with the problem of choosing and implementing a basic response to the new structure of American industry. In theory, at any rate, labor had a number of options. It could have deployed its power to destroy the corporation and substituted a system of cooperative enterprises, to socialize the corporation and thereby the system, to break it up and re-establish the world of the individual entrepreneur, to regulate it through the government, or to organize labor itself within the new framework established by the corporation. If all of its efforts are considered, it can be argued that at least some segment of labor tried each of those solutions. But labor's basic approach was to organize labor on the terms specified by the large corporation: first in segments paralleling management's division of labor, and finally according to the system itself.

The decision to organize within the existing corporation reinforced the influence of the corporation on foreign policy. Since it did not demand a share in investment decisions, labor's policy served to extend and consolidate the position and power of the corporation in the American political economy. The *net* result was to help business organize business. That basic situation was not seriously altered even when labor turned to the government as a tool for regulating such a corporate economy. Not only was the corporation equally influential in politics, but labor's objectives did not challenge—let alone threaten— the key role of the corporation in the economy. In all essentials, therefore, as well as in most particulars, labor foreign policy was (and is) corporation foreign policy. As with the corporation, labor sometimes divided within itself, but it never proposed or fought militantly for a fundamentally different foreign policy.

4. In terms of the extent and character of its interest and influence, the foreign affairs role of the large corporation has developed as a process. There have been conflicts over foreign policy between industrial and financial corporations, and even within some of them; and the institution itself exercised less influence in 1890 than it did in 1900, 1926, or 1969.

Because they have an important bearing on the problem of analysis and interpretation, it also seems wise to review key aspects of the relationship between overseas economic expansion and foreign policy. An apt illustration of the existing confusion on this issue is provided by the assertion that the United States would have to export and invest, on a *pro rata* basis, as much as Great Britain did at the apex of its empire before such overseas economic expansion could be considered crucial to the American economy. Such an analysis may or may not be useful for purposes of personal or public persuasion, but when examined on its own terms it is neither very relevant nor very helpful to an understanding of the political economy of American foreign policy. To consider only the most obvious aspect, it is extremely difficult to establish a valid basis for comparing the two nations. And if, to make an effort to do so, America's industrial regions are treated as the "mother country," then much of what is usually considered domestic commerce and investment has to be classed as foreign or colonial enterprise.

Even in its more moderate versions, that kind of commentary on overseas economic activity is wide of the mark. There are two broad questions at issue with regard to the statistics of overseas economic expansion, and they cannot be mixed up without confusing the analysis and the interpretation. One concerns the overall importance of such expansion to the national economy. The answer to that depends less upon gross percentages than upon the role in the American economy of the industries which do depend in significant ways (including raw materials as well as markets) on foreign operations. Measured against total national product, for example, the export of American cars and trucks seems a minor matter. But it is not possible at one and the same time to call the automobile business the key industry in the economy and then dismiss the fact that approximately 15 percent of its total sales between 1921 and 1931 were made in foreign markets.

The other major point concerns the role of such foreign enterprises and markets in the making of American foreign policy. That effect can be direct in terms of domestic political and economic pressures, or indirect through the results of overseas American economic activity on the foreign policy of another nation. Even in the early part of the century, from 1897 to 1914, the overseas economic expansion of the United States was more impressive than many people realize. Loans totaled over a billion dollars. Direct investments amounted to $2,652,300,000 by 1914. While it is true that the nation also owed money abroad during that period, that point is not too important to an understanding of American foreign affairs. For the loans and investments had a bearing on American foreign policy even though balance of payment computations reduce the net figure. Businessmen with interests in Mexico or Manchuria, for example, did not stop trying to influence American policy (or cease affecting Mexican or Asian attitudes) just because their investments or loans or sales were theoretically and arithmetically cancelled out by the debts other Americans incurred in France or Germany.

Another misleading approach emphasizes the point that

America's overseas economic expansion amounted to no more than 10 or 12 percent of its national production during those years. But 10 percent of any economic operation is a significant proportion; without it the enterprise may stagnate or slide into bankruptcy. In that connection, the most recent studies by economists reveal that exports did indeed spark recovery from the depression of the 1890's. In any event, businessmen, other economic groups, and many intellectuals *thought* the 10 percent made a crucial difference, and most of them concluded that they could get it only by overseas expansion.

All other considerations aside, that reason would make the figure important if it were only 1 percent. Or, to make the point even clearer (and historically relevant), it would still be significant if all an entrepreneur did was to pressure the government to support an effort that failed. In that case the economic indicators would be negative but the relevance to foreign policy might be very high. Such was precisely the case, for example, with the American-China Development Company. It ultimately disappeared from the scene, but before it died it exerted an extensive influence on American policy in Asia.

In another way, overseas economic operations which seem small on paper may mean the difference between survival and failure to a given firm or industry. Faced by the near monopoly control over key raw materials exercised by the United States Steel Corporation after 1903, Charles Schwab had to go to Chile to get the ore supplies that were necessary to sustain the Bethlehem Steel Company. Schwab's investment was only $35 million, but it played a vital role in his affairs and exercised a significant influence on Chilean-American relations. Or, to reverse the example, economic activity which seems incidental judged by American standards is often fundamental to a weaker economy. That aspect of the problem can be illustrated by the situation in Manchuria between 1897 and 1904, where approximately one-tenth of 1 percent of America's national product gave the Americans who were involved a major role in the economic life of that region. And that, in turn, led to crucial decisions in American foreign policy.

It is impossible, in short, to judge the bearing of overseas economic expansion upon American diplomacy in terms of gross statistics. The important factors are the relative significance of the activity and the way it is interpreted and acted upon by people and groups who are at best only symbolized by abstract aggregate figures. And by those criteria there is no question about the great relevance to its foreign policy of America's proposed and actual overseas economic expansion since 1890.

Viewed from those various perspectives, it is possible to discern four overlapping eras, or phases, in the developing role of the large corporation in American foreign affairs: (1) The Consciousness of Maturity and the Specters of Stagnation and Revolution: 1890–1903. (2) The Great Debate over Loans or Exports: 1895–1914. (3) The Triumph of the Corporation and the Internationalization of Business: 1912–1940. (4) The Era of Integration with the State: 1933–1950. And (5) The Crisis of the Corporate Foreign Policy. That framework offers a useful guide for the more detailed examination of the ideas, actions, and influence of the large corporation in connection with American foreign policy since 1890.

I

The crisis of the 1890's was a major turning point in American history. It closed out the Age of Jacksonian Laissez-Faire and unfrocked the individual entrepreneur as the dynamic leader of

American economic life. At the same time, it was the cultural coming-out party of a new corporate system based on the large corporation and similar highly organized groups throughout American society. Initiated in the late 1880's by the Standard Oil Company, the massive centralizing and consolidating movement of the 1890's was undertaken to reorganize, rationalize, and supplant the system of individualistic capitalism which had been dying throughout the long-wave depression touched off by the Panic of 1873. In one sense, therefore, the merger mania of the decade was prompted by the drive to lower production costs. But almost immediately the large corporation leaders and the giant bankers became aware of the disturbing fact that they had more efficiency than they could employ at a satisfactory profit rate. Implicitly or explicitly, therefore, they became equally concerned with markets for their respective goods and services. At the same time, they were challenged on the political front by other Americans who sought either to restore the old system or reform and regulate the new one.

For many years, the domestic side of the resulting debate over the condition and prospects of the political economy was usually described as a struggle between the Progressives and the Conservatives; and the foreign policy side of the conflict was analyzed by transposing those categories as Anti-Imperialists and Imperialists. Recent investigations have challenged that historiography by suggesting that many of the Progressives were themselves Imperialists. Though helpful in some respects, the revisionist interpretation does not really clarify the basic issues. It is true that the imperialist and anti-imperialist nomenclature has some relevance to a short period of eighteen months when the question of what to do with Cuba and the Philippines was hotly debated. But that approach offers very little insight into the period prior to the outbreak of the Spanish-American War, and still less into the resolution of the brief fight over imperialism.

One of the main sources of the confusion is the habit of equating colonialism and imperialism, an approach which tends to hide the fact that a nation can follow a policy of anti-colonialism and still remain the head of a large economic empire. Colonialism is defined by the large-scale emigration of *people* from the mother country to the foreign region. Imperialism is characterized by the *economic* expansion of the mother country, and may or may not involve the establishment of a small colony of administrative and military personnel from the empire country in the weaker area. Furthermore, no more than a soapbox full of Americans advocated colonialism in the true and historic meaning of the institution. The debate about Cuba and the Philippines was an argument over whether or not to adopt the pattern of imperialism developed by Britain after the Indian Mutiny of 1857; and if that system were not followed, what kind of an American program of expansion was to be substituted.

Perhaps another consideration is even more important to a fuller understanding of the debate between the Imperialists and the Anti-Imperialists. Only a tiny and insignificant handful of Americans were against any and all kinds of expansion. The fact is that such men as Grover Cleveland and William Jennings Bryan, who are usually thought of as Anti-Imperialists, actually advocated the expansion of America's economic system and political influence. Bryan favored the kind of imperial anti-colonialism that the British practiced throughout the nineteenth century in such countries as Argentina, and which English historians have recently characterized by the phrases "informal empire" and "the imperialism of free trade."

In essence, therefore, Bryan deserves as much credit as Theodore Roosevelt for launching America's empire. Roosevelt at first favored the traditional imperial policy of establishing formal administrative and military colonies within the subject society, but he ultimately adopted Bryan's approach which was based on extending the Monroe Doctrine to cover the foreign country. That policy, which served as the basis of the Open Door Notes, was in turn founded on the assumption that America's economic and moral power would control the development of the weaker region. Direct military intervention might be necessary to establish American authority (in the case of the Philippines, Bryan called it "restoring order"), and to sustain it in an emergency, but preponderant economic power was the key to such imperial anti-colonialism.

For several reasons, the large corporation played a crucial role in resolving the original conflict between the Imperialists and the Anti-Imperialists. First, it was the source of the overwhelming economic power which made it possible to bypass traditional imperialism. Second, it advocated and took the lead (through such organizations as the National Association of Manufacturers, the National Civic Federation, and the American Asiatic Association) in popularizing the idea that foreign markets provided the solution to the domestic economic crisis and the dangers of political and social upheaval. Shared or adopted by every other special economic group in the country, including the Bryan agrarians, the Gompers labor movement, and the small businessmen, that proposal had mushroomed into a widely accepted panacea by 1897.

Jerry Simpson, a sometimes radical farmer from Kansas, exemplified agrarian agreement in his anguished cry of 1894: "We are driven from the markets of the world!" Other Populists reacted by voting for a big navy. Speaking as president of the NAM, Theodore C. Search provided a candid summary of business thinking: "Many of our manufacturers have outgrown or are outgrowing their home markets and the expansion of our foreign trade is their only promise of relief." Senator Albert J. Beveridge phrased it more majestically: "American factories are making more than the American people can use; American soil is producing more than they can consume. Fate has written our policy for us; the trade of the world must and shall be ours."

Businessman F. L. Stetson voiced the fears of many of getting hemmed-in with his warning that "we are on the eve of a very dark night unless a return of commercial prosperity relieves popular discontent." Others argued that such overseas economic expansion was the only program that would enable them to eke out a profit under the staggering load of welfare legislation. Charles A. Conant, one of the first corporation intellectuals, provided a comprehensive overview: "New markets and new opportunities for investment must be found if surplus capital is to be profitably employed . . . if the entire fabric of the present economic order is not to be shaken by a social revolution."

Then, just as that combined analysis and program for action seemed to be verified by the dramatic jump in agricultural and steel exports during the late summer of 1897, it appeared to be threatened by European counteraction throughout the world. The resulting drive among Americans for militant diplomacy in Latin America and Asia had far more to do with the coming of the Spanish-American War than most historians have allowed. It was the crucial factor in the changing attitude of the large corporation leaders who were hesitant about military intervention in Cuba prior to the summer of 1897. Beginning in May 1897, and becoming very rapid and apparent through the winter of 1897–1898, key economic spokesmen shifted their position.

That movement was further accelerated by their growing

distrust of the Cuban rebels, who appeared increasingly unreliable and generally unsatisfactory as allies, and by the new disposition among Cuban conservatives to accept American overlordship. As a result, a majority of American economic leaders were ready for war by mid-March 1898, some in terms of Cuba as the key to Latin America, perhaps even more with Asia in mind. President William McKinley may have given way to overwhelming pressure for war; but not only was that pressure as much economic as ideological, much of the ideology was counter-revolutionary and characterized by an economic definition of the world. The President made it perfectly clear, moreover, that neither he nor other leaders were going to war to turn the island over to the rebels.

A third influence exercised by the large corporation on the foreign policy of the 1890's was more indirect. Its attitude, policy proposals, and action served as data for influential intellectuals such as Brooks Adams who were driven by the same fear of economic stagnation and social revolution. The same factors reinforced the implicit and explicit conclusions that were drawn from the theory advanced by Frederick Jackson Turner, who explained America's past greatness as the result of such expansion. His frontier thesis stated that prosperity and democracy depended upon expansion; and Turner added a bit later that he was sure Americans would continue the process. Still others, such as the more conservative followers of Herbert Spencer, led by William Graham Sumner, advanced theories that defined such expansion as a natural right (and a natural law) under the principles of laissez-faire.

Those demands of the corporation community and other economic groups were synthesized with the theories of the intellectuals and the ideas of Roosevelt and Bryan by Secretary of State John Hay in his famous Open Door Notes of 1899 and

1900. Hay's policy was designed to secure equal opportunity for American economic power in such areas as China, and to prevent other advanced nations from carving up such regions into new colonies and spheres of influence. It is currently fashionable to dismiss the Open Door Notes as a naive failure, but that approach is seriously misleading in two vital respects.

First, the Open Door Notes ended the debate between the Imperialists and the Anti-Imperialists by subsuming the great majority of both groups in enthusiastic support for the idea that America's preponderant economic power would cast the world in a pro-American mold. A small group of Anti-Imperialists carried on their battle against a foreign policy of expansion for several years, but the issue itself was resolved by the Open Door Notes. The editors of the London *Times* immediately caught that significance of the Notes: "Even protectionist organs are for free trade in China, where freedom is for the benefit of American manufacturers. Even anti-Imperialists welcome an Imperial policy which contemplates no conquests but those of commerce." Seven lean years before, in the first shock of the Panic of 1893, the editors of *Harper's* had advocated the same policy in even blunter terms: "The United States will hold the key, unlocking the gates to the commerce of the world, and closing them to war. If we have fighting to do, it will be fighting to keep the peace."

The second important point about the Open Door Policy is that it became the strategy and tactics of America's expansion and security for the next two generations. If it be judged a failure, the verdict has to be cast in the subtle form of the failure of success. For the mid-century crisis of American diplomacy is in large measure defined by the fact that the Open Door Policy built an empire which is confronted by the specter of general and specific revolt. It may be useful, therefore, to trace the role

of the large corporation in the implementation of the Open
Door Policy.

2

The large industrial corporation was the most important economic institution in foreign affairs until Theodore Roosevelt
failed (during the Russo-Japanese War) in his effort to open the
door to all of Asia in one grand gesture by manipulating Japan
and Russia into exhaustion. It received most of the legislative
attention, as in such matters as reform of the consular service
and reciprocity treaties, and also was favored by the executive,
as in Manchuria and Latin America. Roosevelt's classic blunder
hurt the industrial corporation most in Asia, but it was challenged there and elsewhere by the large bankers for the next decade.

As with the standard interpretation of the debate between
the Imperialists and the Anti-Imperialists, there is some—and
probably more—value in the broadly accepted idea that the
years after 1895 were characterized by the phenomenon of
finance capitalism. Even so, the facts are by no means as clear as
suggested by the stereotype. Rather, the evidence points toward
a relatively short, vigorous struggle in which the bankers won
and then lost the initiative in foreign affairs, though their subsequent actions affected American policy in many ways.

Basically, of course, the financiers were dependent upon the
industrial corporation. The industrialists produced the goods
which made the profits; and even the life insurance companies,
which supplied the bankers with vast funds in the earlier period,
collected their premiums from people with jobs. By 1923, at the
very latest, the industrial corporation had asserted its economic

primacy. Secondly, while the Open Door Policy could have been implemented by working through Japan or Russia, as well as in China directly, its object was to structure and control the development of weaker economies. Fundamentally, therefore, if not immediately, the policy defined the bankers as a tool to help the industrial corporation.

For their part, the bankers naturally stressed operations which would provide them with a steady return on investment. Ideally, and for that reason, they favored direct ties with foreign governments in preference to subordinate collaboration with industrial corporations. Until the Great Depression, therefore, they seldom cooperated directly in the program of overseas industrial expansion. But the crash forced them to accept such an approach, and after the mid-1930's they worked ever more closely with the industrialists, and with the government which pushed an industrial policy.

For those reasons, the struggle between the bankers and the industrialists was a complex and continuing process. In Latin America, Canada, Europe, and most underdeveloped regions, the industrial corporation established and maintained an early predominance: in those areas the bankers succeeded only as they functioned as a means to an industrial end. But the situation in Asia was not that clear. Until his death in September 1909, Edward A. Harriman led the industrialists and outmaneuvered the bankers dominated by the House of Morgan. But none of Harriman's immediate successors (save perhaps John Hays Hammond) was willing to sustain the policy of working through the Russians. Hence the only option was to fall back on the less satisfactory alternative of collaborating with the already entrenched Japanese while at the same time trying to extend America's position in China itself. Even if ultimately successful, that was a slow process because influence had first to be established in Japan. But that approach did give the House of Morgan, which stressed its connections in Tokyo, a kind of *de facto* control of the Open Door Policy in Asia unless and until the industrial corporations or the government committed themselves to a major effort in China proper.

President Woodrow Wilson did get the bankers to finance his chosen White Russians in the battle to overthrow the Bolshevik Revolution and simultaneously open the door into Siberia and Manchuria, but the House of Morgan remained adamant about a clear rupture with the Japanese. Herbert Hoover and Charles Evans Hughes also failed in their later efforts to break the veto wielded by the bankers. For one thing, the industrial corporation was heavily involved at home and elsewhere in the world during the 1920's, and could not undertake a large program in China. For another, China was in the throes of a revolution influenced by the Soviet Union, and that upheaval could be controlled only with the help of Japan. Probably most important of all, however, was the ideological dilemma faced by Hoover and Hughes. For while they wanted to exercise control over the operations of the bankers, and in that way push the Open Door Policy more vigorously in Asia and elsewhere, they did not want to set a precedent of the government defining and limiting property rights to that extensive degree. Expansion itself, after all, was designed primarily to sustain and rationalize the existing system. Forced to choose, they reluctantly acquiesced in Thomas Lamont's financial ties with Tokyo.

Thus there would appear to be four long-term characteristics of the struggle between the industrial and the financial corporation. First, the industrial corporation soon established its leadership in every area except Asia. In those regions the bankers succeeded only as they accepted their subordinate position. Second, the bankers made one major effort, in Latin America, to use foreign loans to strengthen themselves against the industrialists at home. That maneuver not only failed; it no doubt accelerated the bankers' domestic decline. Third, the House of Morgan's pro-Japanese policy became the *de facto* policy of the government in Asia for the next two decades, and was seriously considered as late as 1941. Fourth, the industrial corporation and the government ultimately took over financing the expansion of the Open Door system, and in that fashion settled the conflict in favor of the industrial corporation.

3

Except in Asia, however, the industrial corporation was the key element in the political economy of American foreign policy after 1895—and even there the Open Door Policy was ultimately interpreted from their point of view. A preview of that final emphasis on China proper came in 1913, when Wilson refused to support the bankers in a multi-national consortium loan to the Chinese government. Usually interpreted as a noble retreat from dollar diplomacy, the move was in fact nothing of the sort. The Wilson Administration opposed the loan for two reasons. First, and in the words of Secretary of State Bryan, because the United States would "not have a controlling voice" in it. Second, Wilson thought exports more important than loans to American prosperity and democracy.

Even more revealing, perhaps, was the relationship between the Wilson Administration and the National Council of Foreign Trade. Secretary of State Bryan and Secretary of Commerce William Redfield were the major speakers during the first day of the Council's national convention on May 27, 1914. That date is significant, for it specifies the policy of the Wilson Ad-

ministration at a time when it was clear that America was suffering a serious economic downturn, yet at an hour prior to the
outbreak of World War I. Secretary Redfield, who had been
president of the American Manufacturers Export Association
and a vigorous advocate of overseas expansion before Wilson
called him to the crusade for the New Freedom, led off with a
broad outline of government policy. He assured the corporation
leaders that "because we are strong, we are going out, you and
I, into the markets of the world to get our share." Secretary of
State Bryan spoke next. First he reminded the audience that
President Wilson had already made it clear that it was official
policy to "open the doors of all the weaker countries to an invasion of American capital and enterprise." Having made that
point, Bryan concluded by telling the corporation leaders that
"my Department is your department."

On the next day the convention left its downtown quarters
for a special meeting in the East Room of the White House.
President Wilson, who interpreted the frontier thesis and the
crises of the 1890's and 1913–1914 as proof of the necessity
of overseas economic expansion, had seen fit to take time from
his more official duties to address the delegates. His purpose was
to assure them that he gave full and active support to a mutual
campaign to effect "the righteous conquest of foreign markets."
Perhaps it was because some in his audience seemed startled by
that candid statement of policy, but in any event Wilson went
on to emphasize the point by remarking that such an objective
was "one of the things we hold nearest to our heart." Though
the war intervened to delay the program, the Wilson Administration carried through on such rhetoric with the Webb-Pomerene Law and the Edge Act, both designed to facilitate corporate
expansion overseas, and with vigorous diplomacy to check opposition in Latin America and Asia.

That quiet gathering in the White House symbolized a vital integration of corporation and government thinking on the nature and role of overseas economic expansion. Accelerated and extended by the war itself (which also freed the industrial corporation from the last vestiges of banker control), that consensus asserted the thesis that such expansion was necessary for American prosperity. As was the case in the 1890's, the question of whether or not American leaders were driven by personal economic motives is rather beside the point. Clearly enough, the businessmen *qua* businessmen were, and it is less than helpful to gingerbread the obvious as the complex. As for the corporation leaders who went into the government, the intellectuals, or the more narrowly defined political leaders, they also entertained and acted upon an economic definition of reality. Overseas economic expansion was for them *the* solution for America's problems—be they social, political, or economic.

Of vital importance, therefore, was the concept of trade that had matured since the turn of the century. Far from being defined in the classical sense as the exchange of commodities and services between independent producers meeting in an open market, trade had come to be characterized as the control of markets for American exports and similar authority over raw materials for the production of those exports. In terms of personalities, the consensus was dramatically illustrated by the close and extensive collaboration between Wilson and Herbert Hoover, a corporation leader turned public servant during the war. In Hoover's words, he and Wilson "were always able to find a path ahead upon which to travel successfully together." They agreed upon the crucial importance of economic expansion through the policy of the Open Door, and also shared a preference for securing American objectives through the manipulation of food supplies and by other economic means.

Throughout the 1920's, moreover, American foreign policy was dominated by two corporation men: Hoover and Charles Evans Hughes. Hoover's approach was indicated by his transformation of the Department of Commerce from an organization concerned primarily with domestic affairs into an agency oriented toward overseas expansion; and by his curiously neglected thesis that "the hope of our commerce lies in the establishment of American firms abroad, distributing American goods under American direction, in the building of direct American financing and, above all, in the installation of American technology in Russian industries."

In his efforts to implement the crucial phase of that policy, Hoover tried to shinny on both sides of the street. He refused to let the bankers accept Russian gold but encouraged the large industrialists to take charge of Russia's industrial development. The tactics were less than successful. For one thing, the Russians were quite aware of Hoover's counter-revolutionary objective and interpreted it as verification of Marx's prophecy. For another, the Great Depression made many key industrialists (such as machine tool manufacturers) dependent upon the Russian market and prompted them to pressure Hoover to recognize the Soviet Union. Finally, and most ironic of all, American economic assistance did a great deal to strengthen the very government that Hoover wished to undermine. Neither Hoover nor his successors thought seriously of taking advantage of the pro-American orientation of one segment of Soviet leadership in order to develop and extend that early collaboration.

Hughes revealed his outlook in several ways. He extended the Open Door Policy to all European colonies and Eastern Europe (where such industrialists as W. Averell Harriman became very active). He developed the technique of selecting one large corporation within each industry (as with the Standard Oil

Company) as the chosen instrument of such expansion. He initiated, with the vigorous promptings and assistance of the businessmen, a revision of the practice of military intervention in
Latin America. Economic leaders favored a more moderate policy because, having established themselves in the region, they
found that intervention often cost them more in ill will and the
disruption of the marketplace than it gained them in other
ways. Hoover carried on that work, which culminated in the
Good Neighbor Policy of Franklin Delano Roosevelt and Cordell Hull. And, finally, Hoover and Hughes made it clear to the
bankers that the government viewed loans principally as a device to penetrate and control markets for industrial exports and
to secure control of key raw materials, and secondarily to establish American political authority in Europe.

Choosing in the arrogance of their decline to flout that
warning, Morgan and other bankers tried to restore their earlier
power by financing Latin American nations and Japan's penetration of northeast Asia. The strategy failed in Latin America.
The bankers' desperately effective efforts to seduce unfaithful
borrowers served only to accelerate and deepen their own domestic crisis after 1926. The results were not so clear-cut in
Asia. Supported by some industrialists who found Japan a profitable market, and by various traders, the bankers kept alive the
old alternative of putting the Open Door Policy into operation
by working through and with the Japanese. Though seriously
proposed as late as the summer of 1941 by such intellectuals as
Harry Dexter White, as well as by Thomas Lamont and John
Foster Dulles, that option of the Open Door was ultimately dis-
carded in favor of direct involvement over China.

In the meantime, however, the majority of large corporations extended their overseas operations in Latin America, Europe, the Middle East, and Southeast Asia. First advocated in an

organized and sustained fashion by the agrarians in the 1870's, and then pushed hard by the NAM in 1895, the principle of reciprocal trade treaties as a technique of building and integrating an American world system was finally adopted and legislated into operation by the Roosevelt Administration in 1934. That historic link between the decade of the 1890's and the New Deal was reinforced in several other ways. The principle of the unconditional most-favored-nation clause was a crucial part of the trade agreements program, for example, and New Deal leaders were quite aware that the unconditional most-favored-nation provision was the very crux of the Open Door Policy. It was simply a more austere and legal formulation of John Hay's phrase, "equality of commercial opportunity." And in planning and negotiating such trade treaties, New Deal policy-makers consciously sought to build an integrated American system of export markets and raw material supplies.

In another way, the drift toward formal Keynesian economics which characterized the New Deal served to reinforce the traditional American conception of an Open Door Empire. A Keynesian system need not literally be confined to one nation, but when it is extended it has to be done as a system—in this case an American system. For, by its very reliance upon various controls to stabilize the business cycle, the Keynesian approach cannot by definition even be attempted beyond the limits of such central authority. The climax of that aspect of American policy came in the sharp struggle between Lord Keynes and Harry Dexter White, both of whom understood the principle at stake and sought therefore to define the postwar international monetary organization in terms of their respective Keynesian systems.

Though largely overlooked by historians as well as by supporters of the New Deal itself, the liaison between the Roose-

velt Administration and the large industrial corporation led to
an extensive and intensive expansion of the American foreign
economic system by 1939. It was broadly committed in Latin
America, Europe, and the Middle East; and had defined its rub-
ber and tin supplies (and others as well) almost exclusively in
terms of the resources of Southeast Asia. Beginning in 1935,
moreover, there was a revival of interest in China as the market
of the future. Save for a small group led by Lamont and Dulles,
and the corporations trading with Japan, the large corporation
had by 1939 identified itself with an industrial outlook oriented
more and more toward England and France, toward the depend-
encies still controlled by those nations, and toward other underdeveloped areas penetrated or threatened by the Axis powers.

4

The final integration of government, industrial, and financial
thinking developed in the course of a serious and heated debate
about what to do in response to the expansion of the Axis powers. Most corporation leaders entered the 1930's fearing another
war as the midwife of international and domestic revolution.
Bernard Baruch, for example, thought a war could make the
world safe for democracy as he defined it, but he was impressed
by the dangers of trying that approach a second time. Others
thought a general war would "destroy our Western civilization,"
either directly or by forcing totalitarianism upon even the
United States. For those reasons, as well as because of their initial attraction toward some features of the counter-revolutionary
movements in Italy and Germany, many corporation leaders
thought it wise to work out a compromise with those nations.
The approach was balanced, however, by the feeling that recov-

ery from the depression would enable America to set the terms
of such arrangements and in other ways take the lead in world
affairs and keeping the peace. That attitude, so similar to President Woodrow Wilson's initial response to World War I, seems
also to have been shared at the outset of the 1930's by President
Franklin Roosevelt.

Until about 1935, therefore, there was no serious disagreement over foreign policy between Roosevelt and the leadership
of the large corporation. Even afterward, their differences did
not flare up dramatically. Most corporations, for example, went
along with the principle and practice of the moral embargo that
Roosevelt began to use against the Axis. By 1937, however, the
corporation community had split into two camps on the issue of
foreign policy. That division can be understood most clearly as
the result of three factors. First, the continued economic expansion of the Axis in Central and Eastern Europe, Latin America,
and other underdeveloped areas led some corporation leaders to
conclude that America's Open Door Empire was directly threatened. Second, some of them had realized that the New Deal was
not a devilishly clever strategy of revolution, an awareness no
doubt facilitated by Roosevelt's growing propensity to take them
into his administration. Hence domestic considerations did not
prompt them to resist the President's movement toward more
active opposition to the Axis. Third, and as a direct consequence
of the others, such corporation leaders came to identify democracy as well as economic welfare with the continued existence
and expansion of the American system throughout the world.

Other corporation leaders opposed that estimate of the situation. Though to a lesser extent than earlier in the decade, they
still thought that a compromise with Germany and Japan
would help rather than hurt America's economic and political
position in the world. Perhaps most important was their fear

that victory in a war against the Axis would be purchased at the price of socialism at home. "It is fairly certain," concluded an important spokesman of the group, "that capitalism cannot survive American participation in this war." Others extended the analysis, seeing American involvement as leading to "the end of capitalism all over the world" and the consequent "spread of communism, socialism, or fascism in Europe and even in the United States." Tormented by that nightmare, such corporation leaders argued that America could and should avoid war by building and integrating an impregnable empire in the Western hemisphere, or that it could and should assert America's ultimate supremacy by waiting for the belligerents to exhaust themselves. Senator Harry S. Truman and other political leaders shared the latter view. "The role of this great Republic," explained Truman in October 1939, "is to save civilization; we must keep out of war."

Ultimately, of course, most of those so-called isolationists concluded that such a policy would lead to socialism at home before it produced American predominance in the world. As they did so, particularly after the fall of France, they moved toward an acceptance of American belligerence in the war. In a curious way, the importance of that corporation opposition to an active anti-Axis policy is illuminated by reference to the public opinion polls which have been used by many scholars to justify Roosevelt's behind-the-scenes moves toward military involvement in the war. Such commentators suggest that Roosevelt actually lagged behind the public in acting on a pro-Allied policy. But if the polls are correct, then Roosevelt's hesitation has to be explained either as a misjudgment on his part of the climate of opinion or as the result of his own reluctance to go to war on two fronts.

If the first option is taken, and Roosevelt the master politician judged guilty of a grievous misestimate of public opinion, it would appear that the militant and vocal opposition manifested by the anti-war corporation leadership goes a long way to account for the President's mistake. For by 1939 and 1940 Roosevelt was courting the corporation community more than at any time in the previous five years. If, on the other hand, the fear of a two-front war is emphasized as an explanation for Roosevelt's actions, then the historical and immediate influence of the large corporation appears quite apparent. Approached from the 1890's, the issue became one of waiting to see whether or not the Japanese would move to seal off all of China.

In that context, the question faced by American policy-makers was whether or not to follow the bankers in making a deal with Japan—either in Asia or as a broad strategic move against Germany. In either case the role of the large corporation was very significant. For in failing to take the bankers' option, Roosevelt was left with the original emphasis placed on China by the industrial corporation and those intellectuals who interpreted prosperity and democracy in terms of such overseas expansion of the American economic system.

Perhaps it is wise, in concluding such an analysis, to emphasize the point that there are two questions involved in any discussion of American entry into World War II. The first is whether or not it was necessary for American survival. The second concerns how and why the nation entered it; in what fashion and on what grounds it was determined to be necessary; and the means employed to implement that decision. It may be the greater part of wisdom to conclude that the war was necessary for the survival of American society, but also to conclude that the conception of the world which accounted for the way it was entered was not a definition which strengthened American prosperity and democracy.

Whatever conclusion is preferred on that issue, it seems clear that the large corporation sustained and extended its influence in American foreign affairs after Pearl Harbor. For by mid-1943, when the issue of postwar foreign policy came to the fore and was thrashed out in Congressional hearings and departmental discussions, it was apparent that the Roosevelt Administration was dominated by men whose personal experience and intellectual outlook was conditioned by their careers as leaders or agents or students of the large corporation. Dean Acheson, Averell Harriman, Donald Nelson, Edward Stettinius, Adolph A. Berle, Jr., John Foster Dulles, Eric Johnston, William C. Foster, and James Forrestal are but the most obvious names from the top layer of American leadership in foreign affairs. Those men, and perhaps even Roosevelt himself, had concluded by 1944 that the policy of the Open Door offered the only way to ensure American prosperity and democracy.

Though divided over whether or not to modify America's long-term antagonism toward the Soviet Union and work out a postwar program in conjunction with Russian rulers, American leaders did agree that continued overseas economic expansion was absolutely essential. A few of those men, apparently led by Eric Johnston and Donald Nelson, saw Russia as an enormous market as well as a source of key raw materials. They argued that firm ties with Russia would end the threat of a domestic depression and also pave the way for international peace. From the spring of 1943 through 1944, Russian leaders responded favorably to that approach; first in direct talks with Johnston, then at the Teheran Conference, and finally by submitting a request for a large postwar loan from the United States. Though clearly derived from the axiom that vast overseas economic expansion was necessary to sustain the prosperity of the American system, and not from any romantic or seditious attachment to

the Soviets or their revolution, the Johnston-Nelson program
was blocked by a majority of American leaders. Some opponents
stressed the importance of keeping the Russians weak; others
were more specifically concerned with the problems of building
what Assistant Secretary of State Acheson called "a successfully
functioning political and economic system."

By 1944, indeed, so many American leaders were preoccupied with the specter of another major depression (or sliding
back into the old one) that it is quite surprising to realize how
little attention has been given to that fact in most accounts of
recent American foreign policy. As early as January 1940, for
that matter, representative leaders of America's large corporations began to define the crucial problem of the future in those
terms. Their discussion of American policy in the context of
World War II hinged on the question of how "to organize the
economic resources of the world so as to make possible a return
to the system of free enterprise in every country, and provide adequate economic opportunities to the so-called have not powers." Having had the problem defined for them in those terms,
the editors of *Fortune* devoted the next issue to the questions of
"The Dispossessed" at home and a redefinition of "The U.S.
Frontier."

From the candid admission that the American system was in
serious trouble—"For nearly one-fourth of the population
there is no economic system—and from the rest there is no
answer"—the editors of *Fortune* drew three major conclusions. First, they acknowledged that "the U.S. economy has
never proved that it can operate without the periodic injection
of new and real wealth. The whole frontier saga, indeed, centered around this economic imperative." Second, and in consequence of that fact, the editors defined two new frontiers. A new
emphasis on enlarged consumer sales at home would have to be

paralleled by a tremendous expansion of "foreign trade and foreign investment." Secretary of State Hull's trade agreements program was "a step in the right direction"; but to "open up real frontiers, under a general policy of raising the standard of living of other countries, we shall have to go much further."

In outlining its conception of such a program, *Fortune* argued that "the analogy between the domestic frontier in 1787, when the Constitution was formed, and the present international frontier is perhaps not an idle one. The early expansion of the U.S. was based upon firm political principles; and it may be that further expansion must be based upon equally firm—and equally revolutionary—international principles." *Fortune's* third point emphasized the need for the corporate community to admit its earlier error of opposing the New Deal and go on to more extensive and vigorous leadership inside and outside of the government. Stressing the fact that the New Deal still faced nine million unemployed, the editors concluded that business leadership was essential if the American system was to sustain itself after the war.

Though they did not all agree with the latter specification in that remedy offered by *Fortune* in 1940, by 1943 a broad cross section of American leaders did accept the fact of crisis and did agree that the basic remedy was further overseas economic expansion. Senator Joseph C. O'Mahoney, for example, was highly disturbed by the question of what was to replace the government as the chief consumer of American production after the war. "If that doesn't happen, it is impossible to see how a depression can be avoided much worse than any depression which the country has ever known."

Harold G. Moulton of The Brookings Institution supported that broad analysis, as did the Department of Labor specialist who pointed out that "the thing we have liked to refer to as the

American standard of living is only possible in situations where two people in the family are working." Economist Robert Nathan and Senator Warren Austin also agreed: Avoiding a depression posed "quite a challenge" that could be met only by "assuring markets for the goods and services" produced by America's corporate economy. And William Green, testifying to labor's point of view, concluded that "we will have to, and ought to, find an increased market for much of our surplus production and that will be, I think, one of the problems that ought to be dealt with at the peace conference. I think that we ought to facilitate the sale and shipment of goods between nations to the end that they ought to be able to purchase here and we ought to be able to produce here what they need."

By September 1944, the government had developed a broad synthesis of those various interpretations and proposals. Assistant Secretary of State Acheson presented the analysis during the Congressional hearings on postwar economic policy and planning procedures. His point of departure was the threat of depression and the consequent necessity to sustain full employment. "If we do not do that," he warned, "it seems clear that we are in for a very bad time, so far as the economic and social position of the country is concerned. We cannot go through another ten years like the ten years at the end of the twenties and the beginning of the thirties, without having the most far-reaching consequences upon our economic and social system." "When we look at that problem," he continued, "we may say it is a problem of markets. . . . The important thing is markets. We have got to see that what the country produces is used and sold under financial arrangements which make its production possible. . . . You must look to foreign markets."

In an aside very reminiscent of a similar comment made by Brooks Adams at the turn of the century, Acheson admitted that "you could probably fix it so that everything produced here would be consumed here." But he asserted that such an approach would mean the end of democracy: "That would completely change our Constitution, our relations to property, human liberty, our very conceptions of law. And nobody contemplates that. Therefore, you find you must look to other markets and those markets are abroad." "We cannot have full employment and prosperity in the United States," he summarized, "without the foreign markets." As for the role of economic agreements in the peace settlement, Acheson shared the earlier conclusions of America's corporation leaders. They were vital to such a system because otherwise "it would really mean that we would be relying exclusively on the use of force. I don't believe that would work."

There were almost no references made in those discussions between 1940 and 1944 to the idea of helping poorer nations, or to the relevance of moral standards for foreign policy. The emphasis was on economic expansion and checking the Russians. Acheson had provided, in September 1944, an outline and overview of America's bipartisan foreign policy in the postwar years. While it is true that the program was later presented in a form that emphasized the threat from the Soviet Union more than any other factor, the fact remains that it was conceived in response to quite different dangers. It was originated and sustained as a program to prevent the stagnation of America's corporate economic and political system by industrializing the frontier thesis first advanced by Brooks Adams and Frederick Jackson Turner in 1893.

The American Socialist
(September 1958)

Samuel Adams: Calvinist,

Mercantilist,

Revolutionary

As he was for his contemporaries, Samuel Adams has been a troublemaker for American historians. Thus he has by turns been identified as the "propagandist of the revolution," a "political radical," "the last Puritan," merely the most efficient agitator and organizer of mobs among the outs who wanted little more than to get in, the most important leader of those who sought an extension of popular government, and a "business failure" who became the leader of "the needy Whigs."

All such commentators have had difficulty in accounting for the contrast between his early revolutionary activity and the conservatism of his later years. More than anything else, this apparent discrepancy has made a psychological interpretation particularly attractive. In summary, Adams has been explained and interpreted as everything from a Leveller to a deeply neurotic man haunted by a father image. But the first is untenable on the evidence of his actions as well as his declared philosophy, and the second begs the central question because even if true it fails to explain why his neurosis produced the radical symptom. Other men of that psychological set became Tories; some even literally went home to mother. All these considerations suggest that it might be helpful to start with an examination of Adams himself instead of with a general hypothesis about the Revolution, or with an *a priori* set of psychological categories. This at least has the virtue of making sense out of his career (including his activities in Massachusetts after 1778). And such an approach, it is suggested, offers an important insight into the nature of the Revolution.

Startling as it may seem, what is perhaps the most illuminating analysis of Adams takes the form of a forged document purporting to be a speech he made at the height of his influence in the revolutionary era. Probably written by Joseph Galloway, an extremely perceptive and talented Pennsylvania Nabob who fought it out with Adams day after day down to the last vote on independence and then retreated to London where he handcrafted polemics against the colonies, this manuscript suggests that Adams is best understood as a true Calvinist and thoroughgoing mercantilist.

Whether composed by Galloway or another loyal Nabob, the "speech" presents Adams as a man concerned with "levelling the popery of politics" and establishing "the reign of political protestantism." Attacking those who camouflaged the truth with "a display of words," he insisted that language was *the* tool of thinking and therefore had to be used with care and accuracy. "Let us not be so amused with words," he warned, in commenting on the appeal to colonial well-being advanced by a loyal Nabob. Bringing this method to bear on the economic issues, Adams purportedly concluded that England had changed its policy from one of mutual welfare to unilateral profits: "the extension of *her* commerce was her object." Noting that the conflict would produce an America governed by the true principles of James Harrington and John Locke, Adams supposedly closed his remarks by defining the war as deciding "whether there shall be left to mankind an asylum on earth for civil and religious liberty."

It is such crucial phrases of this forged document which

make it so important despite its literal falseness. They short circuit the stereotypes of Adams in one's mind and produce the new connections which are known as insights. First of all, there is the tone and language of the committed Calvinist. Adams has been called "the last Puritan" a good many times, but there is an appropriately subtle yet crucial distinction between "the last Puritan" and the last Calvinist. It is of the same kind as between Jonathan Edwards and Jonathan Mayhew (who snipped away at Calvin's corporate philosophy until it matched Adam Smith's individualist ideology).*

Since they had captured the name of Puritan, and are even today thought of as the typical example of that group, the New England religious leaders like Solomon Stoddard and Mayhew are known to history (as they were to their contemporaries) as the last Puritans. By setting up an elaborate schema of true Puritanism, which would clarify the position of the men who kept the name and the rhetoric but abandoned the religion, it might be meaningful to speak of Adams as the last Puritan. But it is both simpler and more accurate to think of Adams as a Calvinist who was dedicated to the ideal of a Christian corporate commonwealth. The formal Congregationalism of Adams should not be misconstrued to mean that he was not a Calvinist. Not only was that denomination originally little more than home-rule Presbyterianism, but religion in New England had devalued its theological coin so far by the 1730s that Edwards himself was preaching in a Congregational church. On both counts, therefore, the value of thinking of Adams as a Calvinist seems well established.

* This seems the most appropriate place to acknowledge gratefully my debt to Perry Miller's superb biography of Jonathan Edwards. A re-reading of his study enabled me to integrate the disparate elements of my analysis of Adams.

A parallel similarity between Adams and Edwards is apparent in their common concern with the use of words to achieve accuracy and therefore the morally proper and practically powerful effect. Their common mastery of the science of semantics and the art of propaganda is beyond question. Though the modern connotation of the word propaganda is an invidious one, involving the idea of deception and distortion, it meant in the religious world of the 18th century the literal propagation of the true faith. And here again, Adams as well as Edwards was deeply intent on choosing the right words so that his audience would come to the proper conclusions and hence make the correct commitment. Finally, we have Galloway's open and unforged description of Adams. "He eats little, drinks little, sleeps little, thinks much, and is most decisive and indefatigable in the pursuit of his objects." Though this might be interpretated as meaning that Adams was merely a particularly dedicated Puritan of the Mayhew variety (or as a man guided by Max Weber's version of the Protestant ethic), the other wholly legitimate evidence on Adams belies such an explanation and fills in the image of him as a true Calvinist.

From an early age, Adams received extensive religious training as a strict Congregationalist from his mother who had "severe religious principles." His father was a deacon of Boston's Old South Church. Emerging from this background, Adams participated actively in the Great Awakening and in particular was deeply affected by the personality and writings of Jonathan Edwards. On at least one occasion he heard Edwards deliver one of his powerful sermons. Adams thus matured as a man whose breakfast was opened by grace and whose supper was followed by a family reading from the Bible before he went off to the Caucus Club to discuss and organize the political affairs of Boston.

Adams' views on the relationship between religion and politics were subtle and complex. On the one hand, he staunchly advocated and defended "the free exercise of the rights of conscience," and vigorously opposed any participation by the organized church in secular affairs. Yet he was against allowing Catholics to hold public office because of what he considered their divided loyalties; either their allegiance to Rome was meaningless, in which case they were hypocrites, or they would follow the Pope in a conflict of values with the electorate. At the same time, he defended a modicum of state support to organize Protestantism on the grounds that the church played a vital role in maintaining a firm corporate ethical system and in providing insurance against anarchy.

As with Calvin, Adams was a militant spokesman for the supremacy of civilian authority over military leaders and institutions. And when ethical crises arose he was always willing "to step forth in the good old cause of morality and religion" (as he did, for example, in connection with the Boston theater). As he acknowledged in later years, his central purpose was to make Boston "the *Christian Sparta*" of the world. "I am *in* fashion and *out* of fashion, as the whim goes," he commented in a revealing letter of 1768. "I will stand alone. I will oppose this tyranny at the threshold, though the fabric of liberty fall, and I perish in its ruins."

No Puritan of the Stoddard or Mayhew variety defined his position in those terms. Many of that outlook finally supported resistance to England, but they did so on the basis of very secular economic and class considerations. Adams was quite different. Considered together with the other aspects of this thought, his very candid remarks about "the *Christian Sparta*" and his willingness to pose the issue in terms of an either-or choice indicate that Adams became a revolutionary in the circumstances of his time precisely because he was a Calvinist dedicated to the ideal and the reality of a Christian corporate commonwealth. Calvin himself had followed that course, and his ideas and logic would propel a true follower along the same path.

There seems little doubt that the words (and example) of Jonathan Edwards carried the spirit of true Calvinism into the well-prepared mind of Samuel Adams. Once there, it fused with the ideas of Shaftesbury, Locke, and Harrington to produce a thinker who signed many of his militant polemics, "A RELI-GIOUS POLITICIAN." As with Edwards, Adams mastered Locke's psychology of sensation: he referred to him as "the immortal." Adams also grasped the basically conservative character of Locke's political philosophy and combined it with his own Calvinism. Accepting the assumption that reason "will enable us to discover the designs of Providence," Adams concluded that the "true object of loyalty" is "a well-constituted state" with "a good legal constitution." Sovereignty in such a state was "essentially in the people," and the government itself "nicely balanced" between the legislative houses, the executive, and the judiciary. "Instituted for the common good," its object was "the welfare and happiness of all the people."

At this point Adams went beyond Locke's ambivalence about the state. Though he accepted Locke's statement of natural rights, and based his political theory and practice on that principle, Adams also stressed very explicitly the dangers of individualism. Hence he set himself firmly against men who defined liberty as "nothing else . . . but *their own liberty*." Adams was not a laissez faire individualist who thought that the competition between enlightened self-interests would produce the general welfare. "Liberty no man can truly possess," he amplified, "whose mind is enthralled by irregular and inordinate passions; since it is no great privilege to be free from external violence if the dictates of the mind are controlled by a force within, which erects itself above reason." "Religion and public liberty of the people are intimately connected," he concluded: "their interests are interwoven; they cannot subsist separately."

Education thus became a crucial factor in preserving and improving the commonwealth. Adams laid heavy emphasis on the instruction of *"little boys and girls . . .* , of leading them in the study and practice of the exhalted virtues of the Christian system." Accepting his own responsibilities in this area, he not only supervised the training of his son, but saw to it that a child named John Quincy Adams was instructed in similar principles. Adams thus retained Calvin's corporate Christian meaning for "the general welfare and happiness." By infusing it with a sure definition and delineation, Adams could then accept Locke's insistence on the sanctity of the existing government and at the same time set specific criteria for a just revolution.

Confronting this issue while he was a graduate student at Harvard, Adams apparently worked out the main elements of the answer in dealing with his thesis question: "Whether it be Lawful to Resist the Supreme Magistrate, if the Commonwealth Cannot be Otherwise Preserved." No copy of his disquisition is known to have survived, but by piecing together a number of secondary accounts, and considering them alongside his earliest record writings, Adams' basic themes can be reconstructed. Given the existence of a Christian corporate commonwealth, or the possibility of reforming such a society that had slipped away from the ideal, there is nothing in Adams' thought to justify a revolution.

"The man who dares to rebel against the laws of a republic ought to suffer death," he asserted, because under those circumstances "sedition is founded on the depraved and inordinate passions of the mind; it is a weak, feverish, sickly thing." The same criteria enabled Adams to advocate revolution if such a corporate Christian republic did not exist, or had decayed past the power of internal reform. Indeed, his principles forced him to do so. Thus any opponent of the true commonwealth became a public enemy. Adams ultimately cast Britain, and its agents and allies in the colonies, in that very role.

Flatly declaring that "the Colonies were by their charters made different states by the mother country," Adams concluded that the new British policy was sedition against the original and true principles of the empire commonwealth. Stressing property rights, and hence the crippling economic impact of England's laws after 1763, he demanded immediate and full redress. Here the postwar depression, Boston's decline *vis-à-vis* Philadelphia and New York, and the memories of the enforced failure (and harried bankruptcy) of his father's land bank, reinforced his theoretical and philosophical conclusion.

Absolutely opposed to "utopian schemes of levelling," Adams accepted the causal relationship between property and freedom: "These must stand and fall together." Thus Britain's move to tax the colonists was critically important: it "greatly obstructed" their trade and made the economic situation "very uneasy." Boston in particular "lived by its trade" and therefore had the "deepest concern" about the new policy. For Adams, at any rate, the conclusion was obvious. Acquiescence in such economic restrictions would make every colonist a "bond slave" by depriving him of the basis of his freedom. The Masters of Harvard agreed, asserting in 1765 that the new regulations "made it useless for the people to engage in commerce," and for that reason the laws could "be evaded by them as faithful subjects."

It seems doubtful that Adams sought *immediate* independence prior to 1770. His early polemics and letters stress the idea of reforming affairs in Massachusetts and forcing England

to return to its earlier policy of mercantilism. This does not
mean that he was a British mercantilist. If it is a correct estimate, and his relatively favorable attitude toward the liberal
Governor Thomas Pownall would also seem to substantiate the
analysis, it indicates that Adams was willing to develop Massachusetts within the empire pending final independence. Prior to
1763, when the empire system did change, British mercantilism
did in fact generate the strength and welfare of the colonies as
well as of the mother country. If it had not, the colonists most
certainly would not have developed either the talents or the
substance to stand alone. As compared with the imperialism
that was initiated in 1763, mercantilism helped the colonies at
a relatively low psychic and material cost to them.

Adams understood this. Take the natural and extensive profits of the mercantilist system, he told the British, and be satisfied. "All they desire," he wrote as a spokesman for the colonies
in 1768, "is to be placed on their original authority." On the
other hand, Adams came out in favor of American manufacturing prior to 1763, and there is no question about his basic assumption that the colonies would ultimately become wholly independent. And his penchant for destroying his correspondence
and other records can be interpreted as the careful habit of a dedicated revolutionary. In any event, he clearly sought independence after 1769.

Lest the great importance of Adams be over-emphasized, it
should be made clear that each of the 13 colonies travelled its
own road to independence. There was no nation which roused
itself and went to war; instead there were 13 separate, particularistic states which were usually antagonistic when not uninter-
ested in each other. Adams could no more have singlehandedly
bullied or bamboozled all those colonies into doing the same
thing at the same time than he could have maneuvered his

selection as Pope. He had help, and lots of it, from several sources.

It is very striking to realize, however, that his most reliable and vigorous allies were leaders of the Virginia gentry whose Anglican outlook was in crucial respects similar to his own. They also stressed the ideal of a social and ethical corporate commonwealth, and emphasized the importance of the balanced political economy of mercantilism. For that matter, they made more iron than Massachusetts. There were 82 blast furnaces in Virginia and the rest of the South by 1775, and when added to the output of the other colonies that production surpassed the amount made by England and Wales.

This suggests very strongly that the *Weltanschauung* of the American Revolution was defined by the concept of a corporate, mercantilist society. It makes little difference in this sense whether Adams and his Boston crowd or the Potomac gentry is judged the prime mover of the break with England: both viewed the situation of the colonies from a very similar angle. Much of the sequel to independence in America—similar to Restoration and post-Revolutionary England—can be understood in terms of a conflict between those two groups who had cooperated to effect a revolution.

Despite these considerations, it has sometimes been implied that Adams was psychologically or economically unable to accept the relaxation of tension between England and the colonies that began in 1770; that his will to power or his debts drove him on. Perhaps this was the case in the sense that one of those reasons (or a more sophisticated version of them) was the irreducible last cause of his actions. Yet the form in which those lowest common motives appeared—*and affected other men* —was in a renewed campaign to establish an independent corporate Christian and mercantilist American empire.

Adams was thus a revolutionary without being a radical. He was a Calvinist revolutionary crusading for a Christian corporate commonwealth. Though actually a grave distortion, the cleverest (albeit supercilious) way to attack him would be by calling him a reactionary because he sought such an objective at a time when Western Europe was moving into its epoch of laissez faire. But in fact Adams was correct in understanding that laissez faire was no more appropriate to America in 1770 than it is in 1960. Far better than some of his contemporaries, and many of his later critics, he grasped the truth that America was not unique—it was only behind Europe in its development. It was, in the nomenclature of the mid-20th century, a relatively backward country. As this lag affected the chances to save a corporate Christian society, Adams welcomed it; as it affected the means to employ, both for that social end and for general economic welfare, he quite accurately realized that mercantilism was the appropriate political economy.

Mercantilism is more often argued about than used as an intellectual tool, but several of its essential characteristics seem clear beyond question. As the political economy of a backward country concerned to establish its existence and generate a balanced economic and social growth within the assumptions of private property and capitalism, mercantilism can be described in four basic ways.

First, it clearly began as the idea and program of the trading and commercial interest which argued that it alone could accumulate the capital necessary for the dynamic development of the entire society. Hence it demanded favors and assistance from the government. But, and secondly, that interest idea was soon generalized into a conglomeration of policies and programs which transcended the narrow commercial outlook. The Earl of Shaftesbury caught the essence of the new attitude in a memorandum to Charles II in 1670. "Commerce, as an affair of state, was widely different from the mercantile part," he explained, and went on to recommend a host of old and new policies designed to control, order, and use commerce for the common good.

The third important element in mercantilism was the concept of a common good and general welfare that had religious and secular origins in the Old Testament and the feudalism of the Middle Ages. For this reason, as well as for others, a narrow interest group analysis of mercantilism is very misleading. Fourth, and what was perhaps the most important aspect of all, the mercantilist insisted that neither the immediate ends, a navy and manufactures, nor the long-range goals of the common good, could be attained without conscious effort and direction. He simply did not believe in the Hidden Hand of Adam Smith. God had created the world, but His creatures were responsible for running it. The multiplicity of contradictory self-interests had to be controlled and coordinated if wealth and welfare were to be achieved.

Adams most certainly accepted and acted upon those axioms and the policies that could be deduced from them. "It is the business of America to take care of herself; her situation depends upon her own virtue," he announced in launching his campaign for independence at the end of 1770. "Arts and manufactures, ordered by commerce, have raised Great Britain to its present pitch of grandeur. America will avail herself of imitating her." This emphasis on manufacturing was neither as misdirected nor as ignored as some have concluded. The Boston Society for Encouraging Industry and Employing the Poor (a mercantilist phrase if ever there was one) established a spinning school in 1769. A New York Society for the Promotion of Arts, Agriculture, and Economy began to grant premiums for domestic manufactures and associated apprenticeship schools in 1765. And by 1775 the United Company of Philadelphia for Promoting American Manufactures had 400 female employees. Even more significant was the way Americans reacted to the Tea Act of 1773 as a specific threat to American manufacturing, as well as a general danger to the system.

By granting the East India Company a monopoly of the American tea market, many Americans concluded that the British had designed an economic key that would ultimately open the door to all colonial wealth. Having analyzed the policy to that point, a Pennsylvania mechanic ended on a dreary note. "Thus our merchants are ruined, Ship Building ceases . . . Our Artificers will be unemployed, and every Tradesman will groan under dire oppression." Adams recognized and seized his chance: two months later, in December 1773, his political dock workers threw the stuff into Boston Harbor.

England retaliated in kind, combining the Coercive Acts against Boston *per se* with the Quebec Act directed against all the colonies. The latter law not only took part of the West, north of the Ohio River, and gave it to Canada, but it closed off the rest of the trans-mountain area and granted Catholics in Canada full religious freedom. This combination gave Adams everything he needed: a city as a martyr, a basic religious and ideological issue, and fundamental economic grievances. Calling explicitly for "AN AMERICAN COMMONWEALTH," he warned of English control over colonial Protestant churches, emphasized the danger of Catholic infiltration from Canada, and called flatly for continued westward expansion.

"An empire is rising in America," he exulted, calling for the annexation of Canada, Nova Scotia, and the fishing banks. "We can subsist independently of all the world." Thereafter he concentrated his abilities and efforts on influencing the government of the Confederation to prosecute the war with vigor and to adopt the political economy of mercantilism. In Massachusetts, meanwhile, he pursued the more specific objective of establishing and institutionalizing a corporate Christian commonwealth.

Adams was convinced that England would try "to monopolize our commerce" even after the war. He insisted that trade and land policies had to be chosen with a view to accumulating enough capital at the state and Confederation levels to insure and strengthen actual—as well as formal—independence. "We have not been so long contending for trifles," he commented wryly in 1781. The next year he agitated vigorously for the states to adopt some common set of custom and tariff laws, and for the Confederation government to re-establish America's right to trade with the West Indies. Impost bills, commented a politican of the time, were "the darling child" of Adams. He was particularly adamant about the dangers of uncontrolled trade with England. Correctly estimating Britain's strategy, he warned of its plan "of subjugating America by throwing in upon us a flood of their manufactures." Hence he constantly emphasized the need to enforce all features of an American mercantilist system.

This emphasis on mercantilism and expansion confronted Adams with the same problem that troubled other men of his generation. Their political economy stressed the need for integrated expansion to ward off stagnation and military defeat, and to accumulate the capital needed to produce the general welfare. Yet their political philosophy asserted that republicanism and representative government could only survive in a small state. Like most other American leaders of his time, Adams resolved the contradiction in favor of expansion.

Even so, and despite his concern for mercantilist policies to be unified in a general program, Adams held back from approving the Constitution in the fear that it would subvert democracy and popular government. He had "doubts" based on the anxiety that it would "totally annihilate the sovereignty of the several states . . . and sink [all] into despotism." On the other hand, he thought it was "highly valuable" because of the power the new central government would have to "regulate commerce, to form treaties." In view of his reaction to Shays' Rebellion, it is crucial to note that Adams resolved his ambivalence about the Constitution on the basis of the popular support for the new instrument of government, as well as upon its mercantilist features.

Adams had a similar approach to the sporadic outbreaks of discontent and social unrest that preceded Shays' Rebellion. His advice was "to inquire into the grounds of dissatisfaction; to correct misinformation; to remove groundless jealousies"—in short, to reform and adjust and compromise. At that time, he was far more concerned about the Society of Cincinnati and urged firm measures to break it up. It was "dangerous" because it "might in time, revive the old feudal system."

But Adams reacted militantly when backcountry unrest became armed rebellion against the commonwealth of Massachusetts. "There is decency and respect due to constitutional authority," he had written in 1784, and his proposals for dealing with Shays followed that analysis. "Those men who, under any pretense or by any means whatever, would lessen the weight of government, lawfully exercised, must be enemies to our happy Revolution and the common liberty . . . As we now have constitutional and regular government, and all our men in authority depend upon the annual elections of the people, we are safe without them."

Men far more narrowly conservative than Adams opposed

his demand for harsh sentences including the death penalty against Shays and his supporters, and there is no particular need to review all the weaknesses of his position in the crisis. He made no excuses, and to offer any would be disrespectful of his integrity. He thought violence was a greater risk to the weak, new nation than the conditions which provoked it, and he acted accordingly. Whether or not one agrees with him, his candor is rather refreshing when compared with the behavior of men like Thomas Jefferson.

Shays' Rebellion scared Jefferson. He was initially most disturbed and worried; very little of the spirit of his famous remark about watering the tree of liberty with the blood of patriots can be found in his early letters about the event. It was the work of "mobs" and was "absolutely unjustifiable." Having been reassured by John Adams that the crisis was over, Jefferson began to stress the humanitarian virtues of leniency. But in his most intimate letters the logic was somewhat different. "Unsuccessful rebellions indeed generally establish the incroachments on the rights of the people which have produced them," he reflected. "An observation of this truth would render honest republican governors so mild in their punishment of rebellion, as not to discourage them too much."

As he did in that instance, Jefferson also evaded the real moral and philosophical issues in connection with policy toward the Indians, toward the settlers in Louisiana who did not wish to become citizens of the United States, and concerning political and economic democracy in Virginia. Along with other planter physiocrats like John Taylor of Carolina, Jefferson ruled that state with a benevolent thoroughness quite in keeping with the political and social axioms of Quesnay but quite in contrast with much of his own enlightened and liberal rhetoric. Such considerations raise some interesting questions about Jefferson's substitution of *Happiness* for *Property* in the famous phrase, "life, liberty, and . . .", as it appeared in the Declaration of Independence.

One of them derives from the fact that Adams and his cohorts in Massachusetts had used the phrase long before 1776, but had done so as part of their discussion of a corporate, Christian commonwealth. Perhaps the most striking example occurred shortly after the adjournment of the First Continental Congress in October 1774. Meeting early in December, the Massachusetts provincial congress issued a manifesto for manufactures and was copied by almost every other colony within a year. In this, as in other actions of the congress, Adams played a very influential role and even wrote many of the documents.

Like the private and state papers of Roger Williams, which also reveal a propensity for analogies with the family and shipboard organization, the Massachusetts resolution on manufactures based its argument on the parallel between a society and the filial group. "As the happiness of particular families arises in a great degree from their being more or less dependent upon others; and as the less occasion they have for any article belonging to others, the more independent; and consequently the happier they are; so the happiness of every political body of men upon earth is to be estimated in a great measure upon their greater or less dependence upon any other political bodies; and from hence arises a forcible argument, why every state ought to regulate their internal policy in such a manner as to furnish themselves, within their own body, with every necessary article for subsistence and defense. Otherwise their political existence will depend upon others. . . . For preventing so great an evil, more to be dreaded than death itself, it must be the wisdom of this colony at all times, more especially at this time, when the hand of power is lashing us with the scorpions of despotism, to encourage agriculture, manufactures and economy, so as to render this state as independent of every other state as the nature of our country will admit."

Reflecting on the extent and intensity of the corporate mercantilism of such a document, and on the use of the word happiness in that context, the question arises as to whether Adams did not in fact have a far more mature sense than Jefferson of the relationship between happiness and policy. Adams understood very clearly that mature men do not seek happiness as an end in itself. Rather do they commit themselves to a way of life—a utopia, if you will—that will produce happiness as a by-product. As Adams explained in supporting and advocating such mercantilist measures in 1796, he favored "such legislative aid as may be found necessary for the promoting of useful improvements, and the advancement of those kinds of industry which contribute to their individual happiness as well as that of the public."

Adams was not what is usually meant by the word radical. Attempts to make him into one are misdirected. In a more fundamental sense, however, he was a radical; he was a man who went to the root of the human condition and tried to evolve a program that would sustain and extend that humanity. His utopia was a corporate Christian commonwealth supported by the political economy of mercantilism. And he committed himself to that ideal with the vigor and *élan* of all great revolutionaries.

In doing so, he forced his contemporaries to grapple with a fundamental issue. Is it better, asked Adams, to tell men that they are free individuals responsible primarily to themselves—and then accept the starvation with the riches, and pay the ultimate price of alienation even if the run at success is temporarily rewarding? Or is it better to tell men that they are not in reality free individuals, that they instead have to accept limitans on their liberty and then go ahead and work out a way of living together that will make those limitations as constructive and creative as possible?

Adams thought the second alternative more realistic and more honest, and hence more apt to produce a true commonwealth. Societies can be built by either axiom, of course, but it would be refreshing to have the question asked once again in America. Who knows, men and women with enough imagination and honesty to face that question might well be capable of building socialism in America. Certainly no others will.

Studies on the Left
(1960)

The Cuban Revolution

Assaulted from

Abroad

The United States quickly interpreted Castro's actions of late
1959, and his trade deal with the Soviet Union early in 1960,
as meaning that Cuba had become a totalitarian Communist
satellite. Most commentators have followed that official government line. Neither claim is factually correct. But the ideology which provided that simple, arbitrary explanation of a
very complex reality is nevertheless important because it also
produced the counter-revolutionary invasion of Cuba in April,
1961, almost 63 years to the day after the United States went to
war to pacify Cuba in 1898.

It appears very probable, indeed, that the CIA began before
the end of 1959 to work with counter-revolutionary groups in
Cuba. This activity increased throughout 1960 and into the first
months of 1961. Along the way, it involved active American
military support in providing air cover for the smuggling of
arms and other supplies to Castro's enemies in Cuba. The formal
American decision to arm and train an exile army, however,
was not made until March, 1960.

This chronology of its Cuban operations, along with a great
deal of other evidence, makes it perfectly clear that it is the
CIA—rather than the military—which functions as an independent variable in the formulation and conduct of American
foreign policy. The military does have great influence, both di-

rectly within the government and indirectly through its ties with the industrial complex of the country. Civilians gave the military such influence by defining the world in military terms (both in 1939 and again in 1945), but the military cannot independently conceive and mount an operation having immediate and profound effects on foreign policy.

The CIA not only *can* do that, it *has done* it a good many times. The CIA has originated projects, persuaded the President and other high officials to authorize them on the basis of information provided by the CIA, and then executed the operation through its own agents. It is a self-validating civilian agency with vast areas of independent action in foreign policy. And it was created and is sustained by civilians.

The real points at issue in all this do not concern the wearing of uniforms after being graduated and commissioned from one of the service academies. The questions involve the far more important matters of how one explains America's difficulties and defines its opportunities, and whether or not one is willing to resort to force in solving the problems or exploiting the openings. These subjects are crucial to an understanding of the invasion of Cuba.

The American propensity to externalize evil is at least as well developed as any known to history. We have followed that self-righteous path of least resistance since we won our independence. It is wholly unnecessary to dwell either on the extent or the intensity of the manner in which American leaders and the public at large have done this with reference to the Soviet Union. What is not so generally recognized, however, is the degree to which Americans have also externalized good. The extent, that is, to which they have argued (and finally assumed) that America's political and economic well-being are determined by opportunities that exist outside the United States. This began at least as early as Jefferson's reliance on the frontier to underwrite prosperity and representative government, and has continued to the present day. Americans have always relied on a new frontier.

The United States has furthermore exhibited a pronounced tendency to deal with its difficulties, and to exploit its opportunities, through the use (or the threat) of economic or political force. A rudimentary listing of our wars, quasi-wars, police actions, and interventions makes the point. We have fought, in rough order (and counting only the first conflicts since there are several repeaters), the following nations: various Indian tribes that *we* defined as independent societies, England, France, Spain, Canada, Mexico, Nicaragua, Hawaii, China, Colombia, Germany, Austria-Hungary, various other Latin American governments, Japan, Italy, several Eastern European countries, Koreans, and sundry other Asians. We have applied strong—even massive—economic force as a conscious instrument of policy to every nation with which we have ever had significant relations. None of this makes us unique. Other major powers have their own lists. But that is just the point. We are not unique.

These features of American thought and action in foreign affairs have characterized the policy of the United States toward Cuba not only since 1895, but in particular since Senator Wayne L. Morse's warning to the Cubans on January 12, 1959. By the end of that year, the two official notes on the Agrarian Reform Law (along with many others concerning American property rights), and the increasing agitation to discipline Castro (evil) and thereby re-open Cuba to American influence (good), made it clear that the traditional outlook was as dominant as ever.

On November 29, 1959, for example, Senator Ellender fired

another volley on the sugar quota issue. A bit later, on December 10, Secretary of State Christian Herter made it known that Castro's offer on compensation for American property was no more acceptable than the earlier and similar Guatemalan proposal. And as the Congress reconvened in January, 1960, a consensus began to emerge very rapidly around the idea, as one Representative put it, that "this is a time for action and not pussy-footing."

The outcry that greeted Cuba's barter deal with the Russians in February, 1960, could have been predicted. This bargain was largely the result of three factors. First, Castro's serious economic problems. Second, America's refusal to help solve those difficulties save in a way that would subvert the Revolution. And third, the not particularly astute realization by the Soviets that they could exploit those two conditions in a way that might bring them significant gains. American policy—long-run and short-term—handed the Russians an opening which they promptly exploited. The United States had both the power and the opportunity to avoid that situation. It did not do so.

The greatest gain that Russia ultimately won from its decision to aid Castro concerned the opportunity it finally secured to sit in on the game that the United States had been playing ever since 1945. Moscow could at last talk about its ally on the border of the United States. And it unquestionably began to use Cuba, as it already used other Latin American countries, as a center for the distribution of propaganda and as a base for intelligence operations.

But there was in 1960, and as of September, 1962, there still is, a vital difference. The Russians did not establish Soviet bases in Cuba as the United States has done in such nations as Turkey along the frontiers of the Soviet Union. Moscow constructed no airfields to handle Red Air Force bombers armed with nuclear weapons, built no launching pads for Soviet missiles tipped with hydrogen warheads, and flew no U-2 flights over the United States from Cuba.

The Russians were quite aware of this difference: they understand, even though many Americans seem not to, that their link with Cuba has not changed the essential balance of power which stands in favor of the United States.

American reaction to the Castro-Soviet trade agreement, and to the subsequent development of the tie between the two countries, seems to have been based on the same assumption that produced the policy of containment vis-à-vis the Soviet Union —only this time applied to the United States instead of Russia. It appears to have been grounded, that is, on the axiom that the United States could not continue to exist as a democratic and prosperous capitalist nation if any major European power challenged or blocked or decreased its existing power in, or its potential expansion into, areas and countries along its frontiers.

In any event, President Dwight David Eisenhower's first response was to approve the proposal to arm and train Cuban counter-revolutionaries. The United States next refused to sell helicopters to Castro. Then, on April 20, 1960, the House of Representatives passed a law prohibiting aid to Castro unless a special finding was made to define and authorize such assistance as being in the interests of the United States. The Cubans seem to have interpreted this last act for what it was—the beginning of the shift from letting Castro "go through the wringer" to a policy of speeding up the process. In any event, the revolutionary government made overtures in May to discuss the deteriorating situation.

The United States declined the offer. Instead, on May 26, 1960, it cancelled all aid programs then in operation. This assistance did not amount to very much, but the move indicated how rapidly America was moving to increase its pressure on Castro. Exactly a month later, the House Committee on Agriculture granted the President power to fix the Cuban sugar quota.

After that act, if not indeed from February, the record of American-Cuban relations reads like the script for a crude burlesque on the action-reaction, vicious-circle kind of diplomacy. Castro next seized the Texaco and Esso refineries for refusing to process Soviet crude petroleum. The American note of protest was strong, inaccurate, rather emotional, and filled with portents of retaliation.

That came from both sides on July 6, 1960. Cuba announced Revolutionary Law 851, which established the legal basis for the general nationalization of American and Cuban property. Seizures under the law began almost immediately and continued throughout the year. For its part, the United States reduced the Cuban sugar quota by 700,000 short tons. A bit later, on July 16, it filed "a most solemn and serious protest" against Law 851. It asserted, contrary to the careful opinion of Cuba's best lawyers (given in response to the inquiries of American business interests), that the legislation was "manifestly in violation" of international law.[1] The State Department argument was in essence the same one that had been used in connection with the Agrarian Reform Law. Cuba's action was illegal because it failed "to assure the payment of prompt, adequate, and effective compensation." Despite the grave tone of the American note, Cuba did not rescind the law.

Similar rounds of tit-for-tat continued throughout the summer. And the reality of such clashes was to some extent infused with the kind of mounting anger and small-boy behavior generally associated with the game. The specific timing and tone of some of the exchanges, for example, were undoubtedly guided by that spirit of dare and double-dare. But it is a mistake to *explain* the diplomacy in those terms. Each side had embarked upon a broad course of action which generated fundamental opposition from the other, and the details, timing, and tone of the incidents were secondary and derivative in nature.

. . . Tragedy is defined by the confrontation and clash of opposing truths. And there was truth on both sides. Cuba's truth involved the need for a thoroughgoing social revolution, the right to carry it through, and the legitimate expectation that its former overlord would either help ease the transition or leave it alone to proceed as it could and would on its own. The American truth involved past concern and assistance, existing rights and economic stakes in Cuba per se, and the legitimate expectation that the Revolution would make its transition with consideration for those American equities.

. . . If we accept the broad conceptual approach of thinking about American-Cuban relations within the framework of tragedy—but abandon the theme of inevitability—then we are able to see and raise the central questions. These concern which protagonist had the greater responsibility for acting to change the tragic logic, and what men made the effort.

The United States had the vastly greater responsibility. It took control of Cuban affairs in the period between 1895 and 1902 and never relinquished its final authority. In addition, it asserted and preened itself on a morality which required it to use that power in ways that would have avoided the conditions of the Cuban political economy in 1958, and which would have led to a different approach to the Revolution of 1959 once it had occurred. By its own actions and its proclaimed morality, therefore, the burden was on the United States. . . .

One could make a strong, if never conclusive, argument that the issue of relations with Cuba was one of the two or three cru-

cial elements in the campaign of 1960. A review of all the
speeches and random remarks of the candidates reveals a large
number of references to the problem, and the question became
ever more prominent as the campaign developed. Whatever
part it did play in his election, one thing is certain: John Fitz-
gerald Kennedy raised and pushed the issue. The responsibility
is his.

As in general, so with the Cuban problem: Kennedy's two
most central personal characteristics are his urge to power and
his fear of failure. He obviously wants power very urgently, and
conceives of it in the strikingly narrow terms of himself and his
clan. His propensity to personalize substantive issues, as he did
in connection with the rise in steel prices in 1962, is unusual
even for a man clearly trying to telescope generations into half-
decades. His candid definition of prestige, offered during the
campaign in connection with foreign public opinion of the
United States, is very revealing in this respect. "I define prestige
as influence, as an ability to persuade people to accept your
point of view." Not just esteem and respect, but power over
other people.

Kennedy's concept of power in terms of the clan involves
one of the earliest, indeed one of the most primeval, forms of ex-
ternalizing evil known in human affairs. It is one of the most
rudimentary and intense forms of that phenomenon. This underlying propensity to externalize evil converged in Kennedy with
another characteristic of clan society—the fear of failure.
Those aspects of his outlook reinforced each other, and as they
did so they produced in Kennedy an extremely intense concern
that time was running out and that control of the future was
about to be lost at any moment.

Finally, Kennedy's concept of a New Frontier was very revealing of his outlook even though in reality it was anything

but new. He did enumerate various domestic social welfare issues and scientific problems that needed attention, but his underlying theme was the absolute necessity of continued expansion for the American economic system. This did not involve in
Kennedy's mind any idea or program of colonial or territorial
expansion. It did involve, however, the same kind of overseas
economic expansion that had characterized the thinking of the
vast majority of American leaders ever since—to use a convenient as well as causative event—Frederick Jackson Turner
formulated the frontier thesis in 1893.

Beginning with the proposition that "a prosperous business
community is the measure of our performance," Kennedy moved
directly to support such overseas economic expansion. "I therefore favor expansion of our foreign trade and private investments abroad." "Our exports," he warned, "have not been large
enough." He did enter one reservation to the general axiom
about expansion, but it did *not* concern the unfavorable effects
of such expansion on America's relations with the rest of the
world. It involved only the problem of expanding in such a way
as to "avoid serious adverse effects on domestic industry that can
arise from foreign competition."

Like his predecessors, Kennedy projected this economic expansionism into the political, strategic, and ideological spheres.
"Now in 1960, American frontiers are on the Rhine and the
Mekong and Tigris and the Euphrates and the Amazon. There
is no place in the world that is not of concern to all of us. . . .
We are responsible for the maintenance of freedom all around
the world." "The cause of all mankind," he cried, "is the cause
of America." This approach defined power and the future in
terms of a struggle with the evil of the Soviet Union and other
Communist societies. "Now the question is whether the world
will exist half free and half slave, and if it does not, which way

it will go." "My campaign for the Presidency, therefore, is an effort to mobilize the great strength . . . for the great struggle."

Policy toward Cuba became one of the main examples of the way that Kennedy integrated these personal, economic, and ideological themes. The issue also revealed that Kennedy was aware that there were problems of morality and legality as well as of power and expansion and righteousness. One of the most suggestive indicators of Kennedy's entire outlook was provided by a story concerning Cuba that he told time and again throughout the campaign. Little comment is needed. The way Kennedy changed the story by dropping all reservations about whether it was right for America to control so much of Cuban life indicates Kennedy's underlying approach to resolving the tension between power and morality.

August 24: "Three years ago I went to Havana. I was told that the American Ambassador was the second most powerful man in Cuba. Probably he should not be, but he is not today."

September 2: "I visited Havana three years ago and I was informed that the American Ambassador was the second most influential man in Cuba. He is not today. . . . This is the problem that we face in 1960."

September 5: "Three years ago I went to Havana, Cuba, and I was told that the American Ambassador was the second most powerful man in Cuba. I am not saying he should have been, but he was."

September 15: "I was in Havana three years ago. The American Ambassador informed me on that occasion that he was the second most powerful and influential man in Cuba. Today the American Ambassador is not."

September 20: "Three years ago when I was in Cuba, the American Ambassador was the second most influential man in Cuba. Today the Soviet Ambassador is."

Kennedy's first major speech on Cuba, by which he injected the subject into the forefront of the campaign, was delivered on October 6, 1960. It contained all the basic elements of his analysis and policy recommendations. But he had termed Cuba "a fundamental question in foreign policy" as early as September 6, and the following reconstruction of his views includes quotations from all relevant speeches.

It is noteworthy, first of all, that Kennedy's sense of historical development was limited to the six years prior to the fall of Batista. That was the period during which what he termed the "most serious errors"—or "the basic errors"—were made. He did mention, once, in this connection, the failure "to help Cuba meet its desperate need for economic development." But even then he limited the reference to the same brief period. He was more concerned with the failure to use American power to force Batista to step down in order to block Castro; and his argument suggests—but does not prove—that he was aware of Pawley's plan of December, 1958, to employ that technique. Kennedy's only reference to an earlier phase of American-Cuban relations involved a highly inaccurate and romanticized version of Roosevelt's policy during the 1930's.

The situation in 1960, according to Kennedy, was "critical"—"a disaster." Cuba was "so dangerous" because it represented "the first time in the history of the United States" that "an enemy stands poised at the throat of the United States." Even by the most generous of judgments, this was a gross historical boner. Napoleon stood there in the early years of the 19th century, and Castro is not yet to be compared to Napoleon. Kennedy's argument, of course, was that Cuba was "a new satellite" of the Soviet Union. But he was again gravely inaccurate in describing the island as "a Communist base of operations a few minutes from our coast—by jet plane, missile or submarine." The only foreign base in Cuba was—and remains—the American naval base.

Kennedy's extreme attack prompted the Eisenhower Administration, probably at the insistence of Nixon, to institute export contróls over American trade with Cuba. Kennedy dismissed the action as "too little and too late." His program was to plan "more stringent economic sanctions," to assure the Cubans through a massive propaganda campaign that they would again be free, and to give encouragement and aid to those "who are leading the resistance to Castro"—to those "who offer eventual hope of overthrowing Castro." After all, Kennedy argued, "if you can't stand up to Castro, how can you be expected to stand up to Khrushchev?"

All of this was to be done, however, without breaking American laws or Inter-American treaties. "I have never advocated and I do not now advocate," he asserted unequivocally on October 23, "intervention in Cuba in violation of our treaty obligations." But as so subtly yet convincingly indicated in his telling of the story about the American Ambassador being once but no longer the second most powerful man in Cuba, Kennedy violated his pledge of morality in order to honor his concern for power, his externalization of evil, and his urge to control the future while still in the present.

When Kennedy authorized the invasion, he knowingly violated his avowed morality. In perhaps the single most perceptive and courageous action of his distinguished career, Senator Fulbright bluntly told the President that he was mistaken on moral and pragmatic grounds. He did this not once, but twice. Fulbright's performance was a magnificent display of statesmanship—both absolutely and by comparison with the performance of such liberals as presidential assistant Arthur M. Schlesinger, Jr. As with others, Schlesinger in the crisis valued his future influence more than his present morality. Schlesinger's failure is particularly striking because he has so diligently and haughtily criticized the Communists for just that scale of values—and also because he has stressed the moral issue of slavery in explaining the coming of the American Civil War.

The failure of American leadership was dramatized even more terribly by the failure of Adlai Stevenson to resign his post as Ambassador to the United Nations. Stevenson is a bigger man by far than Schlesinger, Jr. He also stressed morality and responsibility in both his presidential campaigns. Stevenson wept after discovering that he had been lied to so that he would lie to the world. And he apparently gave President Kennedy a verbal thrashing that left the younger man temporarily chastened. But Stevenson went back to his office. Unlike Jefferson, a man he was fond of quoting, Stevenson could not bring himself to resign even with a view to future leadership.

The most perceptive and sobering comment on the American-instigated invasion of Cuba, and upon the conduct of the overwhelming majority of American leaders, was written many years ago by a superb novelist and a profound commentator on human affairs named Joseph Conrad.

"Most of us," Conrad wrote, "if you will pardon me for betraying the universal secret, have, at some time or other, discovered in ourselves a readiness to stray far, ever so far, on the wrong road."

Perhaps it is expecting too much for Americans to thank Castro for offering them an opportunity to learn that lesson. But they should seize the day and do so. They must do so if they are not to stray even further on the wrong road. . . .

The events which occurred after the completion of this manuscript in September, 1962, and particularly those beginning with President Kennedy's speech of October 22nd announcing a blockade of shipping to Cuba, serve only to emphasize and dramatize the central line of argument advanced in the body of this essay.

There would be no missiles of any description or range in Cuba if the actions of the United States toward Cuba since 1898 had followed and honored its professions and promises.

As was pointed out in the closing passages of the essay as completed in September, the United States faced at that time a fateful choice. It could change its policy or risk being confronted in Cuba with a situation comparable with the one posed for the Soviet Union by American power in such countries as Turkey, Formosa, and Okinawa.

The Kennedy Administration did not change its policy. It did *not* respond to Cuban overtures for negotiation. It did *not* relax its economic, political, and military pressure on Cuba. It did *not* stop the provocative and harassing actions of anti-Castro exiles in the United States. It did *not,* in short, honor either its own neutrality laws or its obligations under international treaties.

Furthermore, the Kennedy Administration did *not* initiate quiet, serious discussions with the Soviet Union designed to reach an accommodation whereby an American agreement to tolerate the Cuban Revolution would be matched by a Russian commitment to halt its military aid to the Castro Government. And, in what was perhaps the act that revealed most about its own character, the Kennedy Administration did *not* go to the American public with a candid review of American responsibility for the situation in Cuba, and of the resulting crisis vis-à-vis the Soviet Union, and with a statement of quiet confidence in the ability of the people of the United States to match the restraint and maturity of Soviet citizens during the years they have been confronted with American bombers and missiles but a few minutes flight-time across Russian borders.

Instead, the Kennedy Administration acted unilaterally, and in a manner calculated to dramatize the situation, to establish itself as the sole and arbitrary gate-keeper of all international shipping bound for Cuba. This was by all codes and interpretations of international law an act of war.

The resulting crisis could produce any, or a combination, of several consequences: a nuclear holocaust, a series of American air strikes against targets in Cuba, an all-out American invasion of Cuba, conventional warfare in other areas of the world, or an informal or formal settlement of the Cuban crisis through negotiation. Any effort as of October 24 to predict the specific outcome would be as irrelevant to the purpose of this essay as it would be to the policy decisions being taken by the governments involved in the crisis.

There are three kinds of issues, however, that can be raised by an author whose book will be published approximately six weeks after he scribbles his last word. The first is to point out that American actions of the kind taken by Kennedy toward Cuba have repeatedly offered the Soviet Union an opportunity to finesse the situation against the United States. The usual argument for confronting the Russians with an ultimatum of the kind exemplified by the embargo of October 23–24, 1962 is that it forces them to back down and thereby saves the peace and prevents future crises. But this logic overlooks the truth that the Soviet Union, by reacting with overtures for negotiation and accommodation, immediately preempts the role of the peacemaker. This in turn undercuts the American argument that the Soviet Union is responsible for all the trouble and tension in the world, places the United States on the defensive by having to respond to peaceful alternatives framed by Russia, and ultimately weakens the initial support given America by other countries. The recourse to unilateral, extreme, and bellicose measures offers evidence only about the leaders who employ them, and raises basic questions about the character of that leadership.

If the crisis engendered by such actions does lead to war, then the responsibility is by no means so clearly fixed upon the Russians as the advocates of such a policy maintain. The reason for this involves the second main point that can be made, regardless of the outcome of the crisis. Despite the rhetoric of the Kennedy Administration, missiles are by definition neither offensive nor defensive. A military missile is a high velocity vehicle designed to deliver a warhead on a target. It is offensive if it is used to initiate an attack. It is defensive if it is fired in response to an assault. Missiles are disturbing, it is true, but the feeling induced by their presence exists independently of when they are fired, for the simple reason that they cause the death and the damage in any event.

But the act of defining a missile as offensive before it is used to initiate an attack is a wholly arbitrary and unilateral action. By taking this step, the Kennedy Administration has in effect retaliated before any blow has been struck. This standard justifies Soviet action of a similar kind. The point is important not because it will save any lives if war results, but because it is vital to understand the logic of American policy. From being almost obsessed with fear of another Pearl Harbor, the United States under the Kennedy Administration has moved perilously close to adopting the psychology that produced that attack.

Finally, an author, confronted with a book going to press in the midst of such a crisis, can attempt to define and clarify the crucial factors upon which any analysis and judgment of the issue must depend. These would seem to be the following:

First. The United States enjoyed and exercised, directly and indirectly, preponderant power in Cuba from 1898 until the summer of 1962. The Soviet Union neither caused nor assisted

Castro's Revolution of 1958–1959. The rise of Russian influence in Cuba has been the result of the failure of American policy.

Second. American reaction to increased Russian influence in Cuba has been wholly consistent with the double standard of diplomacy first enunciated in the Monroe Doctrine in 1823. This point should not be confused with the question of whether or not the Monroe Doctrine is still relevant in an age of ICBM's. That is a pseudo-issue which has the effect of obscuring the heart of the matter. The real point about the Monroe Doctrine is that its double standard of judgment has never provided—and does not now provide—a valid moral or pragmatic foundation for a foreign policy.

In the same speech in which he declared the Western Hemisphere off-limits to European powers, President James Monroe openly and officially threw the weight and influence of the United States government on the side of European revolutions against the status quo.[2]

This double standard has been followed by almost every administration since the time of Monroe. And until now, at any rate, it has been the basis of the policy of the Kennedy Administration toward Cuba. But tradition does not make morality. It only makes custom. American policy as exemplified in the Monroe Doctrine is based on a double standard dependent solely upon force for any recognition it may obtain.

Third. President Kennedy's assertion on October 22, 1962, that Russian military aid to Cuba upset the precarious balance of power between the United States and the Soviet Union is false. The charge will not stand up under the weight of facts that have been known publicly for at least a year prior to Kennedy's speech.

There did exist, during the late 1950's, a kind of balance of strength between the United States and the Soviet Union. The United States then enjoyed, as it had since the end of World War II (and as it still does), a vast superiority in nuclear power and in the capacity to deliver that power on target in Russia. The Soviet Union, on the other hand, had managed to conceal the main elements of its nuclear capacity, which in quantitative terms was far inferior. This secrecy, a classic weapon in military strategy, gave the Soviets the potential ability to strike back against the far greater nuclear strength of the United States.

Unilateral American action destroyed this balance. The U-2 flights provided American officials with extensive and reliable information on Soviet nuclear bases. This meant that the United States had the potential to destroy—with the first American attack—the Russian ability to retaliate. Having lost their strategic secrecy, the Russians had only a far weaker nuclear arsenal, and delivery system, with which to confront the awesome power of the United States.

The Russians responded by undertaking nuclear tests to prove-out weapons—such as the 50 megaton bomb, and other warheads that could be launched by smaller, more mobile missiles—that would restore some measure of balance with the United States. Russian military aid to Cuba was another part of the effort undertaken in response to the U-2 flights, and to the American decision to base its nuclear strategy on the ability to destroy Russian missile emplacements in a first attack. By seeking to attain the illusory goal of perfect security, the United States had only moved closer to war.

Fourth. American responsibility for the very great economic and political pressure on the Cuban people, including official encouragement of anti-Castro action, antedates any Soviet influence on the Cuban Revolution. The decision to put Castro "through the wringer" was made in Washington between

March and June, 1959. It was made without any reference to Soviet influence in Cuba. *For that matter, it was made with the clear realization that it might increase Communist influence.* The moral responsibility for the consequences of that decision on the health and welfare of the Cuban people rests squarely upon the United States.

Long years ago, in a moment of exuberance over the use of American power against a vastly weaker nation, Secretary of State John Hay called the Spanish-American War a "splendid little war." That phrase, and the attitude behind it, have haunted the relations between the United States and Cuba for two generations. And it may be that Hay's splendid little war will turn out to have been the first-stage detonator for a horrible, monstrous conflict.

But if not, the first order of business will still remain the changing of American policy toward Cuba. In this matter, as in others, the responsibility of the historian and the citizen are identical. That responsibility is to act on ex-President Dwight David Eisenhower's reminder on October 23, 1962, that "we are free to ask and to learn how we arrived at our present state, even in foreign policy."

That has been the purpose of this essay, and of this post-script.

The United States, Cuba, and Castro
(New York: Monthly Review Press, 1962)

Karl Marx's

Challenge to

America

Marx's work flowed from the methodological axiom that reality and change could be explained, and prognostications offered, by reference to the tension, conflict, and contradictions between the methods of production and the relations of production. By this he meant, fundamentally, the interaction between the way work could be done in any given circumstance and the way men organized themselves to do the work. Sticks and rocks demanded a certain kind of organization for cultivating fields, for example, and that organization begot new ideas about how men ought to be organized, as well as about how the ground might be tilled in different ways. Men acted on these ideas, either in favor of them or against them; that caused changes, and the new conditions generated more ideas.

Men therefore made their own history, but they did so within the limits of existing reality (which of course included old as well as new ideas). It should be clear, though it is often overlooked, that Marx understood and acknowledged the influence of ideas. He did argue, however, that basic ideas changed only very slowly. Hence he insisted that the economic rules, practices, habits, and relationships created by one such set of ideas became and remained the predominant—and even an almost independent—factor in a given situation until new ideas changed the system.

This is often misunderstood as saying that all human action can be, or even must be, explained as flowing from individual, personal economic motives. Marx was no such fool as that. He was quite aware that men could and did act from economic motives, but he also realized that they could and did act on the much broader basis of thinking that the whole network of political and social relationships depended upon maintaining certain economic patterns. They could act, that is, to sustain the marketplace per se as well as an entrepreneur within the marketplace. And Marx explicitly acknowledged the role of passion and chance in affecting the *short-run* development of the system. . . .

It is worth re-emphasizing that Marx did not neglect or discount ideas. This is one of the most common criticisms of him. Its proponents claim he made man into a machine guided by a kind of economic radar. This is simply wrong. He was unequivocal on the point that men could entertain ideas that were broader than those derived from their specific economic role or position. A radical, revolutionary "class consciousness," he pointed out, "can of course also rise in other classes from the observation of the situation of [the proletarian] class."

Marx could not discount ideas for the simple reason that he was principally concerned with the central axioms and dynamic propensities of capitalist development. Indeed, one might argue with considerable effect that it was his very overemphasis on the power of ideas that led him repeatedly, and in a way that contradicted another part of his analysis of ideas, to underestimate the time required for the full evolution of the dynamic features he defined as being the causal engines of the capitalist process. He was very prone to assume that men would perceive the true nature of their condition, and proceed to improve it, much more quickly than they actually did—or have.

Marx's foreshortened sense of time did have the effect of distorting some of his specific projections and predictions. But it seems fair to point out that the problem of understanding and being right about time is a difficulty that plagues all historians and social scientists. Even economists have trouble with time. Those who dismiss Marx have not met this challenge any more effectively than he did. If anything, they have foreshortened time even more drastically. Marx talked about capitalism over a period of at least five centuries, whereas his critics dismiss him as hopelessly wrong on the evidence of less than one. For that matter, most Americans who dispense with him as being irrelevant base their argument on the events of an infinitesimal period between 1941 and 1955.

Finally, it is pertinent to recall Marx's uninhibited praise of capitalist performance. He never intimated, let alone asserted, that capitalism was an unmitigated failure or an unrelieved agony. This seems particularly relevant in connection with America, where the achievement has been great—even if the resources and the favorable circumstances have been grandiose.

The bourgeoisie, Marx commented quite without niggardliness, "has played a most revolutionary part. . . . It has been the first to show what man's activity can bring about. It has accomplished wonders far surpassing Egyptian pyramids, Roman aqueducts, and Gothic cathedrals; it has conducted expeditions that put in the shade all former Exoduses of nations and crusades. . . . [It] has created more massive and more colossal productive forces than have all preceding generations together. . . . What earlier century had even a presentiment that such productive forces slumbered in the lap of social labor?" And, furthermore, the bourgeoisie "has given a cosmopolitian character to production and consumption in every country. . . . National one-sidedness and narrow-mindedness become more and more

impossible, and from the numerous national and local litera-
tures, there arises a world literature."

With these often neglected aspects of Marx clearly in mind,
and hopefully fixed therein for the duration of this discussion, it
is appropriate to begin an evaluation of his critique of capitalism by comparing his general argument about foreign relations
with the record of American foreign policy. . . .

One of the central features of capitalism, Marx argued, was
its splitting of the economy into two principal parts. This
"cleavage between town and country" was not complete, of
course, but the reciprocal relationship between them was heavily imbalanced in favor of the town, or Metropolitan, sector.
Marx was here following Adam Smith, the master theorist of
capitalism, as well as the facts he gathered in his own study of
the system. This was one of the most important instances in
which the theory and the practice of capitalism coincided.

Another such example involved the continued expansion of
the marketplace, first within a country and then beyond its
boundaries. The never-ending necessity to accumulate additional
surplus value, or capital, a process which was essential for the
system as well as to the individual businessman, meant that this
market "must, therefore, be continually extended." Without
such expansion the economic system would stagnate at a certain
level of activity, and the political and social system based upon
it would suffer severe strains leading either to a caste society up-
held by force or to revolution. Hence "the real task of bourgeois
society," Marx explained, "is the establishment of the world
market . . . and a productive system based on this foundation."

As it crossed the national boundary, this process transformed
"the cleavage between town and country" into "the colonial system." The town became the developed, industrial Metropolis,

while the country became the backward, underdeveloped society. It follows both logically and from the evidence that the
periodic crises created and suffered by capitalism intensified the
drive to expand the market. "The conquest of new markets and
the more thorough exploitation of the old ones," Marx pointed
out, served as the principal means whereby the internal crisis in
the Metropolis "seeks to balance itself."

Concerning both the normal and the crisis situations, Marx
was typically succinct and non-euphemistic in describing the
central feature of this expansion of the marketplace. "The favored country recovers more labor in exchange for less labor." It
is worth re-emphasizing, moreover, that Adam Smith reached
the identical conclusion, and based his entire theory and strategy of capitalist success on this essentially imbalanced relationship between the Metropolis and the country society.

Such expansion of the marketplace is directly and explicitly
relevant to an understanding of American foreign relations. It
offers, to begin with, a good many insights into the major periods of American diplomacy. The first of these eras began in the
middle of the eighteenth century and culminated in the 1820's.
The increasing British efforts after 1750 to control and limit the
existing American marketplace, its further agrarian expansion
westward, and its increasing share in international trade, led to
a confrontation with the colonists that lies at the heart of the
American Revolution.

Similar British attempts to restrict American territorial expansion after independence had been won, and to set limits
upon America's international trade (which antagonized the surplus-producing farmers as well as other groups), promoted and
accelerated and intensified the nationalism which led to the
War of 1812. And the American push into the Floridas, and
into the trans-Mississippi region, was obviously expansionist in

origin and purpose. The vision of a great trade with South America and Asia, while not as central to these movements as the concern for land, was nevertheless a significant part of the continuing pressure to expand the marketplace that culminated in the Trans-Continental Treaty of 1819 with Spain.

Throughout this period, moreover, the same underlying thrust to expand the marketplace defined the basic character of American policy toward the Indians. The drive to dispossess the natives of their land, and the campaign to remove all restrictions on trade with the various tribes, combined to drive the Indians further westward while at the same time subverting any efforts to integrate them as full citizens into the white man's society and weakening their ability to resist further encroachments.

In a similar way, Marx's emphasis on the expansion of the marketplace offers major—and in many respects still unexploited—perceptions concerning the struggle between various elements of the country during the 1840's and 1850's to organize the marketplace along one of three alternate axes: a North-South, a South-West, or a North-West alliance. The psychology of fear that became so apparent in all sections of the nation on the eve of the Civil War, for example, is directly related to this increasingly intense conflict.

Farmers in the region north of the Ohio River not only manifested an active desire to control the national government and the Western territories for their own benefit, but developed a corresponding antagonism toward other groups and regions which appeared to be blocking their attempts to win that predominance. Southerners expressed similar hopes and fears, as did still other groups in the Northeastern part of the country. As the economic integration between the Northeastern "town" and the food-producing Northwestern "country" became stronger than an earlier relationship between the Eastern Metropolis and the Southern raw material producing "country," Southerners increasingly defined themselves as members of a potentially independent system sustained and strengthened through connections with non-American Metropolitan areas.

The formerly regional conflicts thus gradually changed into a struggle between two giant sections over the issue of which was to control the trans-Mississippi West. Both blocs viewed that area as what today would be called an underdeveloped, potentially neo-colonial resource that would guarantee their respective prosperity and security. At bottom, both sections viewed slavery as an economic phenomenon that would determine the outcome of the marketplace struggle for final victory. Ultimately, of course, slavery became both a symbol of that conflict and a moral and ideological banner for both sides. If slavery be said to have caused the Civil War, however, it must also be said that it did so more in its economic sense than in its moral respect. For the general response to the abolitionist minority (both positive and negative) was grounded in the economic fears of Northerners and Southerners who saw themselves first of all as combatants in a desperate struggle to control the continental marketplace.

The postwar conflicts between the Eastern Metropolis and the Southern and Western agrarian sectors of the economy can most fruitfully be approached as a clear illustration of the validity of the emphasis placed on "the cleavage between town and country" by Smith and Marx. This provides by far the most accurate guideline to any understanding and interpretation of the Granger, Alliance, and Populist movements. Even a viable psychological interpretation of these protest movements must be grounded upon such a structural analysis.

The general drive to expand the marketplace during these

same years of the late nineteenth century provided the primary energy for the American economic move outward into Europe. Africa, Latin America, and Asia. That expansion has been sustained and intensified in the twentieth century. Nobody but Americans thrust world power upon the United States. It came as a direct result of this determined push into the world marketplace. John D. Rockefeller's comment on the policy of Standard Oil typifies the attitude of both centuries. "Dependent solely upon local business," he explained in 1899, "we should have failed years ago. We were forced to extend our markets and to seek for export trade."

Since the farmer was a capitalist entrepreneur (a vital consideration often neglected or discounted in narrowly psychological interpretations of his behavior), Marx's analysis provides an insight into the policies and actions of the agrarians that most commentators have overlooked. If Marx is correct, that is, then the evidence ought to reveal the farmers participating in the expansionist movement as their production outran domestic consumption. The documents show precisely that: the American farmer's concern with overseas markets played a significant part in initiating and sustaining the momentum of the idea and the practice of such expansion.

Beginning in the early 1880's, the farmers' turn to export markets led directly to diplomatic encounters with England, France, Austria-Hungary, and Germany. It also prompted specific urban business interests, such as the railroads, the flour millers, the meat packers, and the implement manufacturers, to follow the lead of the farmers and undertake their own expansionist efforts. And, more generally, urban business leaders increasingly looked to agricultural export figures as a reliable index of general economic activity.

Politicians likewise responded, and the campaign for reciprocity treaties drew almost as much support from certain agrarian groups (as with Secretary of State James G. Blaine's efforts in 1890 to win reciprocity agreements with Cuba and other food-importing nations) as from the manufacturers. This involvement in the world marketplace also played a central role in the agrarian campaign for unlimited coinage of silver at a ratio of 16 to 1. The farmers, and their leaders like William Jennings Bryan, argued that free coinage would free America from economic control by Great Britain and other European powers and give the United States economic supremacy in the world marketplace. This militant and expansive economic nationalism, which stemmed directly from the experience of the farmers in having to deal through Liverpool and London, not only provided a surprising amount of support for building a new and big navy and taking Hawaii, but was a very significant factor in the coming of the Spanish-American War. . . .

When examined in the setting of one national economy within the world capitalist marketplace, and particularly one of the Metropolitan countries, Marx's argument about increasing misery and increasing proletarianization becomes more difficult to evaluate. His analysis was more complicated and detailed, and he was in many respects ambivalent about one of the central points, namely, whether or not such advanced national capitalism could stabilize the system's inherent tendency toward increasing *economic* misery. It may be helpful, therefore, in order to avoid the most common kind of misunderstanding about this involved issue, to emphasize at the outset that Marx did not define *misery* in exclusively economic terms.

His overriding thesis concerned the *condition* of the lower classes, of which money income he considered only one element. "The lot of the laborer, be his payment high or low." Marx commented, "must grow worse." Hence Marx's argument must be evaluated in terms of the social and psychological aspects of misery, and in terms of how and at what costs the economic record itself was made, as well as upon the narrow economic performance measured in dollars and cents.

A discussion of the economic side of the question should begin with a summary of American gains since 1940. During the last two decades, clearly enough, many citizens have benefited from an increase in real income and in the economic standard of living within the United States. This productive triumph merits every word and inflection of the praise Marx offered to such accomplishments by the capitalist system. There is nothing wrong with being better off in the material, economic sense. Indeed, there is a very great deal to be said in behalf of such improvement. Americans should neither find in that achievement, nor manufacture for it, any sense of shame or guilt. Shame and guilt have to do with moral, not economic, considerations.

The recent nature of this economic improvement is very noticeable. People born after 1925 are not much aware of it, but America suffered a severe, wrenching depression between 1929 and 1940. The yearly per capita real income of non-farm employees was only $4 higher in 1934 than it had been in the 1890's. The comparison is particularly relevant, and illuminating, in that both periods were depression eras, and such cyclic behavior is typical of the capitalist system. It also highlights the question of how long economic gains last under American capitalism. These considerations thus serve to emphasize the point that Marx made about the ways in which capitalism generated its economic growth, and the critique he offered of the quality of life it created. Marx was concerned with the costs, the character, the distribution, and the duration of economic benefits, and with the consequences over time of the manner in which they were secured.

His entire analysis was powered by a commitment to the idea and the ideal of all men becoming modern equivalents of classic Greek citizens, and by his awareness of capitalism's failure to realize the individual's potentialities in either the economic or the political or the social realm. Hence a primary aspect of evaluating Marx's critique concerns the social costs of private enterprise capitalism in the United States. The object of discussing economic gains within this context is not to discount or minimize them, but rather to place them in the same framework established by Marx. The real income in dollars received by a man during a portion of his life is only a part of the measure of even his *net* economic position in the system. And it is an even smaller part of what Marx was talking about when he used the word *misery*.

This is of course a broad subject and shades off into the more general question of whether American capitalism has created an ethical and equitable community. Considered in the more narrow economic sense, however, it is clear that the success of the capitalist system is based on large-scale public assistance. American capitalism functions only through the social accumulation of capital, but that capital is not socially allocated. The citizen-contributor does not even do much proposing, and he most certainly does not participate in any significant way in the process of choosing between the alternatives formulated by those who dispose of the capital. American capitalism, and more particularly the entrepreneurial decision-makers of the system, has had its own tax-supported social security plan ever since the Civil War guaranteed it the opportunity and the protection to extend itself over the entire continent and outward into the world marketplace.

The direct and indirect subsidies provided to capitalist entrepreneurs since that time by non-stockholding taxpayers— past, present, and future—defies accurate and final tabulation. The sum is staggering, even if the account is closed after a rough estimate involving the obvious examples of railroads, steamship companies, automobiles, airplanes, the chemical industry, and agriculture. The private use of public monies has been, and continues to be, a central dynamic element in the success of an American capitalism which nevertheless attributes its achievement to the creative powers of private property and individual enterprise. The competitive market economy of capitalism has not been able to sustain itself without continuing and increasing subsidy from the government—meaning the taxpayer.

A more indirect, but by no means less significant, kind of social cost involves the waste, spoilage, misuse, and depletion of the nation's natural resources. This includes human beings as well as other animal and inanimate wealth. The irony here is that the non-stockholding, non-managerial taxpayer must bear not only the wide costs of the initial phases of such misallocation, but is then taxed additionally to support a belated effort to undo the damage and to hold the line against further decimation. One of the few situations in which the public managed some direct, contemporary return on its inherent title to such resources involved the state of Minnesota's tax on the exploitation of its iron ore deposits by private capitalists. The citizens thereby succeeded in diverting some of the profits into the creation of a major university, thus balancing to some extent the depletion of one social resource through the related and partial creation of another. But that example is almost unique, and serves mainly to dramatize the extent to which American capitalism has been financed by social investment of mammoth proportions.

The most disturbing example of these social costs concerns the relationship between war and the success of American capitalism. The issue is not whether capitalism is a unique cause of war. It is not. The causes of war, including the economic ones, operate within capitalism just as they have within other systems of political economy. It does seem demonstrable, however, that capitalism heightens and intensifies the role and impact of economic factors in causing wars. The essential dynamic engine of capitalism, after all, is held to be a never-ending economic competition within a world marketplace.* It further asserts that such rivalry produces health, wealth, and welfare. The argument thus forges a firm, causal bond between victory in the marketplace and other desirable objectives.

This competition has an inherent tendency to escalate into political tension and conflict, and that exacerbates and reinforces other causes of such contention. For this reason, capitalism reveals a strong propensity to produce or result in organized violence. Capitalists may not want war; and, indeed, the business community is always divided at any moment prior to the outbreak of war over whether or not force should be employed. This division arises out of varying estimates by particular interests, and from a similar disagreement among those who take an inclusive view of the system, over whether it is necessary. But the capitalist outlook structures the world in such a way that capitalist leadership often sees itself as being confronted with a choice between war or defeat in the competitive marketplace. War thus becomes the regrettable but necessary means of avoiding failure in the area of human activity previously defined as being crucial to individual and collective achievement.

This does involve an inherent tendency to violence, but it does not supply a unique cause of war. The distinction is crucial, for Marx's analysis of the relationship between capitalism and

* See Anatol Rapoport. *Strategy and Conscience* (New York: Harper and Row, 1964).

war is often misread or misinterpreted to an erroneous conclusion. All he actually said was that the capitalist qua capitalist operated according to a set of ideas, and under certain practical necessities, that combined to create a momentum which carried competition over into military combat. And this central proposition is supported by psychological as well as other kinds of evidence. . . .

It may be true that American capitalism could have produced its recent gains outside the context of war and cold war. But the record shows that the achievement has occurred only during war and cold war, and that evidence cannot be changed or mitigated by a conditional hypothesis. The only way for American capitalism to prove such a claim would be for it to accomplish similar results without war and cold war. It did not do so between 1876 and 1898, between 1900 and 1914, or between 1920 and 1941. . . .

Consider, for example, President Franklin Delano Roosevelt's famous warning in 1937 that one-third of the nation was "ill-housed, ill-clad, ill-nourished." Beyond the initial shock it caused, the remark was correctly understood by thoughtful observers to carry a devastating (if unacknowledged) judgment of the functioning of American capitalism, as well as of the effectiveness of the New Deal itself. Even so, the criticism was a model of understatement. The figures Roosevelt used were more than 100 percent optimistic. In 1936, that is to say, 68 percent of the multi-person families of the United States existed under conditions of serious deprivation or outright poverty. That 68 percent of the families received but 35 percent of the nation's family income. This was slightly worse than the situation in 1929, when only 65 percent of the families endured such circumstances.

War and cold war provided the dynamism which enabled American capitalism to improve that performance. The families existing in serious deprivation or poverty dropped to 37 percent by 1947, and to 28 percent by 1963. The major portion of those gains came between the Japanese attack at Pearl Harbor and the termination of the economic war effort. The rate of improvement subsequently slowed very markedly. In his contemporary review of the data, *Rich Man, Poor Man,* Herman P. Miller says without qualification that "there has been no appreciable change in income shares for nearly twenty years." And an even more recent study indicates that the poorest one-fifth of the population received 4.9 percent of total income in 1944, compared with 4.6 percent in 1963.* . . .

The people in the lower half of the system have clearly benefited from the increase in total production since 1941, and hence their low relative position does not represent an across-the-board absolute decline. But Marx was primarily and explicitly concerned with the *condition* of such employees, whatever the level of their wages or income; and their relative income position does bear on their condition, as do even more the circumstances surrounding their betterment, and the nature and tone of the society created by the means used to accomplish such improvement.

The same-sized slice of a bigger pie does provide the wage earner with more pie. So, up to a point, does a slightly smaller slice of a bigger pie. But that approach to the question of the condition of the worker begs many of the central issues. It is like saying that having a television set compensates for the lack of modern plumbing and running water in the house. It may, but only if one has accepted a value system that ranks television

* See J. M. Fitzwilliams. "Size Distribution of Income in 1963," *Survey of Current Business* (April 1964).

ahead of sanitation. This attitude ignores the non-economic prices the worker has to pay for the same slice of pie, and the total cost to him of the way it is produced. And the last of these considerations, including as it does the subsidies he provides the system, clearly decreases his net economic share of the general improvement. American capitalism can hardly substantiate its claim to have proved Marx wrong simply because it manages to camouflage its inability to function according to its own axioms. That is success of a kind, to be sure, but it is not of an order sufficient to meet the real issue.

As for non-economic costs, the role of military activities in the overall achievement of American capitalism should be apparent in connection with the years of preparation for and engagement in sustained violence between 1940 and 1945. Today, in the 1960's, economic activity directly connected with the military accounts for 10 percent of the gross national product. This includes, for example, 20 percent of the income of the manufacturing industry, about 50 percent of total production in the electrical industry, and over 60 percent of the work in the shipbuilding sector. Such specifically and directly military employment accounts for 11 percent of the total labor force.

This share, which involves at least 33 percent of American scientists and engineers (and 48 percent of all American research), does not include the men who are employed in the armed forces per se. This military payroll is twice as large as the auto industry's, and one and a half times that of the iron and steel industry. Even when computed with a bias toward underestimation, this direct and indirect military employment accounts for about 20 percent of the total labor force. This figure, which does not include the men who are employed in what passes for the civilian sector of the economy in a cold war environment, comes within 5 percent of the maximum estimates of unemployment in 1933.

Despite this assistance from the military sector, and with the further help provided by the non-military aid programs likewise financed by the taxpayer, American capitalism still has not reduced economic misery to minor levels. . . .

American capitalism has never since 1861 functioned effectively enough to decrease economic misery over any significant period of time, save as it has been stimulated by war or cold war. . . .

The central utility of Karl Marx for Americans in the middle of the twentieth century is that he is a heretic who helps us by bringing our capitalistic ego into a confrontation with our capitalist reality. As with the groom and the horse, the philosopher can lead us to the self-examination, but he cannot make us change our ways. Only we can do that. But there is no doubt as to the value of the philosopher—however we cope with his challenge.

When examined seriously and soberly, the evidence submitted by American capitalism fails to confirm either the popular stereotype or the official myth about Karl Marx. The United States has not proved that Marx was wrong. The overall achievement of American capitalism, even with the peacetime subsidies provided by the non-entrepreneurial taxpayer, and with the further direct and indirect assistance flowing from wars and cold wars, can at most be characterized as a high-level stalemate with the internal forces that Marx identified as driving capitalism toward breakdown under normal circumstances. And, in cybernated production, American capitalism would seem to have fulfilled its axioms and logic in a way that Marx saw as providing both the basis and the reason for a transition to a new order of political economy.

In its non-economic aspects, moreover, which Marx properly insisted were an integral part of the system per se, American capitalism offers countless examples, at both the individual and the group levels, of the harmful and dangerous devolutions that he feared and anticipated. The economic achievement has been purchased at very great costs in human and material resources. The Negro is still not integrated even into the marketplace, let alone the society, a full century after capitalism destroyed the neo-feudal Southern society based on slavery. And possessive individualism operating in a competitive marketplace has increasingly proletarianized and stratified American society.

The individual displays increasing signs, overt and unconscious, of alienation, disorientation, and anti-social behavior. The integrated personality, let alone the integrated group, is produced only in opposition to the status quo, rather than by and through a commitment to the avowed principles of the system. Perhaps the most disturbing evidence of all concerns the way Americans have denied the very conception and idea of Utopia in the name of practicality, pragmatism, and realism. The metaphor of space, which was once a symbol of William Blake's cosmos that awaited man's fertile and creative and transcending genius, has been transformed into a literal area in which to repeat the old frontier habit of conquering a new and virgin territory and then making it over in the image of the old society.

In the realm of foreign affairs, meanwhile, Marx's analysis and predictions have withstood the test of changing reality in an even more dramatic way. From the seventeenth century to the present, the capitalist commitment to expanding the marketplace has guided and set limits upon American foreign policy. It defined relationships with Africa and the Negro, with the

North American continent and the Indian (and even among the whites for control of the continent), and with the underdeveloped societies and nations (and, through them, with other industrial countries).

In each of these cases—the Negro, the Indian, the South, and the underdeveloped areas—the expansion of the American marketplace brought grave and painful consequences to the non-Metropolitan elements. After having been forcibly transferred from his home as a chattel colonial, the Negro was belatedly released from that condition only to be defined and treated as an unequal and hence unfree ego in the marketplace. The Indians who survived suffered a similar fate. The South is even today a depressed, backward, and unequal sector of the Metropolis. And the inherent inequality in the marketplace relationship between the Metropolis and the underdeveloped countries has led, as Marx forecast that it would, to increasing misery for the poor nations and to a determination on their part to break free of that inequitable imperial relationship. . . .

The Great Evasion
(New York: Quadrangle Books, 1968)

The Cold-War

Revisionists

It becomes increasingly clear that many of the policies and actions of the New and Fair Deals, and of the upper-class Daniel Boones of the New Frontier, are producing something less than happiness and security. One of the reactions of liberals within the Establishment is to blame that Nasty Old Populist Lyndon, and to regroup with their own kind. That course has its intellectual and moral difficulties, however, as well as its pragmatic risks, and no one has pointed them out more directly than Daniel P. Moynihan.

One has to respect the integrity and the historical accuracy of his remarks to the A.D.A. on September 24. "The war in Vietnam," he candidly announced, "was thought up and is being managed by the men John F. Kennedy brought to Washington." Then, addressing his audience directly, he remarked that there were few present "who did not contribute something considerable to persuade the American people that we were entirely right to be setting out on the course that has led us to the present point of being waist-deep in the big muddy. It is this knowledge, this complicity if you will, that requires of many of us a restraint. . . . Who are we to say we would have done better?"

Brave words—and largely true.

But also terribly and dangerously misleading. For there is

neither logical nor moral discrepancy between acknowledging responsibility and admitting error. It is neither the act of a trimmer or coward, nor an abstract proposition advanced by an academic. Senator Fulbright and others have done it.

There is no transcendent reason to persist in rationalizing a mistake, or in hanging on to see it through. Explanations can no doubt be found for such action, but they do not speak to the central point. Those who realize that have clearly become increasingly nervous in the service of the Establishment. They know that the primary objective is to discover the where and the why of the mistake, and then rectify it as rapidly and effectively as possible.

A good deal of evidence suggests that Arthur M. Schlesinger, Jr. would like to rectify while at the same time prove that no mistakes were made of major dimensions. His little essays on the war in Vietnam, for example, are interesting exercises in trying to achieve that magical success. He does not succeed because no one can succeed in that enterprise: there are momentum, drift and chance in human affairs, but the initial course determines the effect of the momentum, drift and chance.

The difficulties of Schlesinger's approach are even more evident in his essay on "The Origins of the Cold War," printed in the October issue of *Foreign Affairs* (that *House Beautiful* of the Department of State). The article subtly admits some minor degree of American responsibility for the onset of the cold war as part of a central and overt attempt to modify the attitudes and policies of that era in the knowledge of their clearly dangerous consequences. But he maintains that there were no major American mistakes, and no major American responsibility, because nothing else could have been done. The trouble, he insists, was that "Stalin alone could have made any difference," and Stalin was paranoid.

There is a great book to be written some day explaining how Schlesinger and a good many other historians of his generation came by the power to render such flat-out psychiatric judgments without professional training and without direct access to their subjects. My own candidates for that undertaking are Robert Coles, Abraham H. Maslow or Rollo May, men who somehow acquired a sense of the limits of their approach even as they mastered its discipline.

Meanwhile, the first point to be made about Schlesinger's attempt to fix the origins of the cold war in Stalin's paranoia is that *no major American policy maker between 1943 and 1948 defined and dealt with the Soviet Union in those terms.* Schlesinger offers not the slightest shred of evidence that such was the case. The reason is simple: there is no such evidence.

Even if Schlesinger's characterization of Stalin as a paranoid were granted, the argument would still be unable to account either for the nature or the adoption of American policy. There is only one circumstance in which his proposition would become directly relevant: If a different American policy had been carefully formulated and then seriously tried over a significant period of time, only to fail because of Russian intransigence, then Schlesinger's argument that Stalin's paranoia caused the cold war would bear on the case.

It is particularly important to grasp that point because Schlesinger does not introduce paranoia until after he has demonstrated that Stalin was acting on a rational and conservative basis. Long before he mentions paranoia, Schlesinger notes the ambivalence of Soviet leaders toward an accommodation with the United States, and makes it clear that American leaders were operating on that estimate of the situation—not on the proposition that the Russians were paranoid. While entering the caveat that "no one, of course, can know what was really in the minds of the Russian leaders," he nevertheless concludes that "it is not unreasonable to suppose that Stalin would have been satisfied at the end of the war to secure . . . 'a protective glacis along Russia's western border'. . . . His initial objective was very probably not world conquest but Russian security." And he makes it clear that Stalin kept his word about giving the British the initiative in Greece.

Schlesinger does not resort to explaining Soviet action in terms of paranoia until he has to deal with American efforts to exert direct influence on affairs in Eastern Europe. Then he casually asserts that it was a factor: "given the paranoia produced alike by Russian history and Leninist ideology, [American action] no doubt seemed not only an act of hypocrisy but a threat to security."

That offhand introduction of paranoia as a primary operational factor in historical explanation staggers the mind. It is simply not convincing to hold that a man (in this instance, Stalin) who believes he has negotiated a clear security perimeter is paranoid because he reacts negatively when one of the parties to the understanding (in this case the United States) unilaterally asserts and acts on a self-proclaimed right to intervene within that perimeter. When examined closely in connection with foreign affairs, the most that can be made of Schlesinger's argument is that Stalin may have had strong paranoid tendencies, and that the American thrust into Eastern Europe (and elsewhere throughout the world) could very well have pushed him gradually into, and perhaps through, the psychic zone separating neurosis from psychosis.

The most significant aspect of Schlesinger's argument that emerges at this point is his admission that America's assertion of its right to intervene anywhere in the world, and its action in doing so in Eastern Europe, had a primary effect on Soviet behavior. For in saying that, however he qualifies it later, Schlesinger has granted the validity of one of the major points made by the critics of the official line on the cold war. Many criticisms could be made of his description of the nature and dynamism of American global interventionism, which he labels "universalism," but the most important weakness in his analysis is the failure to discuss the explicit and implicit anti-communism that was a strong element in the American outlook from the moment the Bolsheviks seized power in 1917. That omission gravely undercuts the attempt he makes later to substantiate a vital part of his argument.

For, having admitted the reality and the consequences of American interventionism, Schlesinger faces the difficult problem of demonstrating the truth of three propositions if he is to establish Soviet responsibility for the cold war. First, he must show that a different American policy could not have produced other results. Second, he must sustain the thesis that the Soviet response to American universalism was indeed paranoid. Third, he must prove that the American counter-response was relevant and appropriate.

Schlesinger's argument that an alternate American policy would not have made any difference has two themes. He says that a serious effort to negotiate around the Soviet bid for a $6 billion loan would "merely have reinforced both sides of the Kremlin debate" because "economic deals were merely subordinate to the quality of mutual political confidence." That judgment completely overlooks the impact which a serious American economic proposal would have made on the "quality of political confidence."

In the end, however, Schlesinger falls back on Soviet para-

noia as the reason that a different approach would have made
no difference. Here, however, he introduces a new factor in his
explanation. In the early part of the argument, he holds that the
Soviets "thought *only* of spheres of influence; above all, the Russians were determined to protect their frontiers, and especially
their border to the west, crossed so often and so bloodily in the
dark course of their history." But later Schlesinger suggests that
the paranoia was partially caused, and significantly reinforced,
by the Marxist ideology of capitalist antagonism and opposition.

However, Soviet leaders did not detect capitalist hostility
merely because they were viewing the world through a Marxist
prism. Such enmity had existed, and had been acted upon, since
November, 1917, and anti-communism was an integral part of
the universalism that guided American leaders at the end of
World War II. As Schlesinger demonstrates, willy-nilly if not
intentionally, American leaders were prepared to work with
Russian leaders if they would accept key features of the American creed. It is possible, given that truth, to construct a syllogism proving that Stalin was paranoid because he did not accept
the terms. But that kind of proof has nothing to do with serious
historical inquiry, analysis and interpretation.

The real issue at this juncture, however, is not how Schlesinger attempts to establish Stalin's paranoia. The central question
is whether or not Soviet actions are accurately described as paranoid. The evidence does not support that interpretation. Consider the nature of Soviet behavior in three crucial areas.

First, the Russians reacted to American intervention in Eastern Europe by consolidating their existing position in that
region. Many Soviet actions implementing that decision were
overpowering, cruel and ruthless, but the methods do not bear
on the nature of the policy itself. The Soviet choice served to

verify an important point that Schlesinger acknowledges: Stalin told Harriman in October, 1945, that the Soviets were "going isolationist" in pursuit of their national interests. Russian policy at that time in Eastern Europe was neither paranoid nor messianic Marxism.

Second, the Soviets pulled back in other areas to avoid escalating a direct national or governmental confrontation with the United States. They did so in the clash over rival claims for oil rights in Iran; and that policy was even more strikingly apparent in Stalin's attempt to postpone Mao's triumph in China. In the first instance, prudence belies paranoia. In the second, any messianic urges were suppressed in the national interest.

Third, the Soviets acquiesced in the activities of non-Russian Communist movements. While the term *acquiesced* is not perfect for describing the complex process that was involved, it is nevertheless used advisedly as the best single term to describe the *effect* of Soviet action. Stalin and his colleagues no doubt sought results other than those that occurred in many places —China and Yugoslavia come particularly to mind—and clearly tried to realize their preferences. Nevertheless, they did acquiesce in results that fell far short of their desires.

Schlesinger makes a great deal, as do all official interpreters of the cold war, of the April, 1945, article by Jacques Duclos of the French Communist Party. Let us assume that Duclos wrote the article on orders from Moscow, even though the process that produced the action was probably far more complex than indicated by that simple statement. The crucial point about Duclos' article is that it can be read in two ways. It can be interpreted as a messianic cry for non-Soviet Communist parties to strike for power as part of a general push to expand Russian boundaries or the Soviet sphere of influence. But it can as persuasively be read as primarily a call for non-Soviet Communists to reassert their own identity and become militant and disruptive as part of the Russian strategy of consolidation in the face of American universalism.

Official explanations of the cold war generally imply that American leaders heard the Duclos piece as a bugle call for Communist aid in behalf of Soviet expansion. In truth, no significant number of American leaders feared a Russian military offensive at any time during the evolution of the cold war. When the Duclos article appeared, and for a long period thereafter, they were far more concerned with devising ways to use the great preponderance of American power to further the universalism and interventionism of the United States in Eastern Europe and elsewhere.

But the most astonishing use of the Duclos article by any defender of the official line on the cold war is made by Schlesinger when he employs it to avoid any serious discussion of the impact of the dropping of two atomic bombs in August, 1945. In truth, astonishing is a very mild word for Schlesinger's performance on this point. He says merely that the Duclos article came many months before the bombs were dropped, and then proceeds to ignore the *effect* of the bomb on Soviet leaders. All he adds is a flat assertion that the critics are "not convincing" in their argument that "the bomb was dropped less to defeat Japan than to intimidate Russia" (which is a strained interpretation of what they have said). That is not even to the point, for one could agree that the bomb was dropped only to finish the Japanese and still insist that it had a powerful effect on Soviet thought and action in connection with its future relations with the United States.

The argument could be made, of course, that only a Russia gone paranoid would have been upset by the American act. The issue of psychotic behavior might better be raised about the

Americans. It could also be maintained that the United States had no responsibility for the effects of the bomb on Soviet leaders because the motive in using it was not anti-Soviet. That is about like saying that a man who constantly interferes in the affairs of his neighbors, and who suddenly starts using a 40-millimeter cannon to kill cats in his back yard, bears no responsibility for the neighbors' skepticism about his good intentions. Schlesinger is fully warranted in making a careful examination of the period before the bomb, but he has no justification for so nearly ignoring the role of the bomb in the origins of the cold war.

Finally, there is the question of the relevance and appropriateness of the American response to the Soviet policy of consolidation in Eastern Europe, and the related call for non-Russian Communists to reassert their identity and policies. The answer, put simply and directly, is that the increasingly militarized holy war mounted by American leaders was grossly irrelevant to the situation and highly conducive to producing problems that were more dangerous than those the policy was supposed to resolve.

The fashion of the moment among those who are nervous in the service of the Establishment is to wring one's hands and explain that George F. Kennan did not mean what he wrote in his famous "Long Letter," first filed as a dispatch to the State Department and then printed as the X article in *Foreign Affairs.* Poor Kennan, the argument seems to be, the one time he left his style in the inkwell was unfortunately the time he needed it most.

It is a ludicrous argument. In the first place, Kennan had ample opportunity to revise the document before it was declassified and published. Furthermore, style is an expression of thought, and the intransigent and quasi-military metaphors of the article do accurately express Kennan's deep, abiding and militant anti-communism. In addition, nothing prevented him from immediately revising and clarifying the article if people were getting an erroneous impression of his ideas from an accurate reading of his language; and nothing prevented him from resigning in urgent protest against the rapid emotional militarization of his strategy. Finally, those liberals who enlisted in the cold war had as much to do with that implementation of his policy as did the conservatives. The truth is that Sen. Robert A. Taft made a far more courageous and public fight to prevent that from happening than did either Kennan or those liberals who now wring their hands about the state of the nation and the dangers of the Vietnamese War. And so did the radicals who are now far stronger than they were in 1945, 1946 and 1947—or even 1948.

It is nevertheless true that the contemporary trauma of Establishment liberals is very real. They have come to recognize, or at least sense, the dangerous consequences of American universalism and the global interventionism that it produces. But they cannot wrench themselves free of the false syllogism by which they equate universal interventionism with internationalism, and they cannot tune out the siren call to save the world. They are still practicing the non-intellectualism (and worse) of pinning the label "isolationist" on anyone who has the temerity to point out that universalism is an extremely dangerous *reductio ad absurdum* of internationalism.

Richard H. Rovere spoke to these points in *The New Yorker* of October 28, where he supplied further documentation of the nervousness within the Establishment. In some respects, at any rate, he speaks more directly and candidly about the issues than does Schlesinger. Thus he says that the war in Vietnam is "an application of established policy that has miscarried so dreadfully that we must begin examining not just the case at hand but the whole works."

He also acknowledges the relationship between foreign aid given within that framework and the rise of anti-Americanism and wars. And he bluntly admits that American democracy "is in many ways a fraud." Most important, Rovere speaks directly to the necessity of acting now to change American attitudes and policies before the mistakes of the past lead to very serious disruption and disaffection.

Unless the liberals abandon universalism, they face the serious possibility of being overpowered by the conservatives inside the Establishment at the same time that they are being shunted aside by the radicals in the society at large. One is reluctant to conclude, once and for all, that Schlesinger has allowed his archaic interpretation of American history to blind him to the essential truth that his beloved Vital Center retains its vitality only as it moves left.

That estimate is difficult to accept because of his great intelligence, but it is even more painful to accept because it means that the liberals are becoming mere role players in a Greek tragedy rather than sustaining their activities as protagonists in the Christian tragedy. If that is the case, it could very well mean that America can renounce universalist interventionism only as it is forced to do so.

The Nation
(November 13, 1967)

An American

Socialist

Community?

In moving about the country a good bit the last four years —from the campuses to the metropolis and through the provinces—I have repeatedly been struck by two things. The first is the accuracy of Harold Cruse's observation: "Americans generally have no agreement on who they are, what they are, or how they got to be what they are. . . . All Americans are involved in an identity crisis." The second is that the New Left, or "the movement" as the jargon has it, is not doing very much that is effective in dealing with that dangerous but potentially creative situation.

There is no persuasive evidence that the movement is in the process of becoming a social movement of the kind that can generate and push through major reforms on a continuing basis—let alone institute structural changes—in American society. Whatever the victories of the New Left, there are a good many indications that the activities of the movement are increasing the willingness within the establishment to reform and rationalize the corporate system according to its own adaptation of our criticisms. And some actions of the New Left are creating growing support for repressive policies (as contrasted with suppression in specific crises).

There are two orthodox comments at this point. One maintains that the revolution is being made by people doing their own thing: that if you leave the system it will collapse. But if that is correct, then we either collapse with it or confront the necessity of a new ruthlessness to build the replacement. The other argument maintains that establishment reforms will not —even cannot—go far enough quickly enough to avert a crisis that will open the way for the movement. I do not rule out that possibility, but I do not think it is probable because the analysis overlooks, or discounts, several major considerations:

1. While American society is sick, it is not sick to the verge of rolling over dead, or even to the point that a good push will topple it into History. The will to maintain the system is real and visible and consequential.

2. An establishment trying to reform itself will, for a long period, hold the loyalty of even the least repressive groups in society. This is particularly true so long as the New Left makes no discriminations among other groups in society, makes no sustained effort to involve them as participating equals in a non-elitist movement, and offers nothing to attract them into such a venture.

3. Things may get worse as a short-run prelude to getting better, but they may instead get worse for an indefinite period.

There simply cannot be an era of radical reform, or structural change, without a living conception of community and a clearly developed approach to alternatives to meet the needs of America in an equitable and effective manner. Much of the New Left is operating—consciously or unconsciously— under the illusion that the United States today is comparable to England between 1660 and 1688, France in 1789, Russia in 1917, or one of the many poor and non-industrial countries of the contemporary world. It has become fashionable to call this the New Romanticism, and defend it with orthodox irrationality. It would be better, for the honor of true Romanticism, and for our own well-being (to say nothing of the millions of poor and powerless), to call it ignorance at best—innocent or arrogantly self-righteous as warranted by the specific case—and at worst the most insidious kind of anti-intellectualism.

It flatly will not do, in the last third of the twentieth century, to pretend that we in the United States can indulge ourselves in an indefinite period of willy-nilly-working-out-of-a-new-order. Nor is it meaningful to talk about anarchy or self-contained communes of mutually compatible couples, or of the underground that can provide you with subsistence for a year. There is no more justification for putting people off in that fashion than there is for putting people down. Yet the movement is doing a good deal of both.

Eldridge Cleaver heated up the soul on the issue of goals, with these words: "We start with the premise that every man, woman and child on the face of the earth deserves the very highest standard of living that human knowledge and technology is capable of providing. Period. No more than that, no less than that." That is not really enough, or at least it is seriously open to the charge of mistaking economism for socialism (or whatever other name for the new order you prefer), but it is more than sufficient to end the explicit and implicit nonsense of the movement that mundane matters will take care of themselves come the revolution. They do not now, which is one of our criticisms, and they will not do so even ten years after the revolution if we do not see to it ourselves.

In one of his classic throw-away lines, Schumpeter once remarked that socialism was a post-economic problem. In a strict sense that is true. Socialism is, or at any rate should be, about the nature and functioning of a community, rather than about the failings of the capitalist system. And a community is not created, let alone maintained, by everyone simply doing his own thing. Adam Smith wrote that prescription for heaven on earth in 1776, and after 200 years we ought to be able to recognize the limitations. But Schumpeter's arrow did not hit the center of the bull's-eye. For Marx accurately noted that while capitalism created the means for solving the economic problem it could not organize and use those powers to fulfill its avowed reason for being.

Cleaver, Schumpeter, and Marx. All three were correct. Still are correct. Cleaver's proposition, explicitly expanded to include intellectual, cultural, and interpersonal matters, can stand as the "no-less-than-that" of an American radicalism. But to get on with realizing that objective we have to deal with the implications of Schumpeter's point about socialism. We have, that is, to speak to the nature of a new economy and to the philosophic, physiological, and psychic foundations for a man who is not, as Adam Smith maintained, defined by his propensity to barter and trade in the marketplace. The Left, Old or New, has yet to answer either question.

It is no longer relevant to prove that socialists can operate (albeit more fairly and more efficiently) the centralized and consolidated economic system created by mature capitalism. That would have been very helpful if we had come to power between 1894 and 1914, but the challenge today is to maintain and increase productivity while breaking the Leviathan into community-sized elements. And while the hippies have blasted through some of the walls that capitalism erected around true humanism, they are very largely operating as a self-defined interest group in the classic sense of nineteenth-century capitalism. It is no answer to Smith to define individualism in Freudian terms, or some other human propensity.

So we come down to Marx. It is so obvious as to be the

cliché of the era: capitalism has demonstrated a congenital inca-
pacity to use its literally fantastic powers and achievements to
enable untold members of the lower and middle classes—and
even many in the upper class—to live as human beings. But
Marx also said that the purpose and the responsibility of the
movement is twofold: to extend, deepen, and focus the awareness of that failure, and to organize the people of the society to
use the powers created by mature capitalism in humane and
creative ways.

So far there is less irrelevant about Marx than there is pa-
rochial about the movement. The issues here are not the tactics
of disruption, provocation, and violence. At least not for many
(including myself) who lack the training or guts to be pacifists,
or feel morally queasy about righteously provoking the worst in
other men we know are not prepared to transcend their prejudices in a moment of crisis, or consider non-violent revolution as
a strategy appropriate only for an established socialist society. I
do not think it is possible—even under the best of circumstances
—to move from mature capitalism to established socialism without considerable disruption and some amount of blood.

The central matter, however, concerns when—in what
context and for what purposes—we provoke and disrupt and
spill blood. I think there has been a good deal of bloodletting
that has not produced any *sustained* deepening and focusing of
radical consciousness. It has been my observation, as well as experience, that six months of quiet work in the dormitories, or of
going up to the doorbell for a half-hour conversation, has deeper
and more lasting consequences than the occupation of a building or the provocation of a bust. It was, after all, the teach-ins
rather than the marches that played the major role in generat-
ing the now widespread opposition to the Vietnam War.

And of course that brings us to the nut-crackers: we do not have a meaningful conception of what it is to be an American. We have instead a collection of disjointed notes on what it does not mean, and a vague assertion that all things will be beautiful and lovely come the revolution.

We have never realized that in America the only way to deepen and focus the radical social consciousness of the large numbers of women and men of our time is to tell them in concrete and specific terms how their lives can be richer and more purposeful. There is simply not any time or justification for us to be vague like Marx, technocratically optimistic like Lenin, romantically irresponsible like Trotsky, or latter-day agrarians like Mao and Castro.

If we are going to have a social movement, we will have to build it on the basis of a workable answer to the eminently fair demand from our potential constituency among the lower and middle classes: explain how will socialism be any better than a capitalism without the Vietnam War and with a continuing (and improving) pattern of permissive welfarism. We have, that is, to convince those vast numbers of Americans that we can take the productive apparatus of mature capitalism and reorganize it for their benefit. That means erasing two primary lines in their image of the Left. One is the line that connects radical structural change with things getting worse than they are. The other line connects radicalism with radicals doing their own things at the expense of large numbers of other people.

I am very skeptical that we can meet the challenge through a strategy based on the declining age of the majority of the population; at least not as it is now being attempted by various campus groups. For one thing, most Americans do not define their hopes for a better society in terms of university reform. To use the jargon, that is not relevant to them. Frankly, I sympathize with that for, while campus reform is important to me personally in the short-run and to me as a socialist in the long-run, it is not nearly as central as building an inclusive social movement capable of forcing the Establishment to give large chunks of ground on primary issues affecting the majority of my fellow citizens. Secondly, as presently organized and conducted, the campus wing of the movement is not making any serious reach to its own constituency—witness the rush of student activists to McCarthy and Kennedy.

I think another strategy warrants serious consideration. It has three parts.

1. We must use the campus as a base for reaching the community. This means, in connection with campus action, preparing the ground in the city and the state for the ultimate confrontations on campus. It means, in the broader sense, using the campus as what it is—a generator of ideas—and as a center of serious intellectual activity dealing with the problems of the general society. A radical movement that weakens, or even destroys, the university to gain secondary and symptomatic reforms is not demonstrating a convincing case for general leadership of the society.

2. We must respond to legitimate demands for clear and convincing proposals for the new American community. If we cannot, then we are irrelevant. Evasion of these demands is at best a disingenuous way of putting people down; it is at worst hard evidence of intellectual incompetence. We ought to be able to learn from Russia and China that the lack of clear ideas and programs can lead to all kinds of serious moral and practical troubles.

3. We must start dealing with the large numbers of Ameri-

cans, who have been misled or brutalized as human beings rather than as racists and boobs to be jammed up against the wall. For the self-righteous arrogance in the movement is at least as dangerous to its future as the establishment.

Liberation
(June 1969)

Notes

Brooks Adams and American Expansion

1. H. Adams, *The Education of Henry Adams. An Autobiography* (Boston, 1918), 337–339; compare H. Adams to E. Cameron of August 8, 1893, with same to same of September 15, 1893, *Letters of Henry Adams. Volume II, 1892–1918*, edited by W. C. Ford (Boston, 1938, hereafter cited as *LHA*), 31, 33; B. Adams, "The Heritage of Henry Adams," in H. Adams, *The Degradation of the Democratic Dogma. With an Introduction by Brooks Adams* (New York, 1919), 88–90; B. Adams, *The Law of Civilization* (London, 1895; New York, 1896; New York, 1942, with C. A. Beard's suggestive essay as "Introduction." Citations from 1896 ed. unless otherwise noted).

2. C. Beard, "Introduction," *The Law*, 24, 28.

3. H. Adams, *Education*, 360; H. Adams to B. Adams, June 5, 1895, *LHA*, 69–70; same to same, October 7, 1900, *Henry Adams and His Friends. A Collection of His Unpublished Letters,* compiled by H. D. Cater (Boston, 1947, hereafter cited as *HAF*), 499.

4. B. Adams, *The Law*, viii–xi.

5. B. Adams, *The Law*, vii, xi; H. Adams to B. Adams, June 5, 1895, *LHA*, 69–70; same to same, September [?], 1895, *LHA*, 82–84; same to same, December 27, 1895, *HAF*, 352–353; same to same, January 3, 1896, *HAF*, 354–355; same to same, April 2, 1898, *LHA*, 162–163; H. Adams to E. Cameron, August 21, 1905, *LHA*, 460.

6. B. Adams, *The Law*, 324–325; H. Adams to B. Adams, June 5, 1895, *LHA*, 69–70; H. Adams to Charles F. Gaskell, June 20,

1895, *LHA,* 72; H. Adams to B. Adams, February 18, 1896, *LHA,* 100; H. Adams to C. F. Gaskell, January 7, 1897, *LHA,* 119.

7. H. Adams to B. Adams, December 27, 1895, *HAF,* 353.

8. H. Adams to B. Adams, April 2, 1898, *LHA,* 162–163.

9. B. Adams, "Commercial Future: New Struggle for Life Among Nations," *Fortnightly Review,* LXXI (New Series 65, February, 1899), 274–283. This article became Chapter II of *America's Economic Supremacy* (New York, 1900, 1947); H. Adams to B. Adams, August 20, 1899, *HAF,* 472–473.

10. H. D. Cater, "Preface," *HAF,* lxxxiii, citing Mrs. Winthrop Chandler as his source; H. Adams to B. Adams, January 3, 1896, *HAF,* 354–355; same to same, January 24, 1896, *HAF,* 356–357; H. Adams to E. Cameron, February 26, 1900, *LHA,* 270, and H. Adams to C. F. Gaskell, December 20, 1895, *LHA,* 91, which call attention to Richard Olney's response to *The Law.*

11. H. Adams to Hay, June 18, 1892, November 7, 12, 1892, all in *LHA,* 11–12, 24–26; H. Adams to Hay, December 21, 1891, *HAF,* 259–260; same to same October 18, 1893, *HAF,* 291–294; same to same, January 11, 1898, 143–144.

12. See, as representative, H. Adams to Hay, August 24, 1896, July 28, 1896, October 23, 1896, and October 28, 1896, all in *HAF,* 379, 390–393; and same to same of September 12, 1897, January 11, 1898, May 5, 1898, May 17, 1898, May 26, 1898, May 31, 1899, and December 15, 1899, all in *LHA,* 131–132, 143–145, 175–176, 179–181, 183–184, 230–232, 249–250.

13. H. Adams to Hay, January 4, 1894, *HAF,* 303; H. Adams to Rockhill, October 31, 1898, *HAF,* 451; H. Adams to B. Adams, February 7, 1900, *LHA,* 264.

14. H. Adams to B. Adams, April 2, 1898, *HAF,* 430–431; H. Adams to E. Cameron, April 10, 1898, *LHA,* 165; H. Adams to B. Adams, May 6, 1900, *HAF,* 461–462.

15. H. Adams to Rockhill, August 24, 1898, *LHA,* 187; the maneuvers that secured Rockhill's return can be followed in *HAF,* 452–460; and *LHA,* 207, 214, 218.

16. H. Adams to C. Gaskell, January 23, 1896, October 4, 1898, *LHA,* 93–94, 187; H. Adams to E. Cameron, November 15, 1898,

November 21, 1898, February 26, 1900, April 6, 1902, all in *LHA,* 189, 190, 269, 394.

17. H. Adams to Hay, June 26, 1900, Hay to Adams, July 8, 1900, H. Adams to Hay, September 13, 1900, H. Adams to Hay, December 16, 1900, H. Adams to E. Cameron, February 18, 1901, H. Adams to E. Cameron, March 18, 1901, H. Adams to Cecil Spring Rice, February 8, 1901, all in *LHA,* 289–290, 292, 296–297, 305–308, 315, 316–317, 321–322, and note 10 above.

18. On British policy see J. Chamberlain to Lord Arthur Balfour, February 3, 1898: B. E. C. Dugdale, *Arthur James Balfour* (2 vols., New York, 1936), I, 252–253; Hay's response to this proposal in Hay to Lodge, May 25, 1898: W. R. Thayer, *The Life and Letters of John Hay* (2 vols., Boston, 1915), II, 168, and Hay to C—S—H—, October 29, 1900, "Letters and Diaries of John Hay" (3 vols., Washington, 1908), III, 199; on the influence of Lord Charles Beresford and Alfred E. Hippisley see A. W. Griswold, *The Far Eastern Policy of the United States* (New York, 1938), 48–49, 62–64.

19. C. Denby to R. Olney, February 25, 1895: E. H. Zabriskie, *American-Russian Rivalry in the Far East, 1895–1914* (Philadelphia, 1946), 33; B. A. Romanov, *Rossia v Manchzhurii, 1892–1906* (Moscow, 1928), 102–103; C. Cary, *China's Present and Prospective Railways* (New York, 1899), 14–17.

20. A. Vagts, *Deutschland und die Vereinigten Staaten in der Weltpolitik* (2 vols., New York, 1935), II, 1046–1047, 1040–1058; Griswold, *Far Eastern Policy,* 60, note 4.

21. Denby to Sherman, April 2, 1897: Vagts, *Weltpolitik,* II, 995–996; others pointed out that economic possibilities in Russia were far more important than St. Petersburg's threat to American trade in Manchuria, *Foreign Relations, 1899* (Washington, 1901), 594–599; Vagts, *Weltpolitik,* II, 1046–1047.

22. Adee to Tower, March 8, 1899: Vagts, *Weltpolitik,* II, 1047.

23. B. Adams, "John Hay," *McClure's Magazine,* XX (June, 1902), 180; and see T. Dennett, *John Hay. From Poetry to Politics* (New York, 1933), 289, where Dennett points out that Henry Adams may well have exercised such a critical influence. Dennett seems to have missed the fact that it was Brooks, not Henry, who developed the policy.

24. H. Adams to B. Adams, April 29, 1901, *LHA,* 330.

25. H. Adams to B. Adams, February 8, 1901, same to same, May 7, 1901, *HAF,* 504, 507–509.

26. H. Adams to E. Cameron, April 6, 1902, *LHA,* 383; H. Adams to B. Adams, May 7, 1901, same to same, May 2, 1903, same to same, March 4, 1900, all in *HAF,* 508, 545, 487.

27. B. Adams, "The Heritage of Henry Adams," *Degradation,* 35.

28. *The Letters and Friendships of Sir Cecil Spring Rice. A Record,* compiled by S. Gwynn (2 vols., Boston, 1929), I, 52.

29. *Selections From the Correspondence of Theodore Roosevelt and Henry Cabot Lodge, 1884–1918,* edited by H. C. Lodge (2 vols., New York, 1925), I, 218, 239.

30. T. Roosevelt, "The Law of Civilization and Decay," *The Forum,* XXII (January, 1897), 575, 578, 579, 587; T. Roosevelt to Sir A. Balfour, March 5, 1908: J. B. Bishop, *Theodore Roosevelt and His Time* (2 vols., New York, 1920), II, 107.

31. H. Adams to E. Cameron, February 23, 1902, *LHA,* 374; T. Roosevelt to Mahan, March 18, 1901: H. F. Pringle, *Theodore Roosevelt* (New York, 1931), 374, 171.

32. B. Adams to T. Roosevelt, February 25, 1896, and April 26, 1896: M. Josephson, *The President Makers, 1896–1919* (New York, 1940), 27, 60–61; and see Beard's "Introduction," *The Law* (1942).

33. T. Roosevelt, Speech at the Naval War College, June 2, 1897: *Works. National Edition* (20 vols., New York, 1925), XIV, 182–199; T. Roosevelt to Hay, June 17, 1899: Josephson, *President Makers,* 98.

34. B. Adams, *America's Economic Supremacy* (New York, 1947), 63, 78, 132, 96, 98, 151, 153, 155, 157, 179, 193, 170, 194; Henry advised Brooks that the reviews were "lumps of drivel," H. Adams to B. Adams, February 8, 1901, *HAF,* 504. Prior to the appearance of the volume, Brooks also published another excerpt, "Russia's Interest in China," *Atlantic,* LXXXVI (September, 1900), 309–317.

35. T. Roosevelt, "Expansion and Peace," *The Independent* (December 21, 1899); *The Strenuous Life* (New York, 1904), 23–26; and Adams, *Supremacy,* 179.

36. T. Roosevelt, "Message of the President of the United States to the First Session of the Fifty-Seventh Congress, December 3, 1901," *Congressional Record,* 57th Congress, 1 Session (Washington, 1901), XXXV, 82–83, 84, 86, 88, 89, 92; for passages of striking similarity written by Brooks Adams at an earlier date see "Russia's Interest in China," *Atlantic,* LXXXVI (September, 1900), 310, 317; "The New Industrial Revolution," *Atlantic,* LXXXVII (February, 1901), 165; "Reciprocity or the Alternative," *Atlantic,* LXXXVIII (1901), 154, 155; *Supremacy,* 82, 103, 105, 131–132, 192, 194; and see Roosevelt to B. Adams, September 27, 1901, *The Letters of Theodore Roosevelt,* edited by E. E. Morison (Cambridge, 1951), III, 152–153.

37. H. Adams to B. Adams, April 21, 1902, *HAF,* 524–525.

38. H. C. Lodge, "Some Impressions of Russia," *Scribner's Magazine,* XXXI (1902), 571; J. P. Dolliver, "Significance of the Anglo-Japanese Alliance," *North American Review,* CLXXIV (1901–1902), 594.

39. B. Adams, *Supremacy,* 194.

40. Pringle, *Roosevelt,* 372; T. Roosevelt to L. C. Griscom, July 27, 1905: T. Dennett, *Roosevelt and the Russo-Japanese War* (New York, 1925), 241; B. Adams, *Supremacy,* 179; T. Roosevelt to Hay, July 18, 1903: A. L. P. Dennis, *Adventures in American Diplomacy, 1896–1906* (New York, 1928), 359.

41. T. Roosevelt, conversation with Speck von Sternberg, March 21, 1904: *Die Grosse Politik der Europäischen Kabinette, 1871–1914* (Berlin, 1921–1927), XIX, I, No. 5992; L. Griscom, *Diplomatically Speaking* (New York, 1940), 244–245; Zabriskie, *Rivalry,* 107.

42. T. Roosevelt to Sir G. Trevelyan, March 9, 1905; Pringle, *Roosevelt,* 380; T. Roosevelt to Spring Rice, December 27, 1904; Dennett, *Roosevelt,* 47–50.

43. B. Adams, *Supremacy,* 191; T. Roosevelt to G. von L. Meyer, July 7, 1905; Bishop, *Roosevelt,* I, 399–400.

44. H. Adams to E. Cameron, February 7, 1904, January 10, 1904, August 29, 1905, all in *LHA,* 423, 419, 461.

45. T. Roosevelt to Meyer, July 7, 1905: Bishop, *Roosevelt,* I, 399–400.

46. H. Adams to E. Cameron, August 21, 1905, *LHA*, 460.

47. H. Adams to E. Cameron, August 21, 1905, September 3, 1905, *LHA*, 460, 462.

48. H. Adams to B. Adams, September 20, 1910, *LHA*, 549.

49. Lodge, *Correspondence*, II, 135; T. Roosevelt, "Message of December 3, 1901," *Cong. Record*, 57 Cong., 1 Ses., XXXV, 1, 89; T. Roosevelt to Sir G. Trevelyan: Bishop, *Roosevelt*, II, 249–250.

50. B. Adams, "A Problem in Civilization," *Atlantic*, CVI (July, 1910), 26–32; "The Collapse of Capitalistic Government," *Atlantic*, CXI (April, 1913), 433–443; "The American Democratic Ideal," *Yale Review*, V (January, 1916), 225–233; T. Roosevelt to William Howard Taft, December 12, 1910; Griswold, *Far Eastern Policy*, 132.

51. H. Adams to E. Cameron, September 13, 1912, *LHA*, 603.

52. H. Adams to B. Adams, January 30, 1910, *LHA*, 533.

American Intervention in Russia,

1917–1920

1. Miles to Lansing, April 15, 1919: *National Archives of the United States of America*, Record Group 59, Decimal File No. 861.77/791½. These documents will hereafter be cited by file number alone, save in instances where another Record Group is involved.

2. Summers to Polk, November 2, 1917: 861.00/634½.

3. Francis to Lansing, April 15 and 29, 1918: 814.142/3200, 861.00/1731.

4. The autobiographical remark by Francis is quoted from a personal letter by C. D. Young, "David Roland Francis—American in Russia" (unpublished master's thesis, University of Wisconsin, 1944), 14. Other material on Francis can be found in his manuscript papers, Missouri Historical Society; and in his personal file in the National Archives. Information on the role of trade expansion in his appointment comes from *The Papers of Woodrow Wilson*, Library of Congress; *The New York Times*, February 17, 19, 1916; the *St. Louis Globe-Democrat*, February 23, 1916; National Foreign Trade Convention, *Proceed-*

ings, 1915 (New York: N.F.T.C., 1916), 169; Francis to Wilson, April 8, 1916, and Lansing to Francis, April 10, 1916, both filed as 711.612½.

5. *The Papers of Paul S. Reinsch,* Manuscript Division, Wisconsin State Historical Society, Madison, Wisconsin, contain much interesting and some revealing information previously unused by students of the subject. Reinsch's ideas on American expansion emerge quite clearly in the following published volumes: *World Politics at the End of the Nineteenth Century* (New York: Macmillan, 1904), 310–311, 312, 315; *Colonial Administration* (New York: Macmillan, 1912), 3–4, 7; and *An American Diplomat in China* (Garden City: Doubleday, Page and Co., 1922), xii, 106, 217, 338, 354–355.

6. Unlike Reinsch, Roland Morris was not an intense, professional student of world affairs. His appointment as Ambassador to Japan was more the result of his Princeton associations, his active role in swinging the Democratic Party of Pennsylvania to Wilson, and his personal loyalty to the President. He did have some interest in and knowledge of the area. But he was talented and able, and his performance improved steadily. His major role in intervention came after the decision to commit troops to Siberia had been made, and took the form of making special investigations of anti-Bolshevik forces at the request of Wilson.

7. E. N. Smith to Lansing, December 13, 1917, and Lansing to Smith, December 20, 1917, both in *The Papers of Robert Lansing,* Manuscripts Division, Library of Congress.

8. Lansing to Wilson, March 1, 1915: 793.94/240.

9. Wilson to Lansing, February 7, 1917; Lansing to Wilson, February 7, 1917; Wilson to Lansing, February 9, 1917: all documents filed as 763.72/3261½.

10. These and many of the following quotations come from copies of the President's speeches and articles filed in the *Wilson Mss.* Hereafter they will be cited by date only. These specific remarks come from addresses on May 23, January 3, and August 7, 1912.

11. Wilson, speech of May 23, 1912.

12. Wilson, speeches of September 4 and 9, 1912; also see his remarks of March 4, 1913.

13. Here see Wilson, "The Reconstruction of the Southern States,"

originally published in January 1901 and reprinted in *The Public Papers of Woodrow Wilson*, ed. by R. S. Baker and W. Dodd (New York: Harper and Bros., 6 vols., 1925–1927), I: 389, 393–395; and Wilson, *A History of the American People* (New York: Harper and Bros., 5 vols., 1902), V: 265, 274–275, 292, and 294–296.

14. Wilson, *Public Papers*, I:389.

15. Wilson, speech of May 23, 1912.

16. Wilson, speech of August 7, 1912.

17. Wilson, remarks of December 14, 1914: *Papers Relating to Foreign Relations of the United States, 1914* (Washington: Government Printing Office, 1924), 14. These volumes are hereafter cited as *FR*.

18. Wilson, as quoted by A. S. Link, *Wilson the Diplomatist* (Baltimore: Johns Hopkins Press, 1957), 15.

19. Wilson, public statement of March 11, 1913: *Wilson Mss.*

20. Wilson to W. B. Hale, November 16, 1913: *Wilson Mss.*

21. Wilson, remarks as printed in an interview with S. G. Blythe published as, "Mexico: The Record of a Conversation with President Wilson," *Saturday Evening Post,* Vol. CLXXXVI (May 23, 1914), 4.

22. Wilson to Tyrrell, November 22, 1913: *Wilson Mss.*

23. Wilson, Circular Statement to American Representatives Abroad, March 18, 1913: 893.51/1356a; and also see the remarks by Bryan, after-dinner speech of January 26, 1914, before the American Asiatic Association, reported in the *Journal of the American Asiatic Association*, Vol. XIV (February, 1914), 12.

24. Here see, in sequence: Wilson's memorandum to Japan, March 12/13, 1915: *FR 1915*, 104–111; Wilson to Bryan, February 25, 1915: 793.94/240; and Wilson to Bryan, April 14, 1915: 793-94/294½.

25. On these points first consult H. S. Notter, *The Origins of the Foreign Policy of Woodrow Wilson* (Baltimore: Johns Hopkins Press, 1937), 542–543, 81–82, 278; then Wilson's speeches of September, 1908, and October, 1909, *Public Papers,* II: 54–55, 140–141; and finally his speeches of September 8, 1908, and May 23, 1912, in *Wilson Mss.*

26. Lansing, "Private Confidential Memorandum on the Russian Situation and the Root Mission, August 9, 1917:" *Lansing Mss.*

27. "Memorandum on Strategy of the Present War. Prepared at the Army War College, October 17, 1917 . . . Appendix II: Possible Line of Action Through Russia:" *Lansing Mss.*

28. Lansing to Baker, November 7, 1917: *Lansing Mss.*

29. *The New York Times,* November 10, 1917.

30. *Ibid.,* November 17, 1917.

31. *Ibid.,* November 12, 1917.

32. D. R. Francis, *Russia From the American Embassy, April, 1916–November, 1918* (New York: Scribners, 1921), 173–177.

33. Summers to Lansing, November 26, 1917: 816.00/736.

34. *War Memoirs of David Lloyd George* (London: Nicholson and Watson, 6 vols., 1936), V:2565.

35. House to Wilson, November 28, 1917: *Wilson Mss.*

36. Lansing to Francis, December 1, 1917: 861.00/1008a.

37. *War Memoirs of Robert Lansing* (New York: Bobbs-Merrill, 1935), 331, 339–343. See also the relevant material in the *Lansing* and *Wilson Mss.*

38. *War Memoirs of Lansing,* 345; R. S. Baker, *Woodrow Wilson Life and Letters* (Garden City: Doubleday, Doran, and Co., 8 vols., 1937–1938), II:391.

39. Lansing to Francis, December 6, 1917: 861.00/796a.

40. Wilson, War Message of December 4, 1917: *Wilson Mss.*

41. *The New Democracy: Presidential Messages, Addresses, and Other Papers (1913–1917) by Woodrow Wilson,* ed. by R. S. Baker and W. Dodd (New York: Harper and Bros., 2 vols., 1926), II:2.

42. Colcord to Wilson, December 6, 1917; and Wilson to Colcord, December 6, 1917: *Wilson Mss.*

43. Moser to Reinsch, November 17, 1917: 861.00/963.

44. Reinsch to Lansing, December 6, 1917; and Lansing to Reinsch, December 8, 1917, both filed as 861.00/769.

45. Reinsch to Lansing, December 15, 1917: 861.00/822; and on later developments see J. A. White, *The Siberian Intervention* (Princeton: Princeton University Press, 1950).

46. Lansing, "Memorandum on the Russian Situation, December 7, 1917:" *Lansing Mss.*

47. Summers to Lansing, December 6, 1917: 763.72 / 8033.

48. Lansing to Wilson, December 10, 1917 (enclosing Summers' dispatch of December 6): 861.00 / 807a.

49. Lansing, Desk Diary entry of December 12, 1917: *Lansing Mss.*

50. Lansing, *Ibid.;* and McAdoo to Lansing, December 12, 1917: 861.00 / 804d.

51. Lansing to Wilson, December 12, 1917, enclosing Lansing to Poole (sent December 13, 1917 as 763.72 / 820a); and Wilson to Lansing, December 12, 1917: both filed as 861.00 / 804d.

52. Lansing to Crosby, Confidential, December 12, 1917: 861.00 / 804d.

53. G. F. Kennan, *Russia Leaves the War* (Princeton: Princeton University Press, 1956), 178.

54. Lansing to Crosby, Confidential, December 12, 1917: 861.00 / 804d.

55. Judson to War College Staff, December 17, 1917: Record Group 120, File No. 10220-D-58; and see Lansing's Desk Diary entries for this period.

56. See below for the later assertion of a double game by Francis. I doubt that it is possible to determine absolutely what precisely was in the mind of Francis at this juncture. I am inclined to the conclusion, however, that he was in spite of his prejudices and preferences being influenced by the events and by the interpretation of those developments offered by Robins and Judson.

57. Francis to Lansing, December 24, 1917: 861.00 / 864.

58. Lansing, Desk Diary entry of December 26, 1917: *Lansing Mss.*

59. Lansing, "Memorandum of an Interview with Japanese Ambassador Sato, December 27, 1917:" 861.00 / 877½.

60. Summers to Lansing, December 29, 1917: 861.00 / 894; and Caldwell to Lansing, January 1, 1918 (sent on to Wilson): *Wilson Mss.*

61. Francis to Lansing, December 31, 1917: *Lansing Mss.*

62. Miles, "Memorandum for the Secretary of State, January 1, 1918:" 861.00 / 935½.

63. Wilson to Lansing, January 1, 1918: 861.00/935½.

64. Wilson to Lansing, January 20, 1918: *Lansing Mss.;* Lansing to Daniels, January 3, 1918; and Lansing to Wilson, January 2, 1918, both in *Wilson Mss.*

65. A letter from William Bullitt, enclosing a "Memorandum on the Momentary Hostility of the Bolsheviki . . . [to the] German Government, January 3, 1918" (763.72119/1269½), which suggested the possibility of some kind of short-run collaboration with the Bolsheviks, created a flurry of activity inside the Department. See Phillips to Lansing, January 4, 1918: 763.72119/1269½. It should be kept in mind, however, that Bullitt reaped the labors of Judson and Robins, whose argument along similar lines had been reaching the Departments of State and War, and the White House, for approximately six weeks. Lansing was correct in worrying about Bullitt in terms of an increasing influence of the other men.

66. Lansing, Desk Diary entry of January 4, 1918: *Lansing Mss.*

67. C. Seymour (ed.), *The Intimate Papers of Colonel House* (New York: Houghton Mifflin Co., 4 Vols., 1928), III: 331, Walling's article in *The New York Times,* January 14, 1918. Kennan's handling of this matter of the anti-Bolshevik nature of Wilson's 14 Point Speech contains some of the tightest and best analysis he has offered as an historian.

68. Lansing to Jusserand, January 16, 1918: 861.00/945; Polk to Wilson, January 18, 1918: 861.00/977–998; and Polk to Morris, January 20, 1918 (action dispatch): 861.00/945.

69. Gompers to Wilson, February 9, 1918; Wilson to Gompers, January 21, 1918: *Wilson Mss. The Papers of Samuel Gompers,* Manuscript Division, Wisconsin State Historical Society, Madison, Wisconsin, also contain considerable material on the anti-Bolshevik position taken by Gompers.

70. Wilson to Williams, February 6, 1918: *Wilson Mss.*

71. Other indications of Wilson's struggle with the dilemma can be followed in Page to Lansing, January 15, 1918: *Papers of Ray Stannard Baker,* Library of Congress, a dispatch enclosing a suggestion by Grant Smith (in Denmark) that the United States act as a kind of unofficial agent for the Allies to initiate exploratory talks with the Bol-

sheviks. The reaction to this can be found in Lansing to Wilson, and Wilson's reply, both of January 20, 1918: *Baker Mss.*

72. Lansing to Wilson, February 15, 1918: *Wilson Mss.*

73. Francis to Lansing, February 5 (received the 7th), 1918: 861.00/1064. The disturbed remarks by Miles appear on the dispatch and were sent on up the line. Actually, Francis was also being influenced by American Army Officers Keith and Riggs. Both men concluded that the Bolsheviks were in power to stay, and that the United States should help them resist the Germans. Riggs added, quite accurately, in his report of January 28, 1918, that the Bolsheviks were inclined toward such collaboration with the United States. See also Keith, "Military Report of January 28, 1918:" both filed in Record Group 165:F6497-367.

74. Lansing to Francis, February 14, 1918: 861.00/1064.

75. Lansing, "Memorandum to the British Embassy, February 8, 1918:" 861.00/1097; and Lansing to Page, February 13, 1918: 861.00/1066.

76. Lansing to Page, February 13, 1918: 861.00/1066. In this dispatch Lansing himself emphasized the meaning of the word *now* by explaining that the United States "has not lost hope of a change for the better to be brought about without foreign intervention."

77. Trotsky to Murmansk Soviet, March 1 and 2, 1918: quoted in Strakhovsky, *Origins of American Intervention,* 29, and in his *American Opinion,* 59. Also see Kennan, *Russia Leaves the War,* 491.

78. This material on Sadoul is drawn from sources in the National Archives; and, more recently, from conversations with Harvey Goldberg who has had access to manuscript sources in France. Also see *American-Russian Relations,* 133–135, 140–141.

79. Miles, "Dpt. of State Confidential Periodical Report on Matters Relating to Russia, No. 9, February 19, 1918:" *Lansing Mss.*

80. Lansing's comment is on a copy of the dispatch reporting the French proposal that Phillips sent to Lansing on February 19, 1918: 861.00/1125. Lansing took this document to Wilson for their discussion.

81. Materials as noted in Note 78 above.

82. Francis to Lansing, March 26, 1918: 862.20261/74. See also the dispatches filed by Riggs, some of which are quoted by Strakhovsky, *Origins of American Intervention,* 89, and *American Opinion,* 55.

83. Wilson, Message of March 10, 1918, to the Congress of Soviets: *Wilson Mss.*

84. Also see, on this point, Lansing to Wilson, February 27, 1918: 861.00/1165½ a and b.

85. Lansing to Wilson, February 27, 1918: *Wilson Mss.*

86. Lansing to Page, February 27, 1918: 861.77/307.

87. Lansing to Wilson, February 27, 1918: 861.00/1165½.

88. Sharp to Lansing, February 28, 1918: 861.00/1173; and an even earlier, direct awareness of these matters documented in Lansing to Wilson, February 27, 1918. Also see Jusserand to Lansing, March 12, 1918: 861.00/1676.

89. Lansing to Wilson, February 27, 1918: *Wilson Mss.*

90. Polk to Lansing, in a letter of March 5, 1918, reviewing the events of February 28 and March 1, 1918: 861.00/1246.

91. Reinsch to Lansing, February 21, 1918: 861.00/1138; Lansing to Page, February 24, 1918: 861.00/1136½; Reinsch to Lansing, February 24, 1918: 861.00/1136½; and Summers to Lansing, February 23, 1918: 861.00/1154.

92. Wilson, draft telegram handed Lansing on March 1, 1918: 861.00/1246.

93. Polk to Lansing, March 5, 1918: 861.00/1246.

94. Polk to Lansing, March 15, 1918: 861.00/1285. This is another review of the events of February 27–March 1, 1918, written for Lansing's information.

95. Wilson, Circular of March 5, 1918: *Wilson Mss.* This was sent to Japan as 861.00/1246 at 4 p.m.

96. Long to Reinsch, March 14, 1918: Papers of *Paul S. Reinsch,* Wisconsin State Historical Society, Madison.

97. Lansing, "Memorandum of March 18, 1918:" *Lansing Mss;* and, particularly, Lansing to Wilson, March 19, 1918: *Wilson Mss.* The latter document carries as enclosures a number of telegrams from Knight and others on the scene in Siberia.

98. Lansing to Wilson, March 24, 1918: 861.00/1433½.

99. Wilson to Lansing, March 22, 1918: *Wilson Mss.* The President repeated his judgment when returning Lansing's letter of March 24. Lansing's notation on the document reads as follows: "This was returned to me 3/26/18 by the President who said he quite agreed but did not think the situation yet warranted change of policy." These notations added to various documents by the protagonists seem generally to have been ignored by most students of intervention.

100. Masaryk to Crane, April 10, 1918: *Wilson Mss;* Reinsch to Lansing, April 10, 1918: 861.00/1571; Reinsch to J. V. MacMurray, April 29, 1918: *Reinsch Mss.*

101. "Report of Colonel Speshneff, March 9, 1918"; W. S. Drysdale to Reinsch, March 19, 1918, April 10, 1918; all in *Reinsch Mss.*

102. For example, see Ruggles to War College Staff, April 7, 1918: 861.00/1730½; and his report on April 8, 1918, on his conference with Trotsky of April 8: RG 179: 1240/23. Then consult Francis to Lansing, February 26, 1918.

103. Francis to Lansing, May 11, 1918: *FR, Russia, 1918,* I:526.

104. Lansing to Sharp, April 23, 1918: 861.00/1674.

105. Lansing to Wilson, May 16, 1918: 861.00/1894½; Wilson to Lansing, May 20, 1918: 861.00/1895½.

106. See *American-Russian Relations,* 147–150, 152–153.

107. First consult, on the question of general economic aid, Lansing to Morris, May 22, 1918: 861.00/1819; a dispatch which suggests that the American plan of intervention involved, from an early date, a decision to act unilaterally once the time for action had arrived. This is further borne out by Lansing's response to the request to transport Belgian and Italian troops. In the end, of course, this was the way American intervention was handled. Then see Wilson to Lansing, May 20, 1918 (enclosing Reinsch's dispatch), and Lansing to Wilson, May 21, 1918 (enclosing Miles, "The Military Advance of Semenoff, May 21, 1918"): all in *Wilson Mss.*

108. W. Wiseman to Sir R. Drummond, May 31, 1918: *Papers of Sir William Wiseman,* Yale University Library. This is a long, detailed account of an hour-long conversation with the President.

109. Kennan to Lansing, May 26, and Lansing to Kennan, May 28, 1918: *Lansing Mss.*

110. Page to Lansing, May 28, 1918: 861.00/1901.

111. "Agreement of Allied Ambassadors, May 29, 1918. Confidential:" RG 159:800/1918.

112. Reinsch to Lansing, May 30, 1918: 861.00/1900.

113. Lansing to Francis, June 1, 1918: 861.77/402.

114. Lansing to Page, June 4, 1918: 861.00/1901; and Lansing to Francis, June 4, 1918: 861.00/1955.

115. Long to Lansing, June 7, 1918: 861.00/2008.

116. Lansing to Wilson, June 13, 1918: 861.48/614¾a.

117. Reinsch to Lansing, June 13, 1918: 861.00/2014; Major D. P. Barrows, "Memorandum of April 7, 1918," and especially Drysdale to Reinsch, June 25, 1918: all in *Reinsch Mss.* Also see Moser to Lansing, June 10, 1918: 861.00/1996: Caldwell to Lansing, June 12, 1918: 861.00/2040; same to same, June 14, 1918: 861.00/2021; and Lansing to Morris, July 2, 1918: 861.00/2169.

118. Wilson to Lansing, June 17, 1918: 861.00/2145½; Poole to Lansing, June 12, 1918: 861.00/2053, sent on to Wilson by Lansing, June 19, 1918: 861.00/2053.

119. Wilson to Lansing, June 19, 1918: 861.00/2148½.

120. Wilson to Baker, June 19, 1918 (enclosing a memorandum dated June 17, 1918): *Wilson Mss.*

121. March, "Memorandum" to Baker, June 24, 1918: *Wilson Mss.*

122. Lansing to Wilson, June 23, 1918: *Wilson Mss;* Lansing to Morris, July 2, 1918: 861.00/2168; and Lansing, "Memorandum on the Siberian Situation, July 4, 1918:" *Lansing Mss.*

123. Lansing, "Memorandum of a Conference at the White House in Reference to the Siberian Situation, July 6, 1918:" *Lansing Mss.* Also see Abbott to Wilson, July 10, 1918: *Wilson Mss.*

124. Wilson, Aide-Memoire of July 17, 1918: *Wilson Mss.*

125. Wilson to Lewis, July 24, 1918: *Wilson Mss.*

126. Lansing to Root, October 28, 1918: *Lansing Mss.*

127. Lansing, "Memorandum on Absolutism and Bolshevism, October 26, 1918:" *Lansing Mss.*

128. Lansing to Kennan, "Personal and Secret," February 2, 1920: *Papers of George Kennan,* Library of Congress: Wilson, remarks to the meeting of the Big Five on February 14, 1919: *FR, Paris Peace Conference, 1919* (Washington: Government Printing Office, 1943), III: 1042–1044.

129. Sisson to Creel (drafted by Sisson), sent from Russia as Francis to Lansing, February 19, 1918: 1918 Correspondence, Confidential, Dispatch No. 2388.

130. Lansing, remarks of February 27, 1919: *FR, Paris Peace Conference, 1919,* XI:80.

The Legend of Isolationism in the 1920's

1. F. Bacon, *Novum Organum,* Headlam's translation as revised by C. P. Curtis and F. Greenslet, *The Practical Cogitator* (Boston, Houghton Mifflin Co., 1945), p. 14–16.

2. A. M. Schlesinger, *Paths to the Present* (New York, The Macmillan Co., 1949), p. 69, 201; L. M. Hacker, "American International Relations," in *The United States and Its Place in World Affairs, 1918–1943,* ed. by A. Nevins and L. M. Hacker, (Boston, D. C. Heath and Co., 1943) p. 166; S. F. Bemis, "The Shifting Strategy of American Defense and Diplomacy," in *Essays in History and International Relations in Honor of George Hubbard Blakeslee,* ed. by D. E. Lee and G. E. McReynolds (Worcester, Clark University, 1949), p. 9.

3. In sequence, these quotations come from S. Adler, "The War-Guilt Question and American Disillusionment, 1919–1928," *The Journal of Modern History,* XXIII, NO. 1 (March, 1951), p. 27; A. K. Weinberg, *Manifest Destiny. A Study of Nationalist Expansion in American History* (Baltimore, Johns Hopkins Press, 1935), p. 473; L. M. Hacker and H. S. Zahler, *The United States in the 20th Century* (New York, Appleton-Century-Crofts, Inc., 1952), p. 278, 302; W. Wilson, quoted in Weinberg, *Manifest Destiny,* p. 473; F. D. Roose-

velt, *Foreign Affairs,* VI, No. 4 (July, 1928), p. 577; W. Johnson, *The Battle Against Isolation* (Chicago, Chicago University Press, 1944), p. 132. For similar expressions see S. F. Bemis, *A Diplomatic History of the United States* (3rd ed., New York, Henry Holt and Co., 1950), p. 705; J. D. Hicks, *The American Nation* (Boston, Houghton Mifflin Co., 1949), p. 565; D. Perkins, *The Evolution of American Foreign Policy* (New York, Oxford University Press, 1949), p. 110; and A. Nevins, *America in World Affairs* (London, Oxford University Press, 1941), p. 80.

4. D. F. Fleming, *The United States and World Organization, 1920–1933* (New York, Columbia University Press, 1938), title of Chapter VI.

5. This literature is far too vast to cite, but even a perusal of *The Reader's Guide to Periodical Literature* will indicate the great volume of such material. It is vital to note, however, that the so-called disillusionment writers did not make this mistake—whatever their other errors. They criticized the policies of the time, but documented, in such journals as *The Nation,* the active character of the diplomacy.

6. Quotations, in order, from Weinberg, *Manifest Destiny,* p. 473, 454; H. U. Faulkner, *American Political and Social History* (6th ed., New York, Appleton-Century-Crofts, Inc., 1952) p. 700, 701; J. A. Garraty, *Henry Cabot Lodge. A Biography* (New York, Alfred A. Knopf, 1953), p. 348, 364–65; F. L. Paxton, *American Democracy and the World War. Postwar Years. Normalcy, 1918–1923* (Berkeley, University of California Press, 1948), p. 367. For other examples of this ambiguity see D. Perkins, *The American Approach to Foreign Policy* (Cambridge, Harvard University Press, 1952), p. 26; T. A. Bailey, *A Diplomatic History of the American People* (4th ed., New York, Appleton-Century-Crofts, Inc., 1950), p. 682—where he says that the Harding Administration "retreated into what ex-President Wilson described as 'sullen and selfish isolation' "; H. J. Carman and H. C. Syrett, *A History of the American People* (New York, Alfred A. Knopf, 1952), p. 264–65, and title of Chapter XII; S. E. Morrison and H. S. Commager, *The Growth of the American Republic* (4th ed., New York, Oxford University Press, 1950), Volume II, p. 497; and H. B. Parkes, *The United States of America* (New York, Alfred A. Knopf, 1953).

7. R. W. Van Alstyne, "The Significance of the Mississippi Valley in American Diplomatic History, 1686–1890," *Mississippi Valley Historical Review*, XXXVI, NO. 2 (September, 1949), p. 238; L. L. Leonard, *Elements of American Foreign Policy* (New York, McGraw-Hill Book Co., Inc., 1953), p. 220; among the many others who characterize Lodge in this manner is S. Adler in his recent article on isolation, "Isolationism Since 1914," *The American Scholar*, XXI, NO. 3 (Summer, 1952), p. 340; W. G. Carleton, "Isolationism and the Middle West," *Mississippi Valley Historical Review*, XXXIII, NO. 3 (December, 1946), p. 381–82; C. A. and M. R. Beard, *The Rise of American Civilization* (New Edition. Two Volumes in One. Revised and Enlarged. New York, The Macmillan Co., 1933), p. 681–83; and compare D. Perkins, *The American Approach to Foreign Policy*, p. 26, with D. Perkins, "The Department of State and Public Opinion," Chapter IX in *The Diplomats* 1919–1939, ed. by G. A. Graig and F. Gilbert (Princeton, Princeton University Press, 1953), p. 308. Interestingly enough, both Carleton and Van Alstyne addressed their remarks to meetings of the Mississippi Valley Historical Association, and their articles later appeared as lead articles in the *Review*. On the same program with Van Alstyne, furthermore, was Professor Richard Leopold, whose comments were of a similar nature and whose paper was also printed. This professional audience seems to have ignored their keen suggestions. Professor Weinberg's article, "The Historical Meaning of the American Doctrine of Isolation," *The American Political Science Review*, XXXIV (1940), p. 539–47, offers certain concepts that would go far to resolve the contradictions in his earlier *Manifest Destiny*, but he did not apply the ideas to any later period. H. Feis writes of America's active foreign economic policy in *The Diplomacy of the Dollar, First Era, 1919–1932* (Baltimore, Johns Hopkins Press, 1950), but fails to note that these facts contradict the idea of isolation. The same approach is taken by G. Soule, *Prosperity Decade. From War to Depression: 1917–1929* (New York, Rinehart and Co., Inc., 1947), p. 252–74. Far more stimulating than either Feis or Soule is S. Kuznets, "Foreign Economic Relations of the United States and Their Impact Upon the Domestic Economy," Chapter 11 in his *Economic Change* (New York, W. W. Norton and Co., 1953), p. 296–333. See also the neglected work of A. D. Gayer and C. T.

Schmidt, *American Economic Foreign Policy. Postwar History, Analysis, and Interpretation* (New York, no publisher given, 1939), especially p. 11–17.

8. R. E. Osgood, *Ideals and Self-Interest in America's Foreign Relations. The Great Transformation of the Twentieth Century* (Chicago, University of Chicago Press, 1953).

9. This is strange for a realist trained in the school of Professor Hans J. Morgenthau's *Realpolitik.* For the realists emphasize the fact that the relationship between power and ideals is reciprocal. Not only do ideas fail to have consequences without power, but the sources and the nature of the power have some correlation with the character of the ideals. Thus it would seem doubly unrealistic to slight the sources of power and at the same time discuss the ideas without reference to the private as well as the public record of the groups and individuals in question.

10. C. E. Hughes, "The Centenary of the Monroe Doctrine," *The Annals of the American Academy of Political and Social Science,* Supplement to Volume CXI (January, 1923), p. 7.

11. G. L. Grassmuck, *Sectional Biases in Congress on Foreign Policy* (Baltimore, Johns Hopkins Press, 1951), p. 32, 93, 162, 49.

12. Hamilton to the British Minister, as quoted by S. F. Bemis, *Jay's Treaty. A Study in Commerce and Diplomacy* (New York, Macmillan and Co., 1924), p. 246.

13. R. W. Leopold, "The Mississippi Valley and American Foreign Policy, 1890–1941: An Assessment and an Appeal," *Mississippi Valley Historical Review,* XXXVII, NO. 4 (March, 1951), p. 635; H. C. Lodge, "Foreign Relations of the United States, 1921–1924," *Foreign Affairs,* II, NO. 4 (June, 1924), p. 526.

14. None of the authors cited above makes this association of events central to their discussion of the League issue. Few of them even connect the two. The integration has, of course, been made: most notably by E. H. Carr, *The Soviet Impact on the Western World* (New York, The Macmillan Co., 1947); M. Dobb, *Political Economy and Capitalism. Some Essays in Economic Tradition* (New York, International Publishers, 1945), Chapter VII, and *Studies in the Development*

of Capitalism (New York, International Publishers, 1947), Chapter VIII; H. J. Laski, *Reflections on the Revolution of Our Time* (New York, 1947); Sir L. Namier, *Conflicts. Studies in Contemporary History* (London, The Macmillan Co., 1942), Chapter I; and, of especial significance, H. Hoover, *American Individualism* (Garden City, Doubleday, Page and Co., 1923).

15. W. Wilson, remarks to the Council of Ten, January 16, 1919. *Papers Relating to the Foreign Relations of the United States. Paris Peace Conference* (13 vols., Washington, D.C.), III, p. 583.

16. See the excellent essay by J. H. Foote, "American Industrialists and Foreign Policy, 1919–1922. A Study in Attitudes," Master's Thesis, University of Wisconsin, Madison, 1947; for a typical expression see the remarks of Senator Walter E. Edge—"we wasted, practically wasted, two years of the opportunity presented to us at that time, unequaled, as I say, in the history of the world"—in National Foreign Trade Council, *Official Report of the Eighth National Foreign Trade Convention, 1921* (New York, 1921), p. 553.

17. W. Wilson, remarks to the Big Five, February 14, 1919, *Foreign Relations. Russia, 1919* (Washington, D.C., 1937), p. 59.

18. C. Vevier reviewed these early expansionist sympathies of the Progressives in "The Progressives and Dollar Diplomacy," Master's Thesis, University of Wisconsin, Madison, 1949. W. E. Leuchtenburg later published a summary of his own study of the same question as "Progressivism and Imperialism: The Progressive Movement and American Foreign Policy, 1898–1916," *Mississippi Valley Historical Review,* XXXIX, NO. 3 (December, 1952), p. 483–504. It would seem, however, that Leuchtenburg missed the split within the Progressives over Wilson's foreign policy. For in note 38, page 493, he considers it "remarkable" that the Progressives fought Wilson in view of the degree to which the president "was involved with American imperialist aspirations." This writer's information on the division comes from the manuscript papers of Calvin Coolidge, William E. Borah, William Judson, Samuel N. Harper, Theodore Roosevelt, Alexander Gumberg, Raymond Robins, and Woodrow Wilson; from the materials in the National Archives; and the *Congressional Record.*

19. See, for example, the debates on the Webb-Pomerene Act in

Congressional Record, Volume 56, Part 1, p. 69–71; and the votes on the same legislation, p. 168, 186.

20. Especially pertinent are the remarks of Borah, *Congressional Record,* V54:1:636; V57:1:190; V58:3:3143-44; and his letter to F. Lynch, August 1, 1919, *Papers of William E. Borah,* Library of Congress, Manuscript Division, Washington, D.C. Also important are the comments of Senator Hiram Johnson, *Congressional Record,* V53:1:503, 505. Eric Goldman's penetrating study of the Progressives, *Rendezvous with Destiny. A History of Modern American Reform* (New York, Alfred A. Knopf, 1952), completely misses this development. On p. 273–74, Goldman remarks that the "most striking deviation of American progressivism in foreign affairs from its attitudes in domestic affairs was the enthusiasm for international order in the form of the League of Nations." He proceeds, then, to argue that if the progressives had applied the same criticism to the League as they had to its laissez faire counterpart in domestic affairs "they could hardly have emerged with a favorable attitude." But the key point is that the hard core of the Progressives did exactly this and came out in opposition to the League.

21. This paragraph is based on much the same material cited in note 18. But see, as representative, Cummins' remarks on the loans, *Congressional Record,* V5511:757, 762; Borah on economic factors, V64:1:930-31; and the parliamentary maneuvers over the Liberian Loan, V63:1:287-88.

22. Stimson, Diary entry of December 3, 1919, quoted in H. L. Stimson and McGeorge Bundy, *On Active Service in Peace and War* (New York, Harper and Brothers, 1948), p. 104.

23. H. F. Cline, *The United States and Mexico* (Cambridge, Harvard University Press, 1953), p. 141.

24. H. Croly, *The Promise of American Life* (New York, The Macmillan Co., 1909); H. Hoover, *American Individualism,* p. 43; and Hoover, quoted in Goldman, *Rendezvous with Destiny,* p. 309. Goldman makes this identification between Croly and Hoover, but does not develop it, either as corporatism or in foreign affairs. Other Americans had spoken the language of the community of interest. J. P. Morgan used it to describe his ideal in the economic realm. Brooks Adams

warned Theodore Roosevelt that such coordination at the national level was necessary to insure American supremacy in the world. The Adams argument emphasized the need for an intellectual and political elite chosen from the upper classes to supervise the community of interest through control of the national government.

25. American corporatism is a neglected field. This writer is greatly indebted to Professor Paul Farmer, University of Wisconsin, for many long discussions of the question. Farmer brought to these conversations his intimate and extended knowledge of French corporative theory and practice as it developed to and culminated in the Vichy Government. His insights into the American scene were equally penetrating. At a later date M. H. Elbow, *French Corporative Theory, 1789–1948. A Chapter in the History of Ideas* (New York, Columbia University Press, 1953), was helpful in review. Of other published material, the following were most helpful: S. D. Alinsky, *Reveille for Radicals* (Chicago, University of Chicago Press, 1946); G. A. Almond, "The Political Attitudes of Wealth," *Journal of Politics,* VII, NO. 3 (August, 1945); R. A. Brady, *Business as a System of Power* (New York, Columbia University Press, 1938); R. Bendix, "Bureaucracy and the Problem of Power," *Public Administration Review,* V, NO. 3 (Summer, 1945); J. A. C. Grant, "The Guild Returns to America," *Journal of Politics,* IV, NOS. 3 and 4 (August, November, 1942); W. E. Henry, "The Business Executive: the Psycho-Dynamics of a Social Role," *American Journal of Sociology,* LIV, NO. 1 (January, 1949); E. J. Howenstine, "Public Works Policy in the Twenties," *Social Research,* XII (December, 1946); F. Hunter, *Community Power Structure. A Study of Decision Makers* (Chapel Hill, University of North Carolina Press, 1953); R. S. Lynd, "Power Politics and the Post War World," in *The Postwar World. The Merrick Lectures for 1944* (New York, Abingdon-Cokesbury Press, 1945); and M. Weber, *The Theory of Social and Economic Organization,* trans. by A. M. Henderson and T. Parsons, ed. by T. Parsons (New York, Oxford University Press, 1947). For a revealing glimpse of the later bi-partisan movement toward corporatism, and the consequences thereof, see *The Welfare State and the National Welfare. A Symposium on Some of the Threatening Tendencies of Our Times,* ed. by S. Glueck (Cambridge, Addison-Wesley Press, Inc., 1952); and the last chapter in Goldman, *Rendezvous with Destiny.*

26. *The Memoirs of Herbert Hoover. The Cabinet and the Presidency, 1920–1933* (New York, The Macmillan Co., 1952), p. 36.

27. *Official Report of the 18th Foreign Trade Convention, 1931* (New York, 1931), p. 287.

28. C. E. Hughes, remarks concerning a substitute for Article X of the League Covenant, Union League Club Speech, New York, March 26, 1919.

29. J. Klein, *Frontiers of Trade* (New York, The Century Co., 1929), p. 40, 46.

30. C. Coolidge, Address of May 30, 1928, *Congressional Record,* V69:10:10729.

31. C. E. Hughes, "Centenary of the Monroe Doctrine," *Annals,* p. 17; and Hughes, remarks to the Havana Conference, 1928.

32. The story of the fight over diplomatic immunity for consular officers can be followed in *Foreign Relations, 1925,* p. 211–54; the quote from Hughes is by J. Butler Wright, in *Official Report of the 12th National Foreign Trade Convention, 1925* (New York, 1925), p. 165.

33. Colby to Wright, November 5, 1920, *National Archives of the United States* (hereafter cited as *NA*), 574.D1/240b; Hughes, Memorandum of conversation with Geddes, September 20, 1921, *NA,* 500.A 4/190.5; Stimson, Memorandum of July 20, 1931, *NA,* 462.00 R 296/4594.5.

34. Colby to Russell, August 13, 1920, *NA,* 333.3921 L 96/3; Hughes to Cottrell, April 9, 1923, *NA,* 824.51/174; Hughes to Morales, June 30, 1923, *NA,* 815.00/2609; same to same, May 15, 1923, *NA,* 815.00/2574.

35. Kodding to Hughes, October 10, 1924, *NA,* 375.1123 Coleman and Delong/89; Hughes to Welles, April 10, 1924, *NA,* 815.00/3077a supplement.

36. Stimson, Memorandum of talks with representatives of J. P. Morgan and Co., Paris, July 17, 1931, *NA,* 462.00 R 296/4587.5.

37. G. F. Kennan, *American Diplomacy, 1900–1950* (Chicago, University of Chicago Press, 1951), p. 82; A. A. Berle, Jr., review of H. Feis, *The China Tangle,* in *The New York Times,* Book Review Section, October 4, 1953.

38. Hughes to Judge Hiscock, April 24, 1924, quoted in M. J. Pusey, *Charles Evans Hughes* (2 vols., New York, The Macmillan Co., 1951), II, p. 516; Hughes to Bell, October 22, 1924, *NA,* 893.51/4699; Hughes, Memorandum of conversations with Kato and Balfour, December 2, 1921, *NA,* 500.A4b/547.5.

39. Hughes to Morgan, August 8, 1921, *NA,* 861.77/2184.

40. Stimson, Memorandum of November 21, 1931, *NA,* 793.94/2865; and see Stimson. Memorandum of February 27, 1933, *NA,* 793-94/5953, for a clear review of his changing attitudes.

41. This writer is greatly indebted to Professor Richard N. Current, University of Illinois, for sharing his extended knowledge of the Manchurian Crisis. Professor Current's study will be published in the spring of 1954 by Rutgers University Press.

The Frontier Thesis and American Foreign Policy

1. J. W. Pratt, *America's Colonial Experiment: How the United States Gained, Governed, and in Part Gave Away a Colonial Empire* (New York, 1950), and F. R. Dulles, *America's Rise to World Power, 1898–1954* (New York, 1954) illustrate this ambivalence. F. L. Schuman discusses the problem of characterization in *The Commonwealth of Man: An Inquiry into Power Politics and World Government* (New York, 1952), 209–228. J. J. Servan Schreiber, gifted French commentator, tried to end the semantic quibbling with his remarks in the New York *Herald Tribune,* October 1, 1950: "When a nation, at any given period of history, bears the responsibility for the military security and the economic stability of a geographic zone, that nation is in fact—whether it wants it or not—the head of an empire. From then on it does not serve any purpose, moral or otherwise, to deny the facts and pretend that business is as usual." Refreshingly candid is R. W. Van Alstyne, "American Conceptions of Empire," lecture delivered at the University of Chicago, May 5, 1953, and available from the author.

2. This approach to the problem of opinion and influence stems

from the work of K. Mannheim and W. Dilthey. In addition, it may be ventured that J. A. Schumpeter's concept of the entrepreneur is as useful in studying men in ideas as it is for men in business.

3. This investigation of the role of the frontier thesis in American foreign policy was stimulated by G. Barraclough's long review of W. P. Webb, *The Great Frontier* (Boston, 1952), entitled "Metropolis and Macrocosm," in *Past and Present*, III, No. 1 (Whole Number 5, May, 1954), 77–90. In working back over the voluminous literature on Turner, I found myself most indebted to the work of Charles A. Beard, Lee Benson, Rudolf Freund, James C. Malin, Fulmer Mood, George Wilson Pierson, and Walter Prescott Webb. I also profited from Earl Pomeroy's comments on an early draft of this manuscript. After this manuscript had been completed, my attention was called to L. S. Kaplan, "Frederick Jackson Turner and Imperialism," *Social Science*, XXVII, No. 1 (January, 1952), 12–16: the interpretations diverge at important points. L. Hartz, *The Liberal Tradition in America: An Interpretation of American Political Thought Since the Revolution* (New York, 1955), 288–307; and R. Hofstadter, "Manifest Destiny and the Philippines," in *America in Crisis*, ed. by D. Aaron (New York, 1952), 173–200, discuss the general problem but in quite different fashion.

4. Here see W. Y. Elliott, *The Political Economy of American Foreign Policy: Its Concepts, Strategy, and Limits. Report of a Study Group Sponsored by the Woodrow Wilson Foundation and the National Planning Association* (New York, 1955), 42–54, 338, 391–392; E. H. Carr, *The New Society* (London, 1951), 84–86.

5. L. Benson, "The Historical Background of Turner's Frontier Essay," *Agricultural History*, XXV, No. 2 (April, 1951), 59–82.

6. It should be emphasized that this is not primarily a study of Turner's personal foreign policy. It is an attempt to gauge the nature and extent of the impact which his frontier thesis had on American foreign policy.

7. My understanding of the 1890's has been extended and sharpened by E. H. Phelps Brown with S. J. Hanfield-Jones, "The Climacteric of the 1890s: A Study in the Expanding Economy," *Oxford Economic Papers (New Series)*, IV, No. 3 (October, 1952), 266–307; and B. Weber and S. J. Hanfield-Jones "Variations in the Rate of Eco-

nomic Growth in the U.S.A., 1869–1939," *Ibid.*, VI, No. 2 (June, 1954), 101–131.

8. Of Turner's writings, I returned again and again to the following items, from which all quotations are taken (in sequence). "The Significance of History" (1891), "Problems in American History (1892), "The Significance of the Frontier in American History" (1893), all in *The Early Writings of Frederick Jackson Turner,* ed. by F. Mood (Madison, 1938); "Address on Education in a United States without Free Lands" (January 1, 1896), ed. by F. Mood, *Agricultural History,* XXIII, No. 4 (October, 1949), 254–259; "The Problem of the West" (1896), *Atlantic Monthly,* LXXVIII (September, 1896), 289–297; "Contributions of the West to American Democracy" (1902), *Ibid.,* XCI (January, 1903), 83–96; and Turner to Dodd, October 7, 1919, ed. by W. H. Stephenson, *Agricultural History,* XIX, No. 4 (October, 1945), 249–253.

9. As quoted by T. Anderson, *Brooks Adams, Constructive Conservative* (Ithaca, 1951), 61, 75. Anderson discounts, in somewhat ambivalent fashion, the influence of Adams. For another interpretation, upon which this review is based, see "Brooks Adams and American Expansion," *New England Quarterly,* XXV, No. 2 (June, 1952), 217–232.

10. Eugene, Oregon, *Register-Guard,* July 17, 1955.

11. E. Haycox, *The Earthbreakers* (New York, 1952), 19.

12. Here, among others, see H. N. Smith, "The West as an Image of the American Past," University of Kansas City *Review,* XVIII, No. 1 (Autumn, 1951), 29–39; and H. Schein, "The Olympian Cowboy," *American Scholar,* XXIV, No. 3 (Summer, 1955), 309–320.

13. Letters from Roosevelt to Turner, in *The Letters of Theodore Roosevelt,* ed. by E. E. Morrison, *et al.* (Cambridge, 1951–1954), I, 440, 363, 438.

14. C. P. Nettles, "Frederick Jackson Turner and the New Deal," *Wisconsin Magazine of History,* XVII, No. 3 (March, 1934), 257–265; J. C. Malin, "Mobility and History," *Agricultural History,* XVII, No. 4 (October 1943), 177–191, an interpretation unchanged in *Essays on Historiography* (Lawrence, Kansas, 1953), 36–37; R. Hofstadter, *The American Political Tradition* (New York, 1948),

325–327, 342. D. M. Potter, *People of Plenty: Economic Abundance and the American Character* (Chicago, 1954), 156–157, seems to go along with Malin's view.

15. R. H. S. Crossman seems to sense this in "Towards a Philosophy of Socialism," *New Fabian Essays* (London, 1952), 24. It is also worth recalling, in this connection, that Adams supported the inflationary silverites in 1896.

16. R. E. Osgood, *Ideals and Self-Interest in America's Foreign Relations* (Chicago, 1953), 410; Hofstadter, *American Political Tradition,* 316–317, 539; F. Freidel, *Franklin D. Roosevelt: The Ordeal* (Boston, 1954), 238–241; W. L. Langer and S. E. Gleason, *The Undeclared War, 1940–1941* (New York, 1953), 685.

17. See, for example, the following: *The American Spirit* (New York, 1942), 360–364; "Introduction," for B. Adams, *The Law of Civilization and Decay* (New York, 1943), 3–53; *The Idea of National Interest* (New York, 1934); "A 'Five Year Plan' for America," *Forum,* LXXXVI, No. 1 (July, 1931), 1–11; *The Open Door at Home* (New York, 1934); and *A Foreign Policy for America* (New York, 1940).

18. W. S. Churchill, *Triumph and Tragedy* (Boston, 1953), 73–79, 208–209, 215–216, 219, 227–228; R. E. Sherwood, *Roosevelt and Hopkins: An Intimate History* (New York, 1948), 834.

19. M. W. Childs, "Evaluation," for B. Adams, *America's Economic Supremacy* (New York, 1947), 1–60; and Childs to Williams, June 4, 1955.

20. Perhaps it is significant that Kennan, *American Diplomacy, 1900–1950* (Chicago, 1951), 5–6, cited Childs' edition of Adams; though he may have done this as a convenience to his readers. In any event, compare Adams, *Supremacy* (ed. 1947), 168, 173–174 (where he uses the word "containing") with Kennan's article, "The Sources of Soviet Conduct;" with his remarks at the Department of State's "Round Table Discussion of American Policy toward China, October, 1949," *Hearings on the Institute of Pacific Relations* (Washington, 1952), Part V, 1557–1558; and with Kennan, *Realities of American Foreign Policy* (Princeton, 1954), 27, 64.

21. H. S. Truman, *The American Frontier* (Washington, 1952).

22. Webb, *Great Frontier,* 284–302, 338–347.

23. D. Acheson, remarks of February 21, 1950, *Hearings Before the Committee on Foreign Affairs of the House of Representatives to Amend the Economic Cooperation Act of 1948, as Amended, 1950* (Washington, 1950), Part I, 15–16, 29; remarks of February 21, 1950, *Hearings Before the Committee on Foreign Relations of the United States Senate on Extension of European Recovery, 1950* (Washington, 1950), 14.

24. W. C. Foster, remarks of July 11, 1951, *The Mutual Security Program: Hearings Before the Committee on Foreign Affairs of the House of Representatives, 1951* (Washington, 1951), 197; W. A. Harriman, remarks of July 3, 1951, *Ibid.,* 127; N. Rockefeller, remarks of July 17, 1951, *Ibid.,* 376; W. A. Harriman, remarks of June 6, 1950, *Hearings Before the Committee on Foreign Affairs of the House of Representatives to Amend the Mutual Defense Assistance Act of 1949, 1950* (Washington, 1950), 167.

25. W. A. Harriman, remarks of March 13, 1952, *Mutual Security Act Extension: Hearings Before the Committee on Foreign Affairs of the House of Representatives, March, 1952* (Washington, 1952), 8, 48; D. Acheson, remarks of June 11, 1952, *Hearings Before the Senate Committee on Foreign Relations on the Convention on Relations with the Federal Republic of Germany and a Protocol to the North Atlantic Treaty* (Washington, 1952), 31–32.

26. P. W. Bell, "Colonialism as a Problem in American Foreign Policy," *World Politics,* V, No. 1 (October, 1952), 86, 101–102, 109. On the broader questions involved see J. Gallagher and R. Robinson, "The Imperialism of Free Trade," *The Economic History Review, Second Series,* VI, No. 1 (August, 1953), 1–15; and R. Nurkse, "International Investment To-Day in the Light of Nineteenth-Century Experience," *Economic Journal,* LXIV, No. 256 (December, 1954), 745–758. A most useful bibliography is A. Hazlewood, *The Economics of "Under-Developed Areas,"* (London, 1954).

27. Webb, *Great Frontier,* 2; and F. Mood, "Notes on the History of the Word Frontier," *Agricultural History,* XXII, No. 2 (April, 1948), 78–83.

A Note on Charles Austin Beard's Search for a General Theory of Causation

1. "Charles Beard's Political Theory," in *Charles A. Beard: An Appraisal,* ed. Howard K. Beale (Lexington, Ky., 1954), p. 25. (Hereafter cited as *Beard.*)

2. *Politics* (New York, 1908), p. 32.

3. *The Discussion of Human Affairs* (New York, 1936), pp. 25, 40–41, 87, 92–93.

4. *An Economic Interpretation of the Constitution of the United States* (New York, 1935 ed.), p. xii.

5. *New Republic,* Mar. 31, 1920, pp. 162–63; Feb. 16, 1921, pp. 349–50; May 17, 1933, pp. 22–24.

6. *Forum,* LXXXVI (July, 1931), 1–11.

7. Professor Lloyd Sorenson, a colleague at the University of Oregon, is currently investigating this phase of Beard's career. I am indebted to him for sharing with me his knowledge of the Germans and his estimate of Beard's relationship with their work.

8. Lerner touches upon this point in his essay in *Beard,* p. 44.

9. Conversations with Professor Sorenson.

10. Quoted by Eric F. Goldman in *Beard,* p. 2.

11. Quoted by M. Josephson, "Charles A. Beard: A Memoir," *Virginia Quarterly Review,* XXV (October, 1949), 585–602.

12. The key sentence in B. C. Borning, "The Political Philosophy of Young Charles A. Beard," *American Political Science Review,* XLIII (December, 1949), 1177, would seem to verify this: "At any rate, it is plain that his economic interpretation of American history constituted no sudden break in his developing thought."

13. "The Economic Basis of Politics," *New Republic,* Sept. 27, 1922, p. 128.

14. Douglass Adair, "The Tenth Federalist Revisited," *William and Mary Quarterly,* 3d Ser., VIII (January, 1951), 60–61.

15. *On Re-Reading Marx* (Cambridge, Eng., 1953), p. i.

16. Adair, Lerner, Hofstadter, and Morton G. White all lean toward the view that Beard's theory was based on the economic motive.

17. *The Federalist* (Modern Library ed.), pp. 54–56.

18. *Social Thought in America: The Revolt against Formalism* (New York, 1949), pp. 119, 123–24.

19. Adair, "Tenth Federalist Revisited," p. 60.

20. John Adams, "The Right Constitution of a Commonwealth Examined," quoted by Beard in *Economic Origins of Jeffersonian Democracy,* pp. 300–303; F. W. Gregory and I. D. Neu, "The American Industrial Elite in the 1870's," in *Men in Business,* ed. William Miller (Cambridge, Mass., 1952), pp. 193–211; Donald R. Matthews, *The Social Background of Political Decision Makers* (Garden City, N.Y., 1954); the studies by W. Miller referred to in his "The Business Elite in Business Bureaucracies," *Men in Business,* p. 286; C. W. Mills, "The American Business Elite: A Collective Portrait," *Journal of Economic History,* Supplement, V (December, 1945), 20–44; F. W. Taussig and C. S. Joslyn, *American Business Leaders* (New York, 1932); R. W. Wald and R. A. Doty, "The Top Executives—A Firsthand Profile," *Harvard Business Review,* XXXII (July–August, 1954), 45–54.

21. Albert T. Lauterback, *Man, Motives, and Money: Psychological Frontiers of Economics* (Ithaca, 1954), pp. 24–28; George Katona, *Psychological Analysis of Economic Behavior* (New York, 1951), p. 197.

22. Walter P. Webb, *The Great Frontier* (Boston, 1952).

23. Adair, "Tenth Federalist Revisited," p. 60, and n. 25.

24. "Charles Beard on the Constitution," in *Beard,* pp. 75–92. This concentration on Hofstadter's essay results neither from neglecting nor discounting Eric F. Goldman's essay, "The Origins of Beard's *Economic Interpretation of the Constitution,*" *Journal of the History of Ideas,* XIII (April, 1952), 234–49. Hofstadter's interpretation includes Goldman's more specific thesis that Beard was caught up in the liberal movement that used Darwinism to "oppose Social Darwinism" (pp. 237, 247). Goldman does not, like Hofstadter, stress the Progressive movement's concern with sordid economic motives. But, like Hof-

stadter, Goldman does separate the book on the Constitution from the volume on Jeffersonian Democracy; and, like Hofstadter, does not see either book as primarily an effort to test Madison's general theory. Robert E. Thomas, "A Reappraisal of Charles A. Beard's *An Economic Interpretation of the Constitution*," *American Historical Review*, LVII (January, 1952), 370–75, questions Beard's Progressivism. C. M. Kenyon, "Men of Little Faith: The Anti-Federalists on the Nature of Representative Government," *William and Mary Quarterly*, 3d Ser., XII (January, 1955), 3–6, criticizes Beard. This essay was written before the publication of Robert E. Brown's study, *Charles Beard and the Constitution* (Princeton, 1956). Hence it does not deal explicitly with Brown's analysis of Beard.

25. "Beard on the Constitution," pp. 85–87.

26. "Manifest Destiny and the Philippines," in *America in Crisis,* ed. Daniel Aaron (New York, 1952), p. 173.

27. *An Economic Interpretation of the Constitution*, pp. xix, 14.

28. *Ibid.*, pp. 16–18.

29. *Ibid.*, pp. 324–25.

30. *Economic Origins of Jeffersonian Democracy*, pp. 300–303.

31. *The Economic Basis of Politics* (New York, 1945 ed.), p. 70.

32. *Discussion of Human Affairs*, pp. 25, 40–41.

33. *The United States and the Independence of Latin America, 1800–1830* (Baltimore, 1941), p. 36. Whitaker's best analysis may be found in sections IV and V of chapter 3, pp. 87–99.

34. *The American Party Battle*, pp. 5–11.

35. *The Idea of National Interest*, p. 4, nn. 7 and 8, and continuing through the chapter. For a full review of Beard's work with the Germans see Lloyd Sorenson, "Charles A. Beard and German Historiographical Thought," *Mississippi Valley Historical Review*, XLII (September, 1955), 274–87.

36. *Discussion of Human Affairs*, pp. 40–41, 87; "Written History as an Act of Faith," *AHR*, XXXIX, 222–23.

37. "Currents of Thought in Historiography," *AHR*, XLII, 478.

38. *Discussion of Human Affairs*, pp. 71, 73; "Currents in Historiography," p. 481.

39. *American Party Battle,* pp. 10–11.

40. C. A. and William Beard, *The American Leviathan: The Republic in the Machine Age* (New York, 1930), pp. 4–5, 84; and see C. A. Beard, "The Political Heritage of the Twentieth Century," *Yale Review,* XVIII (March, 1929), 459–60, 463; and "A 'Five Year Plan' for America," *Forum,* July, 1931, pp. 1–11, for further evidence of his interest in technology.

41. *Discussion of Human Affairs,* p. 111.

42. C. A. and Mary R. Beard, *The American Spirit* (New York, 1942), pp. 6–7; but compare all of chapter 1 with Albert Schweitzer, *The Philosophy of Civilization* (American ed., New York, 1949).

43. "Henry Adams," *New Republic,* Mar. 31, 1920, p. 62.

44. Beard's references to Madison's prediction may be found, among other places, in *America in Midpassage* (New York, 1939), II, 936–38; and in *The Republic: Conversations on Fundamentals* (New York, World Book ed., 1943), p. 286.

45. "Henry Adams," pp. 62–63; "Currents of Thought in Historiography," p. 478; "Introduction," to Brooks Adams, *The Law of Civilization and Decay* (New York, 1943 ed.), p. 13.

46. *Federal Licensing of Corporations: Hearings before a Subcommittee of the Committee on the Judiciary on Senate Bill No. 10* (Washington, D.C., 1937), Part I, pp. 70, 72, 79. I am indebted to Professor Orde S. Pinckney, a colleague at the University of Oregon, for calling my attention to this testimony; it is not listed in the bibliography in *Beard.* C. A. Beard, "The Anti-Trust Racket," *New Republic,* Sept. 21, 1938, pp. 182–84.

47. Quoted in *Books That Changed Our Minds,* ed. Malcolm Cowley and Bernard Smith (New York, 1939), p. 19.

48. Comment in *Theory and Practice in Historical Study: A Report of the Committee on Historiography,* Social Science Research Council Bulletin 54 (New York, 1946), p. 13.

49. *America in Midpassage,* II, 921; *American Spirit,* pp. 21, 158–61, 379–83.

50. "Introduction," to Adams, *Law of Civilization and Decay. The*

Republic, chap. XIII, and pp. 273, 284, 324, 336. One cannot but wonder whether Beard's new emphasis, in *The Republic,* on the activities of military leaders after the Revolutionary War did not stem, in part, from his reading of Adams. C. A. and M. R. Beard, *A Basic History of the United States* (New York, 1944), pp. 303, 367, 378–79.

51. *American Foreign Policy in the Making, 1932–1940: A Study in Responsibilities* (New Haven, 1946); *President Roosevelt and the Coming of the War, 1941: A Study in Appearances and Realities* (New Haven, 1948).

52. G. R. Leighton, "Beard and Foreign Policy," in *Beard,* pp. 169–81.

53. Quoted by Goldman, in *Beard,* p. 7.

Charles Austin Beard: The Intellectual as Tory-Radical

1. The story is reported in H. K. Beale, "Charles Beard: Historian," in Beale, *op. cit.,* p. 123.

2. Beard carried on a running battle with many prominent American historians, who accused him of lack of objectivity for his economic interpretations and his interest in contemporary problems. See, for example, the criticisms of him by Theodore Smith, "The Writing of American History in America, from 1884 to 1934," *American Historical Review* (April 1935), XL, 439–449; see also Beard's response to "objective" historians in his review of Arthur M. Schlesinger's *Rise of the City,* in the *American Historical Review* (July 1933), XXXVIII, 779–780. The most strenuous attack on Beard immediately after publication of *An Economic Interpretation of the Constitution* was by Professor Edward Corwin who attributed to Beard the aim of establishing "the truth of socialistic theory of economic determinism and class struggle." *History Teacher's Magazine* (February 1914), V, 65–66.

3. From Beard's letter of resignation of October 8, 1917, cited by Counts, *op. cit.,* p. 245.

4. See the article by Robert E. Thomas, "A Reappraisal of Charles

A. Beard's Economic Interpretation of the Constitution of the United States," *American Historical Review* (January 1952), LVII, 370–375.

The Age of Mercantilism:
An Interpretation of the American
Political Economy, 1763 to 1828

1. Curtis P. Nettels, "British Mercantilism and the Economic Development of the Thirteen Colonies," *Journal of Economic History,* XII (Spring 1952), 105–114; William D. Grampp, "A Re-examination of Jeffersonian Economics," *Southern Economic Journal,* XII (Jan. 1946), 263–282; "On the Politics of the Classical Economists," *Quarterly Journal of Economics,* LXII (Nov. 1948), 714–747; and "The Liberal Elements in English Mercantilism," *ibid.,* LXVI (Nov. 1952), 465–501; Gunnar Myrdal, *The Political Element in the Development of Economic Theory* (London, 1953); Jacob Viner, "Power versus Plenty as Objectives of Foreign Policy in the Seventeenth and Eighteenth Centuries," *World Politics,* I (Oct. 1948), 1–29; Charles Wilson, " 'Mercantilism': Some Vicissitudes of an Idea," *Economic History Review,* 2d Ser., X (Dec. 1957), 181–188. This essay owes an equal debt to the extensive publications of Merrill Jenson and to his generous and helpful interest in this approach to the era. His keen criticisms and perceptive suggestions were invaluable. It also benefited from the interest and intelligence of James Cooper, Lloyd Gardner, Kent Kreuter, Thomas J. McCormick, Walter La Feber, and Martin Sklar. This article is a foreshortened statement of the first section of a longer three-part essay dealing with the characterization and periodization of American history. Together with the other two portions, "The Age of Laissez Moi Faire, 1828–1896," and "The Age of Corporate Capitalism, 1896–1958," it will be published as The Contours of American History by the World Publishing Company.

2. Some readers may feel that the vigor of the subsequent presentation contradicts these caveats. Perhaps they will be reassured by remembering that any tool has to be sharp, though later it may be laid aside out of preference for another.

3. Albert Bushnell Hart, *The Foundations of American Foreign Policy* (New York, 1901), pp. 174–175. The best published study of the early empire outlook is Arthur B. Darling, *Our Rising Empire, 1763–1803* (New Haven, 1940).

4. Gerald Stourzh, *Benjamin Franklin and American Foreign Policy* (Chicago, 1954), p. 54.

5. On Washington see, among others, Charles H. Ambler, *George Washington and the West* (Chapel Hill, 1936), and Curtis P. Nettels, *George Washington and American Independence* (Boston, 1951). Also consult *Letters of Members of the Continental Congress,* ed. Edmund C. Burnett (Washington, 1921), III, 476; Malbone W. Graham, *American Diplomacy in the International Community* (Baltimore, 1948), pp. 9–24; and Max Savelle, "The Appearance of an American Attitude Toward External Affairs, 1770–1775," *American Historical Review,* LII (July 1947), 655–666.

6. *The Revolutionary Diplomatic Correspondence of the United States,* ed. Francis Wharton (Washington, 1889), II, 332.

7. Jedidiah Morse, *The American Geography; or A View of the Present Situation of the United States of America* (Elizabeth Town, 1789), pp. 468–469, quoted in Richard W. Van Alstyne, "American Conceptions of Empire," a lecture delivered at the University of Chicago, May 5, 1953, copies available from the author.

8. See Léon Dion, "Natural Law and Manifest Destiny in the Era of the American Revolution," *Canadian Journal of Economics and Political Science,* XXIII (May 1957), 227–247, as a supplement to Albert K. Weinberg, *Manifest Destiny* (Baltimore, 1935).

9. Of the immense literature on mercantilism, the following items proved most stimulating: Max Beer, *Early British Economics from the Thirteenth Century to the Middle of the Eighteenth Century* (London, 1938); Philip W. Buck, *The Politics of Mercantilism* (New York, 1942); Edgar S. Furniss, *The Position of the Laborer in a System of Nationalism* (Boston, 1920); E. F. Heckscher, *Mercantilism,* rev. ed., ed. E. F. Soderlund (London, 1955), esp. Vol. II; E. A. J. Johnson, *American Economic Thought in the Seventeenth Century* (London, 1932), and *Predecessors of Adam Smith* (New York, 1937); Ephraim Lipson, *The Economic History of England* (London, 1948–49); Gus-

tav F. von Schmoller, *The Mercantile System and Its Historical Signifi-*
cance (New York, 1931); and the items cited in note 1.

10. Here see Oliver M. Dickerson, *The Navigation Acts and the*
American Revolution (Philadelphia, 1951), on the attitude of the colonists toward the Navigation Acts per se. Then consult Oscar and Mary
F. Handlin, *Commonwealth. A Study of the Role of Government in*
the American Economy: Massachusetts, 1774–1861 (New York,
1947); Louis Hartz, *Economy Policy and Democratic Thought: Penn-*
sylvania, 1776–1860 (Cambridge, Mass., 1948); and Merrill Jensen,
The New Nation. A History of the United States During the Confeder-
ation, 1781–1789 (New York, 1950), on the development of an
American mercantilism at the state level.

11. Madison to Jefferson, Mar. 18, 1786, *Letters and Other Writ-*
ings of James Madison. Published by order of Congress (New York,
1884), I, 226–227.

12. Robert L. Ketchum, "Notes on James Madison's Sources for
the Tenth Federalist Paper," *Midwest Journal of Political Science,* I
(May 1957), 20–25; Douglass Adair, " 'That Politics May Be Reduced to a Science': David Hume, James Madison, and the Tenth *Fed-*
eralist," Huntington Library Quarterly, XX (Aug. 1957), 343–360.

13. Madison, Federalist No. 10, *The Federalist,* ed. Henry Cabot
Lodge (New York, 1900), pp. 58–60.

14. Edward Everett, *Orations and Speeches on Various Occasions*
(Boston, 1850–68), I, 210.

15. Here see Charles S. Campbell, Jr., "American Business Interests
and the Open Door in China," *Far Eastern Quarterly,* I (Nov. 1941),
43–58; Nancy L. O'Connor, "The Foreign Policy of the Farmers'
Movements, 1890–1900," unpubl. Masters Thesis, University of Oregon, 1957; William A. Williams, "The Frontier Thesis and American
Foreign Policy," *Pacific Historical Review,* XXIV (Nov. 1955),
379–395, and "The Large Corporation and the Political Economy of
American Foreign Policy: 1890–1958," paper read at the State University of Iowa Conference on Social Sciences, May 1958.

16. Though independently worked out, this analysis is supported
by Charles R. Haygood, "Mercantilism and Colonial Slave Labor,
1700–1763," *Journal of Southern History,* XXIII (Nov. 1957),
454–464.

17. Arthur I. Bloomfield, "The Foreign-Trade Doctrines of the Physiocrats," *American Economic Review,* XXVIII (Dec. 1938), 716–735.

18. William D. Grampp, "John Taylor: Economist of Southern Agrarians," *Southern Economic Journal,* XI (Jan. 1945), 255–268, esp. pp. 258, 263, on Taylor's developing opposition to Jefferson.

19. Joseph Charles, *The Origins of the American Party System* (Williamsburg, 1956), pp. 11–12. Also see John C. Livingston, "Alexander Hamilton and the American Tradition," *Midwest Journal of Political Science,* I (Nov. 1957), 209–224; Arnold A. Rogow, "Edmund Burke and the American Liberal Tradition," *Antioch Review,* XVII (June 1957), 255–265; James O. Wettereau, "Letters from Two Business Men to Alexander Hamilton on Federal Fiscal Policy, November, 1789," *Journal of Economic and Business History,* III (Aug. 1931), 667–686; Samuel Rezneck, "The Rise and Early Development of Industrial Consciousness in the United States, 1760–1830," *ibid.,* IV (Aug. 1932), 784–811. This approach to Hamilton had been worked out in all essentials prior to the publication of the most recent biographies, and for that reason it was deemed wise to present it in the form in which it was originally cast.

20. This section draws heavily on Charles, *Origins of the American Party System,* and on Vols. I and II of Irving Brant, *James Madison* (Indianapolis and New York, 1941—in progress). A more detailed account of these early episodes can be found in Vol. I of Edward Stanwood, *American Tariff Controversies in the Nineteenth Century* (Boston, 1903).

21. Here see Rezneck, "The Rise and Early Development of Industrial Consciousness in the United States, 1760–1830"; and Joseph Dorfman, *The Economic Mind in American Civilization, 1606–1865* (New York, 1946), I, 253–256, 290–293.

22. Stanwood, *American Tariff Controversies,* I, 108–110, 120–121; and for considerable insight into the role of Smith of South Carolina, consult Joseph Ernst, "Growth of the South Carolina Commons House of Assembly, 1761–1775," unpubl. masters thesis, University of Wisconsin, 1958.

23. Eugene P. Link, *Democratic-Republican Socieites, 1790–1800* (New York, 1942), n. 16, p. 49.

24. Charles, *Origins of the American Party System,* p. 97.

25. Quoted in Grampp, "A Re-examination of Jeffersonian Economics," p. 279.

26. On eastern urban votes for war see Warren H. Goodman, "The Origins of the War of 1812: A. Survey of Changing Interpretations," reprinted in *The Shaping of American Diplomacy,* ed. William A. Williams (Chicago, 1956), p. 122.

27. Quoted in Samuel F. Bemis, *John Quincy Adams and the Foundations of American Foreign Policy* (New York, 1949), p. 64.

28. *Ibid.,* p. 180.

29. *Ibid.,* p. 148.

30. *Ibid.,* p. 352; but cf. pp. 364, 127.

31. The traditional neglect of commercial interests and pressures in connection with the formulation and enunciation of the Monroe Doctrine, an approach symbolized in Dexter Perkins, *Monroe Doctrine, 1823–1826* (Baltimore, 1929), is somewhat corrected by Charles L. Chandler, "United States Commerce with Latin America at the Promulgation of the Monroe Doctrine," *Quarterly Journal of Economics,* XXXVIII (May 1924), 466–486. Even more illuminating are Dorothy B. Goebel, "British-American Rivalry in the Chilean Trade, 1817–1820," *Journal of Economic History,* II (Nov. 1942), 190–202; Charles C. Griffin, *The United States and the Disruption of the Spanish Empire, 1810–1822* (New York, 1937); and Arthur Preston Whitaker, *The United States and the Independence of Latin America, 1800–1830* (Baltimore, 1941).

The Cuban Revolution Assaulted from Abroad

1. See R.C. Allison, "Cuba's Seizure of American Business," *American Bar Association Journal,* 47:1 and 2 (January, February, 1961), 48–51, 187–191.

2. The documentary evidence for this is in my volume, *The Shaping of American Diplomacy* (Chicago, Rand McNally Co., 1956; paperback edition 1962), pp. 160–161.

About the Author

William Appleman Williams, the leading American revisionist historian, was born in Atlantic, Iowa. He attended the United States Naval Academy at Annapolis and the University of Wisconsin at Madison, where he also taught for a number of years. He is the author of many books, most notably *The Tragedy of American Diplomacy, The Contours of American History* and *The Rise of the Modern American Empire*. His latest book, *History as a Way of Learning,* is a collection of the most important essays and articles written earlier in his career.

He is at present Professor of History at Oregon State University.